THE PRACTICAL ENCYCLOPEDIA OF
FISH AND SHELLFISH

A COMPLETE GUIDE TO TYPES, THEIR PREPARATION AND COOKING TECHNIQUES, WITH 100 CLASSIC RECIPES SHOWN STEP BY STEP IN OVER 700 PHOTOGRAPHS

KATE WHITEMAN

southwater

This edition is published by Southwater, an imprint of Anness Publishing Ltd,
108 Great Russell Street, London WC1B 3NA; info@anness.com

www.southwaterbooks.com; www.annesspublishing.com

If you like the images in this book and would like to investigate using them for publishing, promotions
or advertising, please visit our website www.practicalpictures.com for more information.

Publisher: Joanna Lorenz
Executive Editor: Linda Fraser
Copy Editor: Jenni Fleetwood
Indexer: Hilary Bird
Designer: Nigel Partridge
Photography: William Lingwood, assisted by Vanessa Davies
Food for Photography: Sunil Vijayakar, assisted by Tonia Hedley (recipes) and
Annabel Ford (reference section)

PUBLISHER'S NOTE
Although the advice and information in this book are believed to be accurate and true at the time of going to press,
neither the authors nor the publisher can accept any legal responsibility or liability for any errors or omissions
that may have been made nor for any inaccuracies nor for any loss, harm or injury that comes about
from following instructions or advice in this book.

bracketed terms are intended for American readers.
For all recipes, quantities are given in both metric and imperial measures and, where appropriate, in standard cups and spoons.
Follow one set of measures, but not a mixture, because they are not interchangeable.
Standard spoon and cup measures are level. 1 tsp = 5ml, 1 tbsp = 15ml, 1 cup = 250ml/8fl oz.
Australian standard tablespoons are 20ml.
Australian readers should use 3 tsp in place of 1 tbsp for measuring small quantities.
American pints are 16fl oz/2 cups.
American readers should use 20fl oz/2.5 cups in place of 1 pint when measuring liquids.
Electric oven temperatures in this book are for conventional ovens. When using a fan oven, the temperature will probably need to
be reduced by about 10–20°C/20–40°F. Since ovens vary, you should check with your manufacturer's instruction book for guidance.
The nutritional analysis given for each recipe is calculated per portion (i.e. serving or item), unless otherwise stated.
If the recipe gives a range, such as Serves 4–6, then the nutritional analysis will be for the smaller portion size, i.e. 6 servings.
The analysis does not include optional ingredients, such as salt added to taste.
Medium (US large) eggs are used unless otherwise stated.

THE PRACTICAL ENCYCLOPEDIA OF
FISH AND SHELLFISH

CONTENTS

INTRODUCTION

Since man evolved as a hunter-gatherer, the world's rivers, lakes and seas have served as an apparently limitless larder, providing a bountiful supply of fish and seafood almost infinite in its variety. From tiny streams to brackish ponds to mighty oceans, all waters yield some kind of fish, shellfish and crustaceans, almost all of them edible, although in many cases you might not guess this from their outward appearance.

Although for many years fish was undervalued in the western world, its importance as a highly nutritious and delicious food is now universally recognized. As controversial farming methods make many other important foods such as meat, poultry, dairy produce and even cereals less attractive than they once were, fish has really come into its own as a healthy alternative.

THE WORLD OF FISH AND SHELLFISH

There is no doubt that fish is good for you. All fish and shellfish is low in fat and high in proteins, minerals and vitamins; oily fish can actually improve your health by lowering cholesterol levels and unclogging arteries. The Japanese, whose diet consists largely of fresh raw fish, have the lowest incidence of heart disease in the world.

Good health is only one of many reasons to eat the fruits of the sea, however. When properly prepared and cooked, they can be among the most delicious foods imaginable. Unfortunately too many of us were brought up on unhealthy and tasteless offerings of heavily-breaded deep-fried scampi (shrimp), or unpalatable, overcooked or watery fish, whose delicate flavour and texture was often reduced to a tasteless

Below: In many areas good fish stalls, like this one in Venice, Italy, are becoming increasingly hard to find.

Right: Octopus and baby squid on sale at Tsukiji fish market in Tokyo.

pulp, or masked with floury sauces. Well-cooked fish and shellfish are quite another matter. Really fresh fish needs little or no cooking or embellishment, and most takes very little time to prepare – a huge bonus for today's time-poor cooks. It is easy to rustle up the most elegant fish dish in under half an hour.

Every fish and shellfish has its own unique flavour, offering something for all tastes. You are unlikely to find a recipe for a piscatorial pudding, but seafood can feature in every other part of meal, including appetizers, soups, main courses, salads and savouries.

Nowadays, however, we are faced with a dilemma. We are constantly told that fish is good for us and that we should eat more of it, but at the same time, we must be aware that thanks to this wonderful food's growing popularity,

an alarming 70% of the world's fish stocks are overfished or severely depleted. Even in the world's deepest oceans, massive trawlers scoop up fish from the depths, plundering the seas for what has become a valuable commodity. Many once common fish, including the mainstays of the fish and chip shop – Atlantic cod, plaice, skate and huss – are now rare, and stocks are at dangerously low levels. To make matters worse, even fish that are sustainable are often caught using methods that are detrimental to other marine species and their habitats. Every year, thousands of dolphins, turtles and sea birds die as a consequence of by-catch, dredging and long-line fishing.

Fish farming may seem to be the obvious solution. After all, the Romans developed oyster farms over 2000 years ago, so it seems logical that in this technological age, we should be able to farm almost any kind of fish and seafood. Many fisheries are ethically run and produce sustainable stocks of excellent, healthy eco-friendly fish, but, when poorly managed, fish farming shares many of the problems of other intensive animal farming, resulting in pollution of the environment, spreading of diseases to wild fish, and the destruction of wildlife and their habitats.

The most obvious benefit of buying farmed fish is that it is often cheap. But cheapness can come at a high price. We must not repeat the mistakes of the

Right: There are fish and shellfish from all over the world on sale on this stall at an indoor market in the Champagne region of France.

past, when demand for ever-cheaper meat and other foods had disastrous consequences in terms of damage to the environment. Fish and shellfish are superb natural foods and should remain so. That said, the products of properly managed fisheries do help to counteract the disastrous effects of over-fishing.

So how can we balance the benefits of including more fish in our diet against the disadvantages of declining stocks and marine mismanagement? The simple solution is to identify which species come from well-managed sources and are caught using methods that minimize damage to the marine eco-system. Befriend your fishmongers and ask them where their fish comes from. If they can't or won't tell you, a simple online search will tell you which species are considered to be sustainably and sensitively harvested. Avoid any that are not.

Surprisingly, fish has not always been so highly valued. Perhaps it has something to do with the fact that it was traditionally eaten on Christian fast days as a substitute for meat, so is associated with self-denial and penance. In times of plenty, readily obtainable seafoods like salmon and oysters were regarded as foods fit only for the poor. Medieval apprentices complained bitterly and refused to eat oysters more than three times a week!

Probably the main reason for eschewing fish, however, was the lack of understanding of how to prepare it. Skinning, filleting, scaling and shelling all seemed like rather hard work. Nowadays, despite the demise of so many fishmongers, there is no need to undertake these laborious processes yourself. Just visit your local supermarket (many now have wet fish counters) and choose ready-prepared fish, or better still, follow the instructions given in this book, which will guide you through the complexities of handling and preparing all kinds of

fish and shellfish. You will find the whole process of preparing and cooking these versatile fruits of the sea extremely rewarding.

The variety of underwater creatures is staggering. I often wonder which intrepid (or desperately hungry) soul was the first to imagine that a hideous lumpfish or multi-limbed octopus might serve as a snack, or spot the potential in a spider crab, spiny sea urchin or slimy sea cucumber for providing a palatable meal. Imagine what pleasures we might have missed had our ancestors been repelled by the appearance of such strange sea creatures. With a few poisonous (sometimes deadly) exceptions, almost everything that swims, crawls, scuttles or merely lurks in the water can supply us with food.

One of the greatest pleasures when travelling is to visit local fish markets and observe the dazzling array of brightly coloured fish and seafood. However strange their shapes and forms, all have a unique beauty and character. Modern methods of fishing and transportation have made sea creatures from all over the world accessible to adventurous cooks, so follow the golden rules of sustainability: don't eat fish from depleted stocks, or undersized specimens; avoid buying fish during their breeding seasons, and always check their provenance. Do all this and you can safely indulge in the pleasure of experimenting with the infinite variety of textures, flavours and colours of the fruits of the sea.

EQUIPMENT

Although it is perfectly possible to prepare and cook fish without special equipment, there are a few items which make the process much easier. Some, such as the fish kettle, take up quite a lot of storage space; other gadgets, such as the fish scaler, are quite tiny, but all will prove invaluable for fish and shellfish cooking.

KNIVES, SCISSORS AND SCALERS

Chef's knife

A large heavy knife with a 20–25cm/ 8–10in blade is essential for cutting fish steaks and splitting open crustaceans, such as crayfish and lobster.

Filleting knife

For filleting and skinning fish, you will need a sharp knife with a flexible blade, which is at least 15cm/ 6in long. This type of knife can also be used for opening some kinds of shellfish. It is essential to keep a filleting knife razor sharp.

Oyster knife

This short, stubby knife – sometimes called a shucker – has a wide, two-edged blade to help prise open the shells of oysters and other bivalves. Make sure that it has a safety guard above the handle to protect your hands.

Kitchen scissors

A sturdy, sharp pair of scissors that have a serrated edge are needed for cutting off fins and trimming tails.

Fish scaler

Resembling a small, rough grater, a fish scaler makes short work of a task that few relish.

Below: Fish scalers

Below: Chef's knife

Below: Filleting knife

Below: Scissors

Left: Oyster knives

PANS

Fish kettle

Long and deep, with rounded edges, this attractive utensil has a handle at either end, and a tightly-fitting lid. Inside is a perforated rack or grid on which to lay the fish. This, too, has handles, and enables the cook to lift out the fish without breaking it. Most modern fish kettles are made of stainless steel, but they also come in enamelled steel and copper with a tin-plated interior. Fish kettles are used on the hob (stovetop) and are invaluable for cooking whole large fish, such as salmon and sea trout. They can also be used for steaming other foods.

Above: A fish kettle takes up a lot of storage space in the kitchen, but if you want to cook whole fish, such as salmon, it is well worth buying.

Right: Oval frying pan

Right: Griddle pan

Right: Chinese bamboo steamers

Above: Stainless steel steamers

Oval frying pan

Such a simple idea, but intensely practical, this large pan enables you to cook whole fish flat instead of bending them to fit a round pan and spoiling their shape.

Griddle pan

A ribbed cast-iron griddle pan is ideal for searing and cooking fish. They can be round, oval or rectangular. Some of the large griddles need to be used over two electric rings or gas burners on top of a stove.

Steamer

If you steam food frequently, a stainless steel steamer set is a good investment. They have a lidded, deep outer pan and a perforated inner basket. Choose the widest type that you can find. Chinese bamboo steaming baskets are an economical alternative. They come in a variety of sizes, from very small dim sum baskets to very wide baskets that are about 35cm/14in across. Chinese steaming baskets can be stacked one on top of the other so that several layers of food can be cooked at one time. Cheapest of all is a small, collapsible, perforated steamer, which unfolds like a flower to fit any pan.

Above: A single-handled wok can be used for steaming and deep-frying as well as stir-frying.

Below: Double-sided hinged rack

Above: Barbecue grilling rack for whole large fish

Below: Sardine rack

Wok

A 35cm/14in wok with a lid will be large enough to cope with most types of fish and will prove invaluable in the kitchen. There's no need to reserve this piece of equipment for stir-frying; a wok also makes an effective steamer and can be used for deep-frying.

SPECIALIST ITEMS

Barbecue grilling rack

A hinged rack in the shape of a fish makes cooking – and turning – a single large fish relatively easy. Also available are shaped racks designed to hold 6–12 sardines. These can be rectangular or round. More useful for general purposes is a double-sided hinged grill rack. These can be square or rectangular and have long handles so that several steaks or fish can be cooked on a barbecue and turned over simultaneously. However, the flat sides do tend to squash the delicate flesh of some fish. Always oil grilling racks before use to prevent the fish from sticking to them.

Smoker

The cheapest home-smoker is a lidded metal box with a rack to hold the fish. Smoke produced by placing dampened aromatic wood chippings or herbs on the coals gives extra flavour. More convenient (and much more expensive) are electric smokers. Stovetop models can be used indoors.

Left: Fish smoker

Right: Fish slices (spatulas)

Right: Fish lifters

Above: Lobster pick and crackers

Right: Tweezers and pins

OTHER USEFUL UTENSILS

Fish lifter

Resembling an elongated fish slice (spatula), the curved and perforated turner is useful for flipping over fish during cooking without breaking them.

Fish slices

Two fish slices (spatulas) with sturdy yet flexible blades will make easy work of turning most fish.

Lobster pick

Choose a pick with a two-pronged fork at the end to extract the flesh from lobster and crab legs.

Lobster crackers

If you eat a lot of lobster or crab, these are well worth having. Lobster crackers look like hinged nutcrackers (often made in the shape of lobster claws) with ridges on the inside to give a good grip. Crackerjack nutcrackers are equally effective.

Mallet

A wooden mallet is useful for cracking crustacean claws and for pounding fish escalopes (fillets).

Pins

Use dressmakers' pins with round heads to extract winkles and whelks from their shells. For safety's sake, stick them in a cork when not using, so that the sharp ends cannot prick the unwary.

Tweezers

Use these to extract small bones and pin bones from fish fillets.

Buying and Preparing Fish

Fish is only worth buying if it is absolutely fresh, and it is best if you eat it on the day you buy it. Fresh fish have shiny skin with a metallic glint and they are covered with a transparent mucus that becomes opaque when the fish is old and stale. The eyes should be clear, bright and slightly bulging. The flesh should feel firm and springy when you press it lightly with your finger; if it feels limp and your finger leaves an indentation, the fish is past its best. Stale fish has an unpleasant "fishy" smell, the skin looks dull, dryish and unattractive and the eyes are sunken.

The best test of freshness for whole fish is to open up the gills; they should be a clear red or rosy colour, not a dull brown. Look for a firm tail and plentiful, shiny close-fitting scales. A fish which has been dead for an unacceptable length of time, or which has not been properly kept, will shed its scales all over the counter. Seafish should have a pleasant odour, redolent of seaweed; freshwater fish should smell of waterweeds. There should never be more than a hint of a "fishy" smell.

Ready-prepared white fish fillets, steaks and cutlets should be neatly trimmed, with moist, firm, translucent flesh. If you must buy frozen fish, make sure that it is frozen solid, with no sign of thawing, and that the packaging is not damaged.

When buying fish, shop with an open mind and be prepared to purchase whatever looks freshest and best on the day. If you want a specific type of fish, it is best to ask the fishmonger in advance so that it can be bought fresh from the market for you. It pays to develop a relationship with one particular fishmonger – if you show that you are really interested in what you are buying, you are sure to get a much better standard of service.

An accommodating fishmonger will gut and clean your fish for you and even scale, skin and fillet it. It is not unreasonable to expect this service, but it does take time. At busy periods, therefore, be prepared to place an order and come back later to collect it. However, if you do have to prepare fish

yourself, don't despair; it is really not difficult, given a sharp, flexible knife and a little dexterity.

Quantities

Allow about 175g/6oz fish fillet, cutlets or steaks per serving for a main course. There is a lot of wastage in whole fish, so allow at least 300g/11oz per person if buying fish this way.

Storing fish

Fresh fish should be eaten as soon as possible after purchase, but most types can be kept in the refrigerator for a day or overnight if necessary. Remove any wrapping or packaging and rinse the fish in very cold water. Pat dry with kitchen paper and place on a plate. Cover with clear film (plastic wrap) and store at the bottom of the refrigerator.

Frozen fish

Although fresh fish is much nicer than frozen, for practical reasons it is not always possible to buy it, and on some occasions frozen fish may be your only option. Of course, you cannot apply the usual tests for freshness – prodding, smelling and judging the colour – so it is important to buy frozen fish from a reputable store with a quick turnover. Transport it in a freezer bag if possible and get it home and into your own freezer without delay. White fish can be kept in the freezer for three months and oily fish for two months.

Commercially frozen fish is frozen extremely rapidly and at a lower temperature than can be attained by the average domestic freezer. This preserves the delicate texture of the flesh. It is not advisable to freeze fish at home, but if you must, it should be kept at −18°C/0°F or below.

Thawing fish

If possible, thaw frozen fish overnight in the refrigerator. If you need it in a hurry, microwave the fish on the defrost setting. Separate the pieces as soon as they are thawed enough and spread out in an even layer. Remove from the microwave while still slightly icy; if fish is over-thawed it will become dry.

ROUND FISH

Scaling

Smooth-skinned round fish, such as trout and mackerel, do not need scaling. For others, such as sea bass, mullet and snapper, it is essential.

First, trim off all the fins with a strong pair of scissors. Take care with the dorsal fins on the back, as they can have sharp spines. Work in the sink, preferably under running water, or the scales will fly all over your kitchen. Otherwise you can cover the fish with a damp cloth to catch the scales. Ideally, you should use a proper fish scaler to do the job, but the back of a round-bladed knife will do almost as well. Always scale fish before filleting if you are going to cook it with the skin on.

1 Wash the fish under cold water. Cut off the three fins that run along the stomach, and the dorsal fins on the back, using strong, sharp scissors.

2 Hold the fish firmly by the tail (a cloth will give a better grip). Using a fish scaler or the back of a knife, and working from tail to head, scrape against the lie of the scales to remove them. Wash the fish again to detach any clinging scales.

Gutting/cleaning

This is a messy job, so always work on several layers of newspaper topped with greaseproof (waxed) paper. There are two ways of gutting a whole round fish: through the belly or through the gills. The former is the more usual method for round fish, but gutting through the gills is preferred if splitting the fish open would spoil its appearance. In either case, the gills should be removed before the fish is cooked, because they taste bitter. Do this by holding the fish on its back and opening the gill flaps. Push out the frilly gills and cut them off at the back of the head and under the jawbone with a sharp knife.

Cleaning through the belly

1 Starting at the site of the anal fin, slit open the belly from tail to head, using a short sharp knife.

2 Gently pull out the innards, severing them at the throat and tail if necessary. Keep any roes and red mullet livers, which are a great delicacy, but discard everything else, having first wrapped the innards thoroughly. Use a tablespoon to make sure the cavity is empty, removing any blood vessels adjacent to the backbone. Wash the cavity thoroughly, then pat the fish dry with kitchen paper.

Cleaning through the gills

1 Lay the fish on its back. Make an incision in the bottom of the belly, near the tail. Locate the end of the innards, and snip through it.

2 Cut through the bone under the lower jaw. Open the gill flaps, insert your fingers into the cavity and gently pull out the innards; these will come away through the flaps, leaving the belly intact. Wash the fish thoroughly and then pat it dry.

Boning bony fish such as mackerel and herring

1 Having removed the fins and cleaned the fish through the belly, open the fish out like a book and lay it on a board, with the skin side uppermost. Press down firmly with your fingers right along the length of the backbone.

2 Turn the fish over and gently pull the backbone away from the flesh. Cut off at the tail and pick out any small loose bones. Rinse the fish and pat dry.

Filleting round fish

1 Lay the fish on a board with the back away from you and the tail towards you. Lift the gill fin and make a diagonal cut behind the fin to the top of the head.

2 Insert the knife about halfway down the fish as close to the backbone as possible. Cut towards the tail, keeping the knife flat to the bone. Lift up the released fillet, turn the knife towards the tail and carefully slide it along the bone to free the fillet completely.

3 Turn the fish over and repeat on the other side. Remove any small pin bones from the fillets with tweezers.

Removing pin bones from fillets

1 There are always some small bones left in a fillet. Run your finger down the fillet to locate them and lift them out with tweezers.

2 Round fish also have tiny pin bones just behind the gill fins. To remove these, make a diagonal cut on either side of the line of bones with a sharp knife. Remove the V-shaped piece of flesh together with the bones.

Flat fish roes

During the breeding season, flat fish contain large roes. In the female fish, these consist of thousands of tiny eggs, which add very little to the flavour of the fish, but weigh quite a lot. So in effect, you are paying for a useless part of the fish.

The soft roes in the male fish, however, are delicious, so do not throw them away. Shallow fry them *à la meunière* in a little butter and serve as a savoury or as a garnish for the cooked fish. They are also excellent dipped in egg and breadcrumbs and then deep-fried in hot oil.

Gutting/cleaning flat fish

Flat fish are generally sold already cleaned, but it is easy to gut them yourself if necessary. Trim off the fins with sharp kitchen scissors. Make an incision just below the gills, then insert your fingers and pull out the innards, including the roe. Wrap the innards in several layers of newspaper before disposing of them. Retain the roe if you like to eat it.

Filleting flat fish

Four fillets can be obtained from flat fish, two from each side. However, the fillets won't be equal in size because the structure of the fish is not regular.

1 Lay the fish on a board with the dark skin facing up and the head pointing away from you. Using a large sharp knife, cut around the head and right down the centre line of the fish, taking the blade of the knife all the way through to the backbone.

2 Working from the head of the fish to the tail, insert the point of the knife under the flesh at the head end. Starting with the left-hand fillet, hold the knife almost parallel to the bones and carefully free the fillet with long stroking movements of the knife.

3 Turn the fish so that the head is towards you and remove the second fillet in the same way.

4 Turn the fish over and repeat the process on the other side.

Skinning whole flat fish

Traditionally, Dover sole are skinned only on the dark side, but other flat fish, such as plaice, flounder or halibut, are skinned on both sides.

1 Lay the fish on a board with the dark skin facing up and the tail towards you. Slit through the skin just below the tail and loosen the skin on both sides.

2 Using a cloth, hold the tail down firmly with one hand. Use the other hand to pull away the skin quickly and firmly towards the head.

Skinning fish fillets

Round and flat fish fillets are skinned in the same way. A really sharp knife is essential for a clean cut.

1 Lay the fillet on a board with the skin side down and the tail towards you. Dip your fingers in a little salt to stop them slipping and grip the tail firmly. Angle the knife blade down at 45° towards the skin and cut with a slight sawing action.

2 Working from the tail to the head, cut along the length of the fillet, folding the flesh forwards as you go and making sure you keep the skin taut.

Filleting fish

Fish fillets are always a popular choice, because there is no wastage, very few bones and, perhaps most importantly, someone else has done all the hard work. But it is often more practical and cheaper to fillet and skin the fish yourself, with the added bonus that you are left with the head and bones for making stock. Remember to wash the fish heads thoroughly first and then remove the gills before using them for stock.

Preparing fish fillets for cooking

Fish fillets can be cooked whole and flat, rolled and secured with a cocktail stick (toothpick), or cut into cubes.

If you are cooking the fillets whole, trim them neatly with a sharp knife, cutting off any very thin flaps of flesh along the edges.

To roll a fillet, lay it on a board skinned-side upwards. Roll the head end (the wider part) towards the tail and tuck the tail underneath. Secure the rolled fillet with a cocktail stick.

To cube a skinned fillet, use a sharp knife to cut along the length of the fillet, making strips of the desired width. This is easier if you follow the natural long lines of the flesh. Then cut each strip across into cubes.

Boning cod steaks

Cod steaks are often cooked with the bone in, or you may wish to remove it for a special meal.

1 Stand the cod steak upright on a chopping board, then insert a sharp knife at the right hand side at the top of the bone.

2 Cut firmly downwards, following the curve of the bone and keeping the knife blade as flat to the bone as possible. Repeat the process on the other side.

3 Lay the steak flat on the chopping board. Carefully lift the flesh away from the bone. Make a small cut across the top to release the bone. Fold the flesh into the middle to make a neat, boneless steak.

COOKING FISH

Fish is an extremely versatile food and there are any number of quick and delicious ways to cook it, "quick" being the operative word, since it is all too easy to overcook the delicate flesh. Almost any cooking method suits fish, except boiling, although simmering is fine for hearty soups. Because fish is so delicate, it is always better to undercook rather than overcook it; you can always give it a little extra cooking, but there is no redressing the dry texture and lack of flavour once it is overdone.

It is impossible to give precise cooking times for fish, because so many factors come into play: the thickness of fillets, for example; whether they are much thinner at one end than the other; the type of fish and so on. Fish is cooked when the internal temperature reaches about 63°C/145°F. You can use a meat thermometer to test this, but with experience you will soon be able to judge by eye.

To test whether fish fillets are cooked, insert a small knife into the centre and part the flesh; it should look opaque rather than translucent. Ease the flesh away from the bone; it should just come away, not fall off easily. Alternatively, press a fork into the thickest part of the fillet. If the prongs go in only halfway, cook the fish for a little longer. If the prongs sink in, meeting a slight resistance near the bone, then the fish is done.

Always take the fish out of the refrigerator at least 30 minutes before cooking to be sure that it cooks evenly.

Cooking without heat

Very fresh fish can be "cooked" without heat by being marinated or soused with lemon juice or white wine vinegar. The acids soften the flesh and turn it opaque. The classic dish of this type is ceviche, where cubes or strips of firm white fish (turbot, cod, halibut, snapper, etc.) are marinated in lemon juice, salt and finely chopped chilli for at least 2 hours, until the flesh turns pearly white.

Cooking "au bleu"

This old-fashioned method of cooking is mainly used for freshwater fish, such as trout, carp, tench or pike, which are still alive or exceedingly fresh. The fish is killed, cleaned through the gills, then sprinkled with boiling vinegar, which turns the slime on its skin a steely blue colour (hence "au bleu").

Enough court-bouillon to cover the fish is heated. The fish is placed in a flameproof dish or fish kettle and the court-bouillon is poured over the fish. The dish or kettle is covered and the fish is simmered gently until it is just cooked. The cooked fish can be served hot or cold. If necessary, the fish should be scaled before being served.

Baking

Whole fish and some chunky fish steaks and fillets, such as cod or halibut, are perfect for baking. Because the flesh is delicate, it is best to bake fish at a lower temperature than would be used for meat, and certainly no higher than 200°C/400°F/Gas 6.

Baking *en papillote* (in a parcel) is an extremely healthy way of cooking, because it uses no fat and retains all the flavour of the fish.

Court-bouillon

This flavoured stock is invaluable for poaching fish or shellfish. The recipe makes about 1 litre/1¾ pints/4 cups.

1 Slice 1 small onion, 2 carrots and the white part of 1 leek.

2 Place the vegetables in a pan and add 2 parsley stalks, 2 bay leaves, 2 lemon slices, 300ml/½ pint/ 1¼ cups dry white wine and 90ml/ 6 tbsp white wine vinegar. Add 30ml/2 tbsp salt, a few white peppercorns and 1 litre/1¾ pints/ 4 cups water.

3 Bring to the boil, lower the heat and simmer for 20 minutes. Strain and leave to cool before using.

Braising

This is another excellent cooking method for whole fish or large fillets.

1 Butter a flameproof dish and make a thick bed of thinly sliced or shredded vegetables, such as a mixture of carrots, onions, fennel and celery.

2 Place the fish on top and pour on enough white or red wine and/or fish or chicken stock to come nearly halfway up the fish.

3 Sprinkle over 15ml/1 tbsp chopped fresh herbs, cover with buttered greaseproof (waxed) paper and bring to the boil. Braise at a low temperature on top of the stove or in a preheated oven at 180°C/350°F/Gas 4, allowing about 20 minutes for a 1kg/2¼lb fish; 10–15 minutes for large fillets.

Fish stock

For many recipes, a good fish stock is essential. It is very simple to make. White fish bones and trimmings make the best stock. Ask the fishmonger for these whenever you buy fish; even if you cannot make stock that day, you can freeze them for later use. To make about 1 litre/1¾ pints/4 cups stock, you will need 1kg/2¼lb white fish bones, heads and trimmings.

1 Wash the fish heads thoroughly then remove the gills. Chop the heads and bones if necessary. Put them in a large pan.

3 Add 150ml/¼ pint/⅔ cup dry white wine. Toss in 6 white peppercorns and a bouquet garni, add 1 litre/ 1¾ pints/4 cups water.

2 Coarsely chop the white part of 1 leek (or ½ fennel bulb), 1 onion and 1 celery stick. Add these to the fish heads and bones in the pan.

4 Bring to the boil, lower the heat and simmer for only 20 minutes (no longer). Strain through a sieve lined with muslin (cheesecloth).

Frying

Shallow frying or pan-frying

For this popular method, pieces of fish (fillets, steaks or cutlets) or small whole fish are cooked in a little fat in a shallow pan to caramelize and colour the outside. This can either be a prelude to another cooking method or the fish can be fully cooked in the pan. Before frying, the fish can be coated with flour, breadcrumbs or oatmeal. Plain fish can be fried without fat using a non-stick pan, but it will have to be cooked carefully to prevent drying out.

Frying in butter gives the best flavour, but it burns easily, so should be combined with a small amount of oil. Alternatively, use clarified butter or just oil. Heat the fat in the pan until very hot, put in the fish and seal briefly on both sides. Lower the heat and cook the fish gently until done. If the pieces of fish are large or the recipe is more complex, it may be necessary to finish cooking in a moderate oven.

Deep-frying

Because fish is delicate, it must be coated in flour or some kind of batter before being deep-fried. This seals in the flavoursome juices, so that the fish is deliciously crisp on the outside and moist inside. Most fish is suitable for deep-frying, from tiny whitebait to large chunky fillets.

Use plenty of oil and make sure that it is really hot (180–190°C/350–375°F) before putting in the fish. Use an electric deep-fryer, or test by carefully dropping a cube of bread into the hot oil; if it browns within 30 seconds, then the oil is hot enough. Larger pieces of fish should be cooked at a slightly lower temperature than small pieces like goujons. This allows the heat to penetrate to the centre before the outside burns. Do not cook too many pieces of fish at the same time, or the temperature of the oil will drop. Oil used for frying fish should never be used for any other purpose, as it will inevitably impart a fishy flavour.

1 Heat the oil in a deep-fryer to 180°C/350°F. Dip the fish in seasoned flour, add to the oil and cook until golden.

2 Drain the fish on a double thickness of kitchen paper before serving.

Goujons of sole or plaice

The name goujon comes from the French for gudgeon, which are small freshwater fish often served crisply fried. Goujons are strips of fish, such as sole, plaice or flounder; which are deep-fried and served with tartare sauce. They are ideal for persuading children to eat fish, especially if they can eat them with their fingers.

SERVES FOUR

INGREDIENTS
   8 sole, plaice or flounder fillets
   120ml/4fl oz/½ cup milk
   50g/2oz/1 cup plain (all-purpose) flour
   vegetable oil, for deep-frying
   salt and ground black pepper

1 Skin the fish fillets and cut them into 7.5 x 2.5cm/3 x 1in strips. Season the milk with a little salt and pepper. Pour it into a shallow bowl, and place the flour in another bowl or spread it out on a plate.

2 Dip the fish strips first into the milk, then into the flour. Shake off the excess flour.

3 Fill a large pan one-third full with vegetable oil. Heat to about 185°C/360°F or until a small cube of bread dropped into the oil turns brown in 30 seconds.

4 Carefully lower the fish strips into the hot oil, adding 4 or 5 at a time. Fry for about 3 minutes, turning them occasionally using a slotted spoon, until the strips rise to the surface and turn golden brown in colour.

5 Lift out each piece of cooked fish with a slotted spoon and drain them on a double thickness of kitchen paper. Keep the cooked goujons hot in the oven while you cook successive batches.

Stir-frying

This quick-cooking method is perfect for fish, prawns (shrimp) and squid.

1 Cut the fish or squid into bite-size strips; leave prawn tails whole, with the tail shells intact. Toss them in a little cornflour (cornstarch).

2 Heat a little oil in a wok over a very high heat, add a few pieces of fish or shellfish and stir-fry for a few moments.

Searing

This method is best for thickish fillets that have not been skinned or small whole fish, such as sardines and red mullet.

1 Smear the base of a heavy frying pan or griddle with a little oil and heat until smoking. Lightly brush both sides of the fish with oil and put it into the hot pan.

2 Sear for a couple of minutes, until the skin is golden brown, then turn the fish over and cook on the other side.

Grilling and Cooking on the Barbecue

Fish steaks, thick fillets and relatively small whole fish, such as sardines, red mullet or trout, can be grilled (broiled) or cooked on a barbecue, as can crustaceans. The grill (broiler) should be preheated to a very high heat so that the fish juices are sealed in quickly. Griddle pans are better than overhead grills, but either will do. Grilling on a barbecue can be a little more tricky, as bastes or marinades used to keep the fish moist can drip and cause flare-ups.

All grilled fish will benefit from being marinated for 1 hour in a mixture of oil and lemon juice before being cooked. If the fish is to be cooked whole, make several slashes down to the bone on either side to make sure that the fish cooks quickly and evenly. Brush the grill rack and fish with oil to prevent sticking. Thin fillets need only be grilled on one side, without a grill rack. Brush the grill pan with oil. Place it under the grill until hot, then pass both sides of the fish through the oil before grilling on one side only; the underside will cook at the same time.

Microwaving

Fish can be cooked successfully in a microwave oven. As long as it is not overcooked, it will be moist and full of flavour. Always cover the fish with clear film (plastic wrap). Cook it on full power (100 per cent) for the shortest possible time recommended in your handbook, then give it a resting period to allow it to finish cooking by residual heat. Cooking time depends on the thickness and density of the fish. The following are general guidelines for 500g/1¼lb fish, but test before the end of the given time to check that the flesh is still succulent.

Whole round fish, thick fillets, steaks and cutlets: cook for 4–5 minutes, then leave to stand for 5 minutes.

Flat fish, thin fillets: cook for 3–4 minutes, then rest for 3–4 minutes.

Fish with denser flesh (monkfish, tuna, skate, etc): cook for 6–7 minutes, then leave to stand for 5 minutes.

Cook fillets in a single layer, thinner parts towards the centre, or tuck a thin tail end underneath a thicker portion.

Fish can also be microwaved whole, provided that they will fit in the oven. Slash the skin in several places to prevent it from splitting. Turn the fish over halfway through cooking.

Poaching

Cooking in a stock or court-bouillon brings out the flavour of fresh fish.

1 A whole fish can be poached in a fish kettle, provided it is not too large, while portions are best placed in a single layer in a shallow heatproof dish.

2 Cover with cold court-bouillon or stock, add a few herbs and flavourings.

3 Lay some buttered or greaseproof (waxed) paper on top and heat until the liquid just starts to tremble. At this point, thin pieces of fish may be done. Continue to cook thicker pieces at a bare simmer either on top of the stove or in the oven, until the flesh is just opaque. For 1kg/2¼lb fish allow 7–8 minutes. To serve the fish cold, leave it to cool in the poaching liquid.

Butter sauce for poached fish
Poached fish needs very little enhancement other than a simple sauce that has been made from the poaching liquid.

1 Remove the cooked fish from the poaching liquid and keep it hot while you make the sauce.

2 Strain the liquid into a pan and place it over a medium heat. Simmer gently until the liquid has reduced by half.

3 Whisk in some cold diced butter or a little double (heavy) cream to make a smooth, velvety sauce. Season to taste. Pour the sauce over the fish and serve.

Roasting

This is more usually associated with meat, but it is an excellent method of cooking whole fish and "meaty" cuts, such as monkfish tails or swordfish steaks. The oven should be preheated to very hot – 230°C/450°F/Gas 8 – with the roasting pan inside. The fish will then be seared by the heat of the pan, and the juices will not escape.

Drizzle a little olive oil over the fish before roasting. For extra flavour, roast it on a bed of rosemary, fennel or Mediterranean vegetables.

Smoking

Although most of the smoked fish we buy has been commercially smoked, it is easy to smoke your own, adding a new dimension to bland tastes.

Hot smoking

This method cooks and smokes the food at the same time, using a special smoker filled with fragrant hardwood chips (hickory and oak are popular), which give the fish a delicious flavour. Domestic smokers are quite small and very easy to use. Some can be used indoors, but on the whole they are best suited to outdoor use, where the smoke can dissipate easily. For large quantities you can use a kettle barbecue. Heat the wood chips to 80–85°C/176–185°F, place the fish on the rack, put on the lid and smoke until the fish looks like pale burnished wood.

Cold smoking

This method cures but does not cook the fish. It must first be salted in dry salt or brine, then hung up to drip dry before smoking at 30–35°C/86–95°F.

Tea smoking

This Chinese method of smoking is usually used for duck, but imparts a wonderful flavour to oily fish, such as mackerel and tuna, and shellfish such as scallops and mussels.

1 Line a wok with foil and sprinkle in 30ml/2 tbsp each of raw long grain rice, sugar and aromatic tea leaves.

2 Place a wire rack on top of the wok and then arrange the fish in a single layer on the rack. Cover the wok with a lid or more foil and cook over a very high heat until you see smoke.

3 Lower the heat slightly (some smoke should still escape from the wok) and cook until the fish is done. A mackerel fillet takes 8–10 minutes, large prawns (shrimp) 5–7 minutes.

Steaming

Many people assume that steaming will result in bland, flavourless fish. Far from it; this method of cooking enhances the natural flavour and the fish remains moist and retains its shape, even if you overcook it.

Steaming is the healthiest way of cooking fish. It uses no fat and because the fish is not in contact with the cooking liquid, fewer valuable nutrients are lost in the process.

1 Half-fill the base pan of a steamer with water and bring it to the boil. Place the fish in a single layer in the steamer basket, leaving room to enable the steam to circulate freely.

2 Lower the fish into the steamer, making sure that the insert stands well clear of the boiling water.

3 Lay a sheet of greaseproof (waxed) paper over the surface of the fish, then cover the pan tightly with a lid or foil and steam until the fish is just cooked.

4 Fish cooks very quickly in a steamer, but take care that the level of the water does not fall too low. Check once or twice during cooking and keep a supply of boiling water on hand to add more.

Alternative steamers

There are plenty of purpose-made steamers on the market, which range from the hugely expensive stainless steel models to modest Chinese bamboo baskets. However, you can easily improvise with a pan, any perforated container (a colander or sieve, for example) and some foil. Make sure that the pan is large enough to hold a good depth of water.

Whatever the type of steamer, remember that the golden rule of steaming is not to allow the boiling liquid to touch the steamer basket or the fish or shellfish.

A Chinese bamboo steamer, which can be used in a wok or on top of a large pan, is ideal for steaming fish or shellfish. If you like, arrange the fish on a bed of aromatic flavourings, such as lemon or lime slices and sprigs of fresh herbs. Alternatively, before adding the fish or shellfish, you can place finely shredded vegetables, seaweed or samphire in the base of the steamer to give extra flavour.

BUYING, PREPARING AND COOKING SHELLFISH

The term "shellfish" is loosely applied to seafood other than fish. Strictly speaking, it means aquatic invertebrates with shells or shell-like carapaces. This includes the crustaceans – lobsters, crabs, prawns (shrimp) and similar creatures – as well as some molluscs, such as clams, mussels and oysters. For convenience, however, the category extends to other molluscs too, such as the cephalopods (octopus, squid and cuttlefish) and lesser known sea creatures, such as sea urchins.

When discussing shellfish, it is impossible to divorce preparation and cooking techniques, since one is bound up so closely with the other. Lobsters and crabs, for instance, are cooked live; mussels are opened and cooked in one simple process.

Crustaceans and molluscs need very little cooking to enhance their already superb flavour. Indeed, many molluscs can be eaten raw, provided they are extremely fresh and come from unpolluted waters. Crustaceans of all types must be cooked; unlike fish, the larger specimens can be boiled. Many of the methods used for cooking fish are suitable for shellfish – poaching, frying, grilling (broiling) and steaming.

CRUSTACEANS

Lobsters and crabs

Buying

Live lobsters or crabs should smell very fresh and still be lively and aggressive when picked up. The tails of lobsters should spring back sharply when they are opened out. Crabs should feel heavy for their size, but you should make sure this is not because there is water inside the shell. Shake them – any sloshing sounds are a bad sign. The shell should neither be soft nor should it contain any cracks or holes.

Lobsters in particular command a high price, which reflects the effort involved in catching them. It is a good idea to check that lobsters and crabs have both claws, as one may often be lost in a fight. If a claw is missing, make sure the price is reduced accordingly.

Preparing and cooking a live lobster

1 The most humane way to kill a live lobster is to render it unconscious by placing it in a freezerproof dish or tray and covering it with crushed ice. Alternatively, put the lobster in the freezer for 2 hours.

2 When the lobster is very cold and no longer moving, place it on a chopping board and drive the tip of a large, sharp heavy knife or a very strong skewer through the centre of the cross on its head. According to the experts, death is instantaneous.

3 If you can't face stabbing the lobster, put it in a large pan of cold, heavily salted water and bring slowly to the boil. The lobster will expire before the water boils.

4 Alternatively, you can add the comatose lobster to a large pan of boiling water. Plunge it in head first and immediately clamp on the lid. Bring the water back to the boil.

5 Lower the heat and simmer the lobster gently for about 15 minutes for the first 450g/1lb and then allow 10 minutes more for each subsequent 450g/1lb, up to a maximum of 40 minutes.

6 When cooked, the lobster will turn a deep brick red. Drain off the water and leave to cool, if not eating hot.

If cooking two or more lobsters in the same pan, wait until the water comes back to the boil before adding the second one. More than two lobsters should be cooked separately.

Always buy cooked lobsters or crabs from a reputable supplier who cooks them fresh every day. The colour should be vibrant and the crustaceans ought to feel heavy for their size. Cooked lobsters should have their tails tightly curled under their bodies; avoid specimens with floppy tails, which may have been dead when they were cooked.

Quantities

When calculating how much you should buy, allow about 450g/1lb per person.

Storing

For practical reasons you will wish to cook live lobsters or crabs on the day you buy them, unless you want them live in your bathtub.

If you cannot pop them straight into the pot, live crustaceans can be wrapped in wet newspaper or covered in a very damp dishtowel and kept in the coldest part of the refrigerator. If you intend the crustaceans to be unconscious when you kill them, you may want to put them in the freezer for a couple of hours or submerge them in crushed ice.

Removing the meat from a boiled lobster

1 Lay the lobster on its back and twist off the large legs and claws.

2 Carefully crack open the claws with a wooden mallet or the back of a heavy knife and remove the meat, keeping the pieces as large as possible. Scoop out the meat from the legs with a lobster pick or the handle of a small teaspoon.

3 On a chopping board, stretch out the body of the lobster so that its tail is extended. Turn it on to its back and, holding it firmly with one hand, use a sharp, heavy knife to cut the lobster neatly in half along its entire length.

4 Discard the whitish sac and the feathery gills from the head and the grey-black intestinal thread that runs down the tail.

5 Carefully remove all the meat from each half of the tail – it should come out in one piece.

6 Keep the greenish tomalley (liver) and the coral (roe), which are delicious. This roe is only to be found in the female or "hen" lobsters. Like the tomalley, it is usually added to a sauce. The creamy flesh close to the shell can also be scraped out and used in a sauce.

Grilling lobster

Preheat the grill (broiler) to high. Boil the lobster for 3 minutes only, then drain, split in half and clean.

Lay the halves of the lobster cut side up in a grill pan, brush generously with melted butter and cook for about 10 minutes, spooning on more melted butter halfway through.

If the lobster has already been killed by stabbing, it can just be split and cooked for about 12 minutes.

Cooking lobster on the barbecue

Prepare the lobster as for grilling (broiling). Brush the cut sides with butter seasoned with garlic or cayenne. Grill cut side down over moderately hot coals for about 5 minutes, then turn the halves over and grill them on the shell for 5 minutes more. Turn the lobster halves over once more, brush the flesh with more melted butter and grill it flesh side down for 3–4 minutes more.

Preparing a live crab

To kill a crab humanely, chill it by submerging it in ice, or leave it in the freezer for a couple of hours until it is comatose (see Preparing and cooking a live lobster, page 24). When the crab is no longer moving, lay it on its back on a chopping board, lift up the tail flap and look for a small hole at the base of a distinct groove. Drive an awl or sturdy skewer into this hole, then carefully push the skewer between the mouth plates between the eyes. The crab is now ready for cooking.

Alternatively, if stabbing a crab does not appeal to you, the live crab can be killed and cooked simultaneously. There are two ways of doing this. Either plunge the crustacean into a large pan of salted, boiling water, bring back to the boil and cook for 10–12 minutes; or place it in a pan of cold salted water and bring it slowly to the boil. The latter method is reckoned to be the more humane, because the crab becomes sleepy as the temperature rises and succumbs well before the water reaches boiling point. Whichever way you choose, calculate the cooking time from the moment that the water boils, and do not boil the crab for more than 12 minutes, whatever its size.

Removing the meat from a cooked crab

1 Lay the cooked crab on its back on a large chopping board. Hold the crab firmly with one hand and break off the tail flap. Twist off both the claws and the legs.

2 Stand the crab on its head and insert a heavy knife between the body and shell. Twist the knife firmly to separate them so that you can lift the honeycomb body out.

3 Alternatively, hold the crab firmly and use your thumbs to ease the body out of the shell.

4 Remove and discard the feathery, grey gills (these are unattractively but descriptively known as "dead men's fingers"), which are attached to either side of the body.

5 Press down on the top shell to detach the spongy stomach sac – this is found directly behind the mouth. Cut the honeycomb body into quarters with a large, heavy knife.

6 Carefully pick out the white meat, using a skewer.

7 Use a teaspoon to scoop out all the creamy brown meat from the back shell, then scoop out the thin solid brown meat from inside the flaps.

8 Crack open the claws and legs with a mallet (or use the back of a heavy knife), then remove the claw meat in the largest possible pieces. Pick or scrape out the leg meat with a lobster pick or a skewer. The smallest legs can be kept whole and used to make a delicious shellfish stock.

Prawns, Shrimps, Langoustines and Crayfish

Buying

There is some confusion over the terms prawn and shrimp. In America, the word shrimp refers to all sizes and types of prawns, but in most countries shrimps are a tiny separate species.

Prawns and shrimp are not sold alive, but crayfish must be as their flesh deteriorates quickly after death and can become poisonous. All fresh raw prawns and shrimp should have crisp, firm shells and a fresh smell. Do not buy any that smell of ammonia. If you cannot buy fresh prawns or shrimp, buy frozen. Transport them in a freezer bag and get them into your freezer as quickly as possible. Do not buy frozen prawns or shrimp that have been thawed.

Quantities

If you buy them with the shells on, allow about 300g/11oz prawns or shrimp per serving. Some crustaceans – Dublin Bay prawns, for example – tend to be sold shelled, without the heads. If you buy these in the shell, remember that there will be a lot of wastage (up to 80 per cent) so buy a generous amount. Keep the shells to flavour sauces and stocks.

Storing

Fresh prawns and shrimp should be eaten as soon as possible after purchase. Crayfish – including the yabby – are the exception. They are none too fussy about what they eat, so it is best to purge them after purchase. Place them in a bowl, cover with a damp dishtowel and leave in the coldest part of the refrigerator for 24 hours.

Poaching langoustines or prawns

Raw langoustines or prawns are best poached in sea water. Failing that, use a well-flavoured *nage* (fish stock) or heavily salted water. Bring the poaching liquid to the boil in a large deep pan, drop in the crustaceans and simmer for only a minute or two, depending on their size. Be careful not overcook the shellfish, or the delicate flesh will become tough.

Peeling and deveining raw prawns

Raw prawns and large shrimp are often peeled before cooking. Raw prawns must have their intestinal tracts removed before cooking, a process that is known as "deveining". It is not necessary to devein very small shrimp.

1 Pull off the head and legs from each prawn or shrimp, then carefully peel off the body shell with your fingers. Leave on the tail "fan" if you like.

2 To remove the intestinal vein from prawns, make a shallow incision down the centre of the curved back of the prawn using a small sharp knife, cutting all the way from the tail to the head.

3 Carefully pick out the thin black vein that runs the length of the prawn with the tip of the knife and discard.

Grilling or cooking langoustines or large prawns on the barbecue

This method is also suitable for crayfish. The shellfish can be raw or cooked.

1 Preheat the grill (broiler) or barbecue to hot. Butterfly the shellfish by laying them on their backs and splitting them in half lengthways, without cutting right through to the back shell.

2 Open the shellfish out like a book and brush the cut sides all over with a mixture of olive oil and lemon juice.

3 Lay the shellfish in a grill (broiler) pan or on a barbecue rack. Cook for 2–3 minutes on each side; cooked shellfish for about half this time. To make sure they keep their shape, you could thread the butterflied shellfish on to skewers before cooking.

Peeling cooked prawns, langoustines and crayfish

1 Twist off the heads and, in the case of langoustines, the claws.

2 Squeeze the shellfish along their length and pull off the shell and the legs with your fingers.

3 To keep the tail fan, carefully peel off the last piece of body shell, otherwise, squeeze the end of the tail and remove.

Fantail or phoenix prawns
This way of serving large prawns (shrimp) comes from China. The cooked prawns, with their bright red tails, are supposed to resemble the legendary phoenix, which in China is a symbol of dignity and good luck.

1 Remove the heads from the prawns and peel away most of the body shell with your fingers. Leave a little of the shell to keep the tail "fan" intact.

2 Make a long shallow incision in the back of each prawn and remove the black intestinal vein with the point of the knife.

3 Hold the prepared prawns by the tails and dip them lightly in a little seasoned cornflour (cornstarch), and then in a frothy batter before deep-frying them in hot oil until the tails, which are free from batter, turn red.

Potted Shrimp
These are very simple to make and will keep for several days. If possible, use fresh, not frozen, brown shrimp. They are tedious to peel, but worth the effort. Serve with buttered brown bread or toast and lemon wedges.

SERVES FOUR

INGREDIENTS
    350g/12oz/1^{1}/2 cups butter
    225g/8oz cooked peeled shrimp,
        thawed if frozen
    1 bay leaf
    1 large blade of mace or 2.5ml/
        ^{1}/2 tsp ground mace
    ground black pepper and
        cayenne pepper

2 Clarify the remaining butter, by placing it in a small pan and heating very gently over a low heat until melted and foaming. Strain through a sieve lined with muslin (cheesecloth) into a small bowl, leaving the milky solids at the base of the pan.

1 Melt 250g/9oz/generous 1 cup of the butter in a pan. Add the shrimp, bay leaf, mace and seasoning. Heat gently, then discard the bay leaf and mace. Divide the shrimp between four ramekins and leave to set.

3 Spoon the clarified butter over the potted shrimp, making sure they are completely covered. When cool, transfer the ramekins to the refrigerator and chill for up to 2–3 days, until ready to serve.

MOLLUSCS

Bivalves (mussels, clams, oysters and scallops)

Buying

Like other types of shellfish, molluscs deteriorate rapidly, so you must make sure that they are alive when you cook them. Scallops are an exception, as they are often sold already opened and cleaned. Bivalves such as mussels, clams and oysters should contain plenty of sea water and feel heavy for their size. Do not buy any that have broken shells. If the shells gape, give them a sharp tap on a hard surface. They should snap shut immediately; if they don't, do not buy them as they will either be dead or moribund.

Quantities

When buying mussels, clams or similar shellfish, allow about 450g/1lb per person, as the shells make up much of the weight. Four or five scallops will serve one person as a main course.

Storing

Mussels, clams and other bivalves must be eaten within one day of purchase, but will keep briefly stored in the refrigerator. Tip them into a large bowl, cover with a damp cloth and keep them in the coldest part of the refrigerator (at 2°C/36°F) until ready to use. Some people advocate sprinkling them with oatmeal and leaving them overnight to fatten up. Oysters can be kept for a couple of days, thanks to the sea water contained in their shells. Store them cupped side down. Never store shellfish in fresh water, or they will die. Ready-frozen bivalves should not be kept in the freezer for more than 2 months.

Preparing

Scrub bivalves under cold running water, using a stiff brush to remove any sand or dirt. Open the shellfish over a bowl to catch the delicious juice. This will be gritty, so must be strained before being used. Cockles (small clams) usually contain a lot of sand. They will expel this if left overnight in a bucket of clean sea water or salted water.

Cleaning mussels

1 Wash the mussels in plenty of cold water, scrubbing them well. Scrape off any barnacles with a knife.

2 Give any open mussels a sharp tap; discard any that fail to close.

3 Pull out and discard the fibrous "beard" that sprouts between the two halves of the shell.

Moules Marinière

1 Chop 1 onion and 2 shallots. Put in a large pan with 25g/1oz/2 tbsp butter and cook over a low heat until translucent.

2 Add 300ml/½ pint/1¼ cups white wine, a bay leaf and a sprig of fresh thyme. Bring to the boil. Add 2kg/4½lb cleaned mussels, cover the pan tightly and steam over a high heat for 2 minutes. Shake the pan vigorously and steam for 2 minutes more. Shake again and steam until all the mussels have opened. Discard any closed ones.

3 Stir in 30ml/2 tbsp chopped fresh parsley and serve immediately.

Steaming mussels

This method opens and cooks the shellfish all at once. It is also suitable for clams, cockles and razor-shells.

1 Put a few splashes of white wine into a wide pan. Add some finely chopped onion and chopped fresh herbs, if you like, and bring to the boil.

2 Add the mussels, cover the pan and shake over a high heat for 2–3 minutes. Remove the mussels that have opened.

3 Replace the lid and shake the pan over a high heat for another minute or so. By this time all the mussels that are going to open should have done so; discard any that remain closed.

4 Strain the cooking liquid through a sieve lined with muslin (cheesecloth).

5 The cooking liquid can be reheated and used as a thin sauce, or heated until it has reduced by about half. For a richer sauce, stir in a little cream.

6 The mussels can be eaten as they are, or the top shell can be removed and the mussel served on the half shell. Alternatively, they can be grilled (broiled), but take care not to overcook.

Grilling mussels and clams

Steam open the molluscs and remove the top shell. Arrange in their half shells in a single layer on a baking sheet. Spoon over a little melted butter flavoured with chopped garlic and parsley. Top with fresh breadcrumbs, sprinkle with a little more melted butter and cook under a hot grill (broiler) until golden brown and bubbling.

Opening clams and razor-shells

The easiest way to open clams or razor-shells is by steaming them, in the same way as you do for mussels. However, this method is not suitable if the clams are going to be eaten raw like oysters.

1 Protect your hand with a clean dishtowel, then cup the clam in your palm, holding it firmly. Work over a bowl to catch the juices.

2 Insert a sharp pointed knife between the shells. Run the knife away from you to open the clam, twisting it to force the shells apart.

3 Cut through the hinge muscle, then use a spoon to scoop out the muscle on the bottom shell. This part of the mollusc should be discarded.

Opening small clams in the microwave

1 Thin-shelled molluscs like small clams can be opened in the microwave. Place them in a bowl and cook on full power (100 per cent) for about 2 minutes.

2 Remove the open molluscs and repeat the process until all have opened. Do not try to open large clams, oysters or scallops this way, as the thick shells will absorb the microwaves and cook the molluscs before they open.

Opening scallops in the oven

The easiest way to open scallops is to place them, rounded side down, on a baking sheet and place them in an oven preheated to 160°C/325°F/Gas 3 for a few moments until they gape sufficiently for you to complete the job by hand.

1 Spread the scallops in a single layer on a baking sheet. Heat them until they gape, then remove them from the oven.

2 Grasp a scallop in a clean dishtowel, flat side up. Using a long, flexible knife, run the blade along the inner surface of the flat shell to cut through the muscle that holds the shells together. This done, ease the shells apart completely.

3 Lift off the top shell. Pull out and discard the black intestinal sac and the yellowish frilly membrane.

4 Cut the white scallop and orange coral from the bottom shell and wash briefly under cold running water. Remove and discard the white ligament attached to the scallop flesh.

Cooking scallops

Scallop flesh is very delicate and needs barely any cooking; an overcooked scallop loses its flavour and becomes extremely rubbery. Small scallops need to be cooked for only a few seconds; larger ones take a minute or two.

Scallops can be pan-fried, steamed, poached and baked au gratin. They are also delicious grilled (broiled).

Wrap scallops in thin strips of bacon or pancetta before grilling (broiling) them to protect the delicate texture and add extra flavour.

Opening oysters

You really do need a special oyster knife if you are to open – or shuck – oysters successfully. If you haven't got one, use a strong knife with a short, blunt blade.

1 Scrub the shells under cold running water. Wrap one hand in a clean dishtowel and hold the oyster with the cupped shell down and the narrow hinged end towards you.

2 Push the point of the knife into the small gap in the hinge and twist it to and fro between the shells until the hinge breaks. Lever open the top shell.

3 Slide the knife along the inner edges of the top shell and sever the muscle that joins the oyster to the shell. Lift off the top shell, leaving the oyster in its juices in the bottom shell.

Cooking oysters

Oysters are best eaten raw with just a squeeze of lemon or a dash of Tabasco sauce. If you prefer to cook them, do so very briefly. They can be poached or steamed for a minute or two and served with a white wine sauce; grilled (broiled) like mussels or clams; deep-fried in cornmeal batter; or added to meat, fish or shellfish pies or casseroles.

Gastropods (winkles, whelks and abalone)

Small gastropods such as winkles (also known as periwinkles), whelks and limpets need little preparation other than a quick rinse under cold running water. They are removed from the shell after cooking, either with a small fork or, in the case of winkles, with a dressmakers' pin. Larger gastropods, such as abalone (or their cousins, the ormers) and conch, must be removed from the shell and beaten vigorously to tenderize them before cooking. In some fishmarkets, especially those in California, tenderized abalone is sold in slices.

Cooking abalone or ormers

There are two schools of thought when it comes to cooking abalone. One claims the best way is to marinate the flesh, then cook it briefly in butter; the other claims that if abalone is to be truly tender, it needs long, slow cooking. Both methods work equally well, but only if the abalone has been thoroughly beaten first.

Boiling winkles or whelks

Ideally, these shellfish should be boiled in sea water, so if you gather them yourself, take home a bucket (pail) of water in which to cook them. Otherwise, use heavily salted water. Bring this to the boil in a pan, add the winkles or whelks and simmer for about 5 minutes for winkles; 10 minutes for whelks.

To test whether winkles or whelks are ready, use a fork or dressmakers' pin to remove the body from the shell. It should come out easily. If not, cook for a little longer, but do not overcook, or the winkles will become brittle and the whelks tough.

Cephalopods (octopus, squid, cuttlefish)

Buying

You may have seen Mediterranean fishermen flailing freshly caught octopus against the rocks to tenderize them. It is said that they need to be beaten at least a hundred times before they become palatable. Fortunately for the consumer large octopus are usually sold already prepared, so we are spared this unpleasant task. Small octopuses can be dealt with in much the same way as squid, but even they have tough flesh which needs to be beaten with a wooden mallet before being cooked.

Most fishmongers and supermarkets now sell ready-cleaned squid, but cuttlefish are more usually sold whole. Both are easy to clean, and are prepared in similar ways. When buying fresh squid, look for specimens that smell fresh and salty, have good colour and are slippery. Avoid squid with broken outer skins, or from which the ink has leaked.

Quantities

The amount of octopus or squid that will be required will depend on how substantial a sauce you are going to serve. As a general guide, 1kg/2¼lb octopus, squid or cuttlefish will be more than ample for six people.

Storing

As for fish.

Cleaning and preparing octopus

1 Cut the tentacles off the octopus and remove the beak and eyes. Cut off the head where it joins the body and discard it. Turn the body inside out and discard the entrails.

2 Pound the body and tentacles with a mallet until tender, then place in boiling water and simmer very gently for at least 1 hour, or until tender. Serve with a flavoursome sauce.

Baby Octopus and Red Wine Stew
Baby octopuses are tender and delicious, particularly cooked in a stew with the robust flavours of red wine and oregano. Unlike large octopuses, they need no tenderizing before cooking.

SERVES FOUR

INGREDIENTS
  900g/2lb baby octopuses
  450g/1lb onions, sliced
  2 bay leaves
  60ml/4 tbsp olive oil
  4 garlic cloves, crushed
  450g/1lb tomatoes, peeled
    and sliced
  15ml/1 tbsp each chopped fresh
    oregano and parsley
  salt and ground black pepper

Put the octopuses in a pan of simmering water with a quarter of the sliced onion and the bay leaves. Cook gently for 1 hour. Drain the octopuses and cut into bitesize pieces. Discard the heads. Heat the olive oil in a pan, add the remaining onions and the garlic cloves and cook for 3 minutes. Add the tomatoes and herbs, season with salt and pepper and cook, stirring, for about 5 minutes until pulpy, then cover the pan with a lid and cook very gently for 1½ hours.

Cleaning and preparing squid

1 Rinse the squid thoroughly under cold running water. Holding the body firmly in one hand, grasp the tentacles at the base with the other, and gently but firmly pull the head away from the body. As you do this the soft, yellowish entrails will come away.

2 Use a sharp knife to cut off the tentacles from the head of the squid. Reserve the tentacles but discard the hard beak in the middle.

Squid ink

This can be used as a wonderful flavouring and colouring for home-made pasta and risotto, or to make a sauce. Having removed the ink sac, put it in a small bowl. Pierce it with the tip of a knife to release the thick, granular ink. Dilute this with a little water and stir until smooth. Use the ink right away, or freeze it for later use.

There is ink in an octopus too. It is found in the liver and is very strongly flavoured. Like squid ink, it should be diluted in water before being used.

3 Remove and reserve the ink sac, then discard the head.

4 Peel the purplish-grey membrane away from the body.

5 Pull out the "quill". Wash the body under cold running water.

6 Cut the body, flaps and tentacles to the required size.

Cooking squid

Squid is often cut into rings and deep-fried. It can also be stewed, stuffed and baked, or sliced and stir-fried.

1 For stir-frying, slit the body from top to bottom and turn it inside out. Flatten it and score the inside lightly with a knife to make a criss-cross pattern.

2 Cut each piece lengthways into ribbons. These will curl when stir-fried.

Cleaning and preparing cuttlefish

Cut off the tentacles and remove the beak from the cuttlefish. Along the length of the body you will see the dark line of the cuttle bone. Cut along this line and remove the cuttle bone. Prepare in the same way as squid. The body is usually left whole.

Sea urchins

There are several edible varieties of sea urchin. They are particularly popular in France, where they are served raw, or lightly cooked in salted water and eaten like boiled eggs. The tops are sliced off and fingers of bread are then dipped into the coral flesh.

A CATALOGUE OF FISH AND SHELLFISH

The almost infinite variety of edible sea and freshwater fish has always been an inspiration to cooks, who love them for their fresh flavour, versatility and nutritious qualities. There is a host of delicious shellfish, each with its own unique flavour and all evoking the unmistakable tang of the sea. Once, we were limited to eating only fish and shellfish from local waters, but now, thanks to modern transportation methods, a whole new world of exciting species is available to cooks. This chapter is designed to help you to identify the fish and shellfish you may find on the fishmonger's slab and to give you an indication of how it can be cooked.

SEAFISH

There are two main categories of seafish: round and flat. Those that live on or near the sea bed are known as demersal fish. Flat fish are demersal fish, spending most of their time on the sea bed and doing very little swimming. Consequently they have delicate white flesh with little muscle tone. The nutritious oil of "white" fish is concentrated in the liver.

In "oily" fish, this oil is dispersed throughout the flesh. Oily fish tend to swim in shoals near the surface of the sea; they are known as pelagic fish.

ROUND WHITE FISH

THE SEA BASS AND GROUPER FAMILY

This large and important family of fish is known as *perciformes* because they all share some of the characteristics of perch. They have at least some spiny fins, a V-shaped tail and pectoral fins set high on the body. The pelvic fins have one spiny ray each.

Various species of perciformes are found in the Indian and Pacific oceans and the Caribbean, and also in Mediterranean and Atlantic waters.

Right: Sea bass

Sea bass *(Dicentrarchus labrax)*

Among the finest of all fish, sea bass have an elegant, sleek shape rather like salmon, and a beautiful silvery body with a darker back and a white belly. They can grow to a length of 90cm/36in and weigh up to 7kg/15½lb, although the average weight is 1–3kg/2¼–6½lb.

Habitat Sea bass are voracious predators that live in small shoals close to rocky coasts in Great Britain and the Mediterranean. They can also be found in salt water lakes and large river estuaries. Because wild sea bass are in such demand, they have become prohibitively expensive. Avoid buying trawled fish, which deplete stocks and often entangle dolphins in the nets, and go for the more eco-friendly line-caught fish. Sea bass can also be farmed successfully and there are fisheries all over the Mediterranean and in Cornwall, England.

Other names The French for sea bass is *bar*; owing to their ferocity, they are also known as *loup de mer* (sea wolf). In Italian, they are *spigola* or *branzino*; their Spanish name is *lubina*.

Buying Wild sea bass are in season from late April to December, while farmed fish are available year-round. Allow about 200g/7oz per serving. Avoid buying Chilean sea bass; these large, meaty specimens are vulnerable to overfishing as they are very slow-growing and have a low reproductive capacity. Their numbers are declining at an alarming rate.

Cooking Sea bass have very few small bones and fine, firm flesh that holds its shape well during cooking. They are versatile fish with a delicate flavour and can be cooked by almost any method – grilled (broiled), baked, braised, poached, shallow or stir-fried, or steamed over seaweed or samphire. A whole poached sea bass, skinned and served cold with mayonnaise, makes a wonderful party dish. Plainly cooked sea bass can be served with any number of sauces, from *beurre blanc* to fresh tomato coulis and Asian sesame dressing. A classic French dish is *bar au fenouil*; grilled sea bass served on a bed of fennel twigs flamed with Pernod. Sea bass are highly prized in China, where they are braised with ginger and spring onions (scallions), while the Japanese slice the flesh wafer-thin and use it raw.

Alternatives Few fish can equal sea bass for flavour, but good substitutes in most recipes are grey mullet, sea bream (porgy), grouper and John Dory.

Scaling sea bass

The skin of sea bass is excellent to eat, and it becomes deliciously crisp when grilled (broiled) or pan-fried. It does, however, have very hard scales, so it is essential to scale sea bass before cooking. Ask your fishmonger to do this, or follow the instructions in the section on Buying and Preparing Fish.

Other varieties
Dicentrus punctatus (speckled bass) takes its Latin name from the small black spots on its back and sides. It is found mainly in the southern Mediterranean and is very similar to sea bass. Two other varieties come from North America and southern seas; striped bass and black bass. Both are excellent fish, but neither tastes quite so fine as sea bass.

Stone bass/Wreckfish *(Polyprion americanum)*

This ugly cousin of the sea bass lives in deep Atlantic waters, often amid wrecked ships at the bottom of the sea, which is how it came by its alternative name. This makes it difficult to catch; it can only be line-fished at a depth of more than 150m/500ft, so it is seldom found in stores and markets. Its Italian name is *cernia di fondale* (bass from the deep). It has dark skin and large, bony fins, and the end of its tail is straight, not V-shaped like the tails of other types of bass.
Cooking If you do find stone bass for sale, it is likely to be as fillets or steaks, which can be cooked in the same way as any other white fish.

Comber *(Serranus)*

These smaller members of the grouper family have reddish or brownish skin with wide vertical markings. *Serranus scriba* is so called because its markings are said to resemble scribbles.
Cooking Comber have delicious firm white flesh. The whole fish can be poached, steamed, braised or baked. Fillets and steaks can be grilled (broiled), pan-fried or steamed.

THE SEA BREAM FAMILY

There are approximately two hundred species of sea bream, some of which, unusually for seafish, are vegetarian. They have tall, compact bodies and slightly snub noses.
Habitat Sea bream are found in all warm and temperate coastal waters, including the Atlantic, up to the Bay of Biscay.

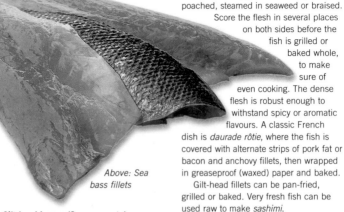

Above: Sea bass fillets

Gilt-head bream *(Sparus aurata)*

This beautiful fish is considered the finest of all sea bream. It has silver scales, a gold spot on each cheek and a golden crescent in the middle of its head from which it takes its name. Its dense, juicy white flesh has been highly prized for thousands of years; the ancient Greeks and Romans considered it a fish fit for feasting, and it was sacred to Aphrodite, the goddess of love. One wonders what she would have made of the fact that gilt-head breams are hermaphrodite, starting as male and becoming female as they mature.
Other names Gilt-heads are also known as royal bream. Sometimes in English they are called *daurade* (also spelt *dorade*), as in French. The Italian name is *orata*, the Spanish is *dorada*.
Buying In the wild, gilt-heads can live for up to 11 years and grow to a length of 70cm/34in, weighing up to 3kg/6½lb. They are sold whole or as fillets. There is a high percentage of wastage, which makes them expensive. Nowadays they are successfully farmed throughout the Mediterranean, particularly in Greece, so they have become a little less costly and are available all year. Fresh gilt-head bream should have bright, silvery scales.
Cooking All bream have numerous wide scales that must be removed before cooking, or the diner will experience a most unpleasant mouthful. Whole gilt-head bream can be treated like sea bass

or sole – baked, grilled (broiled), poached, steamed in seaweed or braised. Score the flesh in several places on both sides before the fish is grilled or baked whole, to make sure of even cooking. The dense flesh is robust enough to withstand spicy or aromatic flavours. A classic French dish is *daurade rôtie*, where the fish is covered with alternate strips of pork fat or bacon and anchovy fillets, then wrapped in greaseproof (waxed) paper and baked.
Gilt-head fillets can be pan-fried, grilled or baked. Very fresh fish can be used raw to make *sashimi*.

Red bream *(Pagellus bogaraveo)*

This tall rosy-red fish has a pronounced black spot above the pectoral fin on each shoulder. It grows to about 50cm/ 20in and is usually sold already filleted. Red bream lives deep in the sea and feeds on crustaceans and molluscs, which make it particularly tasty. It is found in northern European waters, but swims southwards in winter to spawn, and is a much sought after fish in Spain and Portugal.
Other names Young red bream have small blue spots on their backs and are sometimes known as blue-spotted bream. In French, red bream is rather rudely called *dorade commune* (common bream); the Italians call it *pagro*, *pagello* or *occhialone*, meaning "big eye". The Spaniards call it *besugo*.
Cooking Extremely fresh red bream can be eaten raw as *sashimi*. Whole fish and fillets should be cooked in the same way as snapper, bass or red mullet.

Black bream *(Spondyliosoma cantharus)*

This large bream is sometimes found in the North Sea. It is actually dark grey, with beautiful golden stripes running from head to tail. Unlike the gilt-head, it is unisexual and monogamous. Like gilt-head bream it can be baked, broiled, poached, steamed in seaweed, or braised. The flavour and the texture are similar but not as fine.

Ray's bream *(Brama brama)*

These large shoaling fish live in depths of 100m/328ft and below, but come up to the surface in summer, sometimes with tragic consequences, as the eponymous John Ray found when he discovered huge quantities of the fish stranded on the coast of Britain in the 17th century. Ray's bream are brownish-grey, with firm flesh and a good flavour. They should be cooked in the same way as other bream.

Dentex *(Dentex dentex)*

These relatives of the sea bream are particularly popular in Mediterranean countries, in whose waters they are found. They are also found to a lesser extent in the East Atlantic. Their colour varies with their age; young dentex are grey, changing first to reddish pink, then to a beautiful steel blue with a sprinkling of dark spots.

Above, from front: gilt-head bream, red bream and black bream

Other names *Denté* in French, *dentice* in Italian and *dentón* in Spanish.
Cooking Dentex can grow up to 1m/39in in length, but they are best eaten when 30cm/12in long. Fish this size can be grilled (broiled) whole or baked with herbs. Larger specimens should be cut into steaks and grilled or fried.

Porgy *(Pagrus pagrus)*

The eponymous hero of *Porgy and Bess* took his name from these rosy-tinted North American relatives of the bass, variations of which are also found in the Atlantic coastal waters around Africa. Porgies grow to a length of up to 75cm/30in and can be cooked whole or as steaks – baked, grilled (broiled), poached, steamed or braised, using any of the recipes for bream.

Unusual species of bream
Among the many varieties of bream, there are a number whose names describe their appearance.

The **two-banded bream**, a fish which makes very good eating, has two distinct vertical black bands fore and aft.

Annular bream, which is the smallest of its group, has a dark ring round its tail, as does **saddled bream**, while **sheepshead bream** has an upturned snout.

The small varieties, such as annular bream and saddled bream, are used for making soup.

A classic Tuscan dish, *sarago e parago*, uses two different kinds of small bream, boned and stuffed with raw ham and rosemary, then grilled (broiled) over a wood fire.

THE COD FAMILY

This large family includes haddock, hake, ling, pollack, whiting and many other related species of white-fleshed fish. Most come from the Atlantic and other cold northerly waters, including the Pacific Ocean. Hake is also found in the warmer Mediterranean and is highly prized by the Spanish and Portuguese.

Cod *(Gadus morruha)*

Long, torpedo-shaped fish with vibrant yellowish-brown mottled skin and a whitish belly, cod have a large head with a snub nose, a protruding upper jaw and a whiskery barbel on the chin which acts as a sensor as they search for food on the sea bed. They can live for over 20 years and grow to a length of 6m/20ft (weighing up to 50kg/110lb), although such specimens are sadly rare and most commercially fished cod weigh between 3 and 8kg/6½ and 17½lb.
Habitat Cod live in cold water with a high salt content. They hatch in huge numbers close to the surface of the water, but gravitate down to the sea bed where they feed on crustaceans, molluscs and worms. Large cod also feed on smaller fish. Cod can be caught in trawler nets or line-caught.

Today, overfishing of Atlantic cod has severely depleted stocks, which are now only one-tenth of what they were 30 years ago. There is some evidence that they are beginning to show a slight recovery in the North Sea, but unless the fishing industry gives them time to replenish themselves properly, they will remain well below sustainable levels. Because of its comparative rarity, cod has become more highly appreciated

than before, as the great French chef Auguste Escoffier predicted in the 19th century: "If cod were less common, it would be held in as high esteem as salmon;" (at that time, regarded as the king of fish) "for, when it is really fresh and of good quality, the delicacy and delicious flavour of its flesh admit of its ranking among the finest of fish".
Other names In France, cod is called *cabillaud*. In Italy, *merluzzo* and in Spain, *bacalao* (which can also mean salt cod).
Buying Cod is most commonly trawled or netted. Both these methods can damage the delicate flesh and adversely affect the marine environment, so always ask for line-caught cod. The worst affected areas for overfishing of cod are the North and Irish Seas, the West of Scotland, Greenland and Norway, so avoid fish from these areas and buy Pacific cod which comes from well-managed fisheries and is available all year round. Organic cod farming is a new development in Shetland; the flesh of these farmed fish is firmer and whiter than wild-caught cod, but don't expect them to be a cheaper option; at present, they are still extremely pricey.

There is a lot of wastage in whole cod, which makes these fish very expensive, so they are more usually sold as steaks and fillets. Try to buy thick cuts from the shoulder or middle of the fish and always check that the flesh is very white. The fresher the fish, the firmer and flakier the flesh will be.
Cooking Cod holds its texture well and can be cooked in many different ways, but it is important not to overcook it. The flavour is robust enough to take strong and spicy flavours. Whole fish can be poached in a court-bouillon and

Above: Cod fillet and steaks

served cold with mayonnaise, green sauce or tartare sauce. Cod can also be baked or roasted in the oven or braised in white wine.

Most cooking methods are suitable for cod fillets and steaks, except for grilling (broiling), which can destroy the flaky texture. They can be poached, steamed, braised in tomato sauce or topped with a crust of breadcrumbs and herbs and baked. They are delicious floured and sautéed, or coated with batter and deep-fried. Cod makes an excellent substitute for more exotic fish in curries. Fresh and smoked cod fillets can be used to make fish cakes, fish pies, salads and mousses.

Cod can be salted or dried (see Dried and Salted Fish). The roe is often smoked and used to make *taramasalata*. Frozen cod is almost always frozen at sea, ensuring that it retains its freshness and flavour. It is available as steaks, fillets and breaded cuts. The liver produces cod liver oil, which tastes disgusting but is good for you.
Alternatives Any firm-fleshed white fish can be substituted for cod, including flat fish such as brill, halibut and turbot.

Above: Cod

Above: Haddock

Coley (Pollachius virens)

Traditionally regarded as cod's poor relation, coley has unappealing greyish flesh, which is responsible for its low price. Long and slim, the fish has a protruding lower jaw and no barbel. The skin on the back is dark grey, lightening to mottled yellow on the sides and almost white on the belly. Coley generally weigh 5–10kg/11–22lb, but smaller fish do appear on the fishmonger's slab.

Habitat Coley live in huge shoals in both deep waters and near the surface. They prefer cold, very salty water. They are voracious predators who prey on herring and have cannibalistic tendencies.

Other names Coley are also known as saithe, coalfish and pollock. In French, they are *lieu noir*, in Italian *merluzzo nero* and in Spanish *abadejo*.

Buying Coley are sometimes sold whole, weighing 1–4kg/2¼–8¾lb, but are more usually sold as steaks, cutlets and fillets. The unattractive grey flesh whitens during cooking. It should feel firm to the touch. Coley must be extremely fresh, or the flesh will become woolly and unpleasant.

Cooking Coley is less fine than cod in texture and flavour. Rubbing the greyish flesh with lemon juice helps to whiten it, but the colour can also be masked by coating the fish in batter. It will withstand robust flavours and can be baked, braised, grilled (broiled) or fried. Smoked coley has an excellent flavour, but is seldom available commercially. It is worth smoking at home.

Alternatives Pacific cod, haddock or any firm-fleshed white fish can be substituted for coley.

Haddock (Melanogrammus aeglefinus)

These are generally smaller than cod, growing up to 1m/39in long and weighing 1–2kg/2¼–4½lb. They have dark brownish-grey skin with a black lateral line and a black spot above the pectoral fin. Their eyes are large and prominent. They live close to the sea bed and prefer water with a high salt content.

Haddock is often considered to be interchangeable with cod, but its flesh has a more delicate flavour and a softer less flaky, texture.

Habitat Haddock are shoaling fish which live at the bottom of cold northern seas in Europe and North America. They feed on molluscs, worms and other small fish and spawn in the coldest, saltiest water they can find.

Other names In North America, young haddock are known as scrod. In French, the fish is called *aiglefin* (from the Latin name).

Confusingly, the French for smoked haddock is *haddock*. In Italian, haddock is *asinello*; in Spanish it is *eglefino*.

Buying Fresh haddock is at its best in winter and early spring, when the cold has firmed up the flesh. Line-caught specimens have the best flavour. You may find whole small haddock (weighing 450g–2kg/1–4½lb) at the fishmonger's, but the fish is usually sold as fillets. Before you buy, prod the flesh to make sure that it is firm.

Cooking Fresh haddock is a versatile fish, which can be cooked in the same way as cod. When cooking whole haddock, leave the skin on to hold the delicate flesh together.

Haddock is the perfect fish for deep-frying and it makes wonderful fish and chips (French fries). It also makes excellent lasagne and pie, especially when the fresh fish is mixed with an equal quantity of smoked haddock.

Hake (Merluccius merluccius)

This most elegant member of the cod family is a long, slim fish with two spiny dorsal fins, bulging eyes and a protruding lower jaw without a barbel. The head and back are dark steely grey and the belly is

Below: Haddock fillets

silvery white. The inside of the mouth and gills is black. A mature fish can grow up to 1m/39in, but the average length is 30–50cm/12–20in.

Habitat Hake are found in most temperate and cold waters. By day, they live near the sea bed, but at night they move to the surface to hunt oily fish such as herring, mackerel and sprats.

Other names The French have several names for hake: *merlu*, *colin* and *merluchon* (small immature fish). The Spanish call it *merluza*. In Italian, it is *nasello*. In North America, hake is often known as ling or whiting, although it is far superior to the European whiting.

Buying Due to overfishing, hake have become quite scarce and expensive. There are two main stocks for European hake – northern and southern. Southern stocks have been severely depleted, so avoid buying these. Hake can be trawled or caught on long lines; line-caught fish have a better texture. Hake must be very fresh, or it becomes flabby. The flesh will always feel quite soft to the touch, but should never feel limp. Whole fish should have bright eyes and smell of the sea.

When calculating how much hake to buy, allow for 40 per cent wastage for whole fish. Keep the head, as it makes particularly delicious soup or fish stock.

Hake is usually sold as cutlets or steaks. The fish has few bones and these are easy to remove. Avoid buying fillets, as they tend to disintegrate when cooked.

Cooking Whole hake can be poached, baked or braised in wine, lemon juice and fresh herbs or tomato sauce. Like all fish, it should never be overcooked. Steaks can be grilled (broiled), coated in egg and breadcrumbs and deep-fried, or sautéed in olive oil and garlic. They can also be layered with potatoes and onions, or with tomatoes and cheese and baked *au gratin*. Light buttery sauces go well with hake, as does caper sauce. Shellfish such as mussels and clams are perfect partners. A popular Spanish hors d'oeuvre is *escabeche* – marinated hake served cold.

Above: Ling

Alternatives Haddock and cod can be substituted for hake in any recipe.

Other varieties North American silver hake is a small, streamlined fish with an excellent flavour. Varieties of hake are also found in the warmer waters of South America and southern Africa.

Ling *(Molva molva)*

This fish has a long, slender greenish-brown body with a silver lateral stripe, no scales and a barbel on the lower jaw. It is the largest relative of the cod, growing to a length of 1.8m/6ft.

Habitat Ling are found in the Atlantic, from shallow coastal waters to the deep sea. They are often found near rocks, where they feed on round and flat fish, small octopus and crustaceans. Deepwater ling are beginning to suffer from overfishing, and often occupy habitats that are vulnerable to the impacts of trawling.

Other names Mediterranean ling are sometimes known as blue ling. They have larger eyes and a shorter barbel than common ling, and are esteemed for their superior flavour. Both varieties are known as *lingue* in French, *molva occhiona* in Italian and *maruca* in Spanish. Rock ling are available in Australia. In Scandinavian countries, ling is salted, dried and sold as *lutfisk* or *klipfisk* (see Dried and Salted Fish).

Buying As with all fish, the best ling are line-caught. Ask for fish from coastal waters and avoid buying fish from deepwater

stocks. Ling are generally sold as fillets or middle-cut cutlets. You may find small whole fish on the fishmonger's slab; if they measure under 90cm, they are immature and you should not buy them. Ling are available from September to March. Don't buy them in summer, which is their breeding season.

Cooking Ling has firm flesh with a good flavour and is sometimes substituted for monkfish. Whole fish can be baked or braised, or made into casseroles, soups and curries. Fillets and cutlets can be grilled (broiled) or pan-fried.

Alternatives Any sustainable member of the cod family can be substituted, or try conger eel for a change.

Pollack *(Pollachius pollachius)*

These attractive temperate members of the cod family have steely grey backs and greenish-yellow bodies with a curved lateral line. They have a protruding lower jaw and no barbel. They are smaller than cod, although they can reach a length of 1.3m/4ft.

Habitat Pollack live in shoals near the surface of the sea, feeding on sprats and herrings, or close to the bottom where they eat deep-sea prawns (shrimp).

Other names Its yellow colour gives pollack the name of *lieu jaune* in French. It is also known as *merluzzo giallo* in Italian and *abadejo* in Spanish.

Buying Pollack are at their best in autumn (fall) and winter. They are usually sold as fillets, cutlets or steaks. If you need a whole fish, look for a superior line-caught specimen.

Above: Hake

Above: Pouting

Cooking Pollack has a drier texture and less pronounced flavour than cod, so it benefits from a creamy, highly flavoured sauce. It is good for fish pies and soups and can be baked, braised, deep-fried or sautéed. It is suitable for any recipe for cod, haddock, hake or ling.

Pouting (Trisopterus luscus)

This sulky-sounding fish is a poor (and cheap) relation of the whiting. It is comparatively small (about 25cm/10in long), with light brown papery skin.
Habitat Pouting are found in inshore waters, particularly in rocky areas and around wrecks and reefs.
Other names Also known as bib or pout. In French it is *tacaud*, in Italian *merluzzo francese* and in Spanish *faneca*.
Buying Pouting goes off quickly and must be eaten very fresh. Your nose will soon tell you if it is past its best. Try to buy locally caught whole fish and avoid them in February and March, their spawning season. Ask your fishmonger to fillet the fish, and cook them as soon as possible, as the fillets will rapidly deteriorate.
Cooking As for whiting.

Whiting (Merlangus merlangus)

Similar in appearance to haddock, whiting are small fish (generally about 30–40cm/12–16in long). They have greenish-grey skin, a silvery belly and a black spot at the base of the pectoral fin. The head is pointed, with a protruding upper jaw and no barbel.

Habitat Whiting are found all over the Atlantic. They feed on crustaceans and small fish such as sand-eels and herrings and are often found near rocky shores.
Other names Its old name was merling. The French call it *merlan*, the Italians *merlano* and the Spanish *merlán*.
Buying The fact that it is abundant all year and has soft, rather unexciting flesh means that whiting is cheap and undervalued. However, really fresh whiting is well worth buying. Whole fish should be scintillatingly shiny. Fillets

Below: Whiting

should be pearly white and feel soft but definitely not flabby. Stale whiting may have a woolly texture and taste unpleasant, so make sure that you buy only absolutely fresh fish. Whiting are small, so allow two fillets per serving.
Cooking The whiting's meltingly tender flesh makes it an ideal basis for a soup, as it contributes a velvety texture. It is also excellent for quenelles and fish mousses. Whiting is a versatile fish that can be coated in breadcrumbs or batter and fried. It can also be pan-fried, grilled (broiled) or gently poached in wine or court-bouillon and served with a lemony sauce or flavoured butter. Whatever cooking method you use, make sure the whiting is well seasoned.
Alternatives Plaice, flounder or sole can be used, and all of the cod family.

Whiting en colère

A once immensely popular dish was *merlan en colère* ("angry whiting"). Whole fish were baked with the skin on, then curled around so that their tails could be stuck through their eye sockets or into their mouths. Presumably the name came from the assumption that the fish was chasing its own tail in anger. Mercifully, this method of serving whiting has fallen out of favour.

THE GURNARD FAMILY

Gurnards belong to a group of fish known as the Triglidae family. These curious, prehistoric-looking fish have cylindrical bodies, high armour-plated heads with wide mouths, and strange pectoral fins with the three lowest rays divided into "fingers", which they use to explore the sea bed. They emit a curious grunting noise, caused by vibrating their swim bladders, possibly as an aid to keeping

Below: Red gurnard

schools together. Gurnard weigh between 100g/3¾oz and 2kg/4½lb. There are several types, which are distinguished by their colour; all have lean white flesh with a firm texture but rather insipid taste. They are rich in iodine, phosphorus and protein.
Habitat Gurnard are found in the Atlantic and Mediterranean. They live on or near the sea bed, using their "fingers" to seek out crabs, prawns (shrimp) and small fish in the sediment.
Other names Also known as sea robin and gurnet. The French call them *grondin*, the Spanish, *rubios*.

Grey gurnard *(Eutrigla gurnardus)*

These fish have brownish-grey backs and silvery bellies. They grow to a maximum length of 45cm/18in. The lateral line is scaly and should be removed before cooking. Avoid eating immature fish measuring less than 24cm/10in.

Red gurnard *(Aspitrigla cuculus)*

The most attractive member of the gurnard family, this pinkish-red fish has bony extensions to the lateral line, which give it the appearance of vertical

Above: Tub gurnard

stripes on its back. It has the finest flavour of all the gurnards and is sometimes substituted for red mullet. Red gurnard are fast growing and mature at a large size. Avoid eating those that measure less than 20cm/8in.

Tub gurnard *(Trigla lucerna)*

This larger gurnard is orangey-brown with orange pectoral fins. It is an excellent swimmer and sometimes leaps right out of the water, high above the surface.
Buying Gurnard are bony fish with an unexceptional flavour, so they tend to be cheap. They are usually sold whole – ask the fishmonger to remove the spiny fins and the skin. Beware of buying red gurnard masquerading as red mullet (*rouget*). The latter is vastly superior.
Cooking Small gurnard are best used in soups and stocks. Larger fish can be braised or baked on a bed of vegetables with a little white wine. Take care when eating whole gurnard, as they are very bony. Fillets can be coated in breadcrumbs and fried, or steamed and served with a Mediterranean sauce.
Alternatives Red or grey mullet can be used in any gurnard recipe, and will generally give a better result.

Scorpion fish *(Scorpaena scrofa, Scorpaena porcus)*

Like gurnard, scorpion fish have huge heads and armour-plated cheeks. Their enormous scaly heads have loose folds of skin above and between the eyes. The dorsal fin is made up of large poisonous spines. The smaller brown scorpion fish has a finer flavour than its larger cousin.
Habitat Scorpion fish are found throughout the Mediterranean and off the coast of North Africa. They also live in Atlantic waters, ranging from the English Channel to Senegal.
Other names The French for scorpion fish is *rascasse* (*chapon* in the south of France). Italians call it *scorfano*; in Spanish it is *cabracho* or *rascacio*.
Buying Scorpion fish are usually sold whole. You should allow for a huge amount of wastage; a 2kg/4½lb fish will serve only four people.
Cooking Scorpion fish is best known as an essential ingredient in bouillabaisse. Whole fish can be baked or braised with fennel; scorpion fillets can be cooked *à l'antillaise*, braised with tomatoes, potatoes and red (bell) peppers.
Alternatives Monkfish, snapper, John Dory or gurnard can be used in a pinch.

Above: Scorpion fish

THE MULLET FAMILY

Over a hundred species of mullet are found in temperate and tropical seas. These belong to two main groups, grey and red, which are unrelated and very different in appearance and flavour.

Grey mullet *(family Mugilidae)*

Varieties of grey mullet are found all over the world. These beautiful silvery fish resemble sea bass, but have larger scales and small mouths, suited to their diet of seaweed and plankton. They are shoaling fish that live in the vicinity of the muddy sea bed, so they sometimes smell and taste rather muddy. A good grey mullet has lean, slightly soft, creamy white flesh with quite a pleasant flavour.

Habitat Grey mullet are found in coastal waters and estuaries all over the world.

Varieties The finest is the golden mullet (*Liza aurata*), which has a thin upper lip and gold spots on its head and the front

Below: Red mullet are considered one of the finest seafish.

Above: Silver-skinned grey mullet are found all over the world.

of the body. It is one of the smallest mullets, growing only to about 45cm/18in. In French, it is known as *mulet doré*. Thick-lipped mullet (*Crenimugil* or *Chelon labrosus*) has, as its name suggests, thick lips and a rounded body. This mullet is sometimes farmed. The thin-lipped mullet (*Liza ramada*) has a golden sheen, a thin upper lip and a pointed snout, which gives it its French name of *mulet porc*. The largest mullet is the common or striped grey mullet (*Mugil cephalus*), which can grow up to 70cm/28in. This fish has a brown body, silvery back and a large head. Its eyes are covered by a transparent membrane. In French it is called

mulet cabot. There is also a small Mediterranean mullet whose main claim to fame is its ability to leap out of the water to escape predators. This is the leaping grey mullet (*Liza saliens*).

Buying Except in France, you are unlikely to find any differentiation between the varieties of grey mullet at the fishmonger. If possible, choose fish that come from the sea rather than estuaries, as the latter often have a muddy taste and can be flabby. Grey mullet are usually sold whole – ask the fishmonger to scale and skin them for you. Keep the roes, which are delicious. Larger fish may be sold filleted.

Cooking Grey mullet must be scaled before being cooked. Any muddiness can be eliminated by soaking the fish in several changes of acidulated water. Whole fish are very good stuffed with fennel and grilled (broiled). Slash the sides and add a splash of aniseed apéritif before cooking the fish, and serve with a buttery sauce. Mullet roe is a delicacy and can be eaten fresh, fried in butter or used in a stuffing for a baked fish. When salted and dried, mullet roe is the authentic basis of taramasalata and *bottarga* or *boutargue*, which is delicious served wafer-thin on country bread as canapés, or grated over pasta.

Red mullet *(Mullus surmuletus and Mullus barbatus)*

These are among the finest of all seafish. They are small (up to 40cm/ 16in long), with pinkish-red skins streaked with gold. Their heads have two long barbels on the chin. They have lean, firm flesh. The flavour is robust and distinctive.

Other varieties *Mullus surmeletus* is more correctly known as *surmullet*; it has rosy red skin and is larger than *Mullus barbatus*, which has three yellowish stripes along each side and grows to a length of 30cm/12in.

Goatfish Types of red mullet known as goatfish because of their long, beard-like barbels are found in the warm Pacific and Indian Oceans. They are smaller (up to 20cm/8in) and less colourful than cold-water mullet, and they have drier, less tasty flesh.

Habitat Red mullet are found in Atlantic and Mediterranean waters. They live on sandy or rocky areas of the sea bed, feeding on small sea creatures.

Other names Red mullet are usually cooked complete with their livers and sometimes all their guts. These impart a gamey flavour, giving the fish the nickname "woodcock of the sea". In America, all red mullet are known as "goatfish", regardless of size or place of origin. The French for mullet is *rouget*; depending on the variety, it is *rouget barbet*, *rouget de roche* or *rouget de vase* (*Mullus barbatus*). In Italian, red mullet is *triglia*; in Spanish, *salmonete de roca* (*Mullus surmuletus*) or *salmonete de fango* (*Mullus barbatus*).

Buying Red mullet have delicate flesh that is highly perishable, so it is essential to buy extremely fresh fish. They should have bright skin and eyes and feel very firm. The scales should be firmly attached, not flaking off the skin. Because they are small, red mullet are usually sold whole, but large fish are sometimes filleted. The flesh is quite rich, so a 200g/7oz fish will be ample for one person. Ask the fishmonger to scale and gut it for you, and keep the liver, which is a great delicacy.

Cooking The best ways to cook red mullet are grilling (broiling) and pan-frying. Slash the sides before grilling a whole fish to be sure of even cooking. Red mullet marry superbly with many Mediterranean flavours, such as olive oil, saffron, tomatoes, olives, anchovies and orange. They can be cooked *en papillote* with flavourings or made into mousses and soufflés. Very small, bony red mullet are used in bouillabaisse.

THE WRASSE FAMILY

This large family of fish is notable for its varied and dazzling colours. Wrasse range from steely blue to green, orange and golden; in some species, the sexes have different colours. All wrasse have thick lips and an array of sharp teeth. They are small fish, seldom growing larger than 40cm/16in in length.

Habitat Wrasse are found in both Atlantic and Mediterranean waters. They live near rocky coasts, feeding on barnacles and small crustaceans.

Varieties The most common is the ballan wrasse (*Labrus berggylta*), which has greenish or brownish skin, with large scales tipped with gold. Male and female cuckoo wrasse (*Labrus mixtus*) have strikingly different coloration; the males are steely blue with almost black stripes, while the females are orangey-pink with three black spots under the dorsal fin. The name of the five-spotted wrasse (*Symphonus quinquemaculatus*) is self-explanatory, while the brown spotted wrasse is completely covered with spots. Rainbow wrasse (*Coris julis*) have spiny dorsal fins and a red or orange band along the body.

Right: Common wrasse

Below: Brown spotted wrasse

Other names In French, wrasse is variously known as *vielle*, *coquette* and *labre*. In Italian, it is *labridi*; in Spanish *merlo*, *tordo* or *gallano*.

Buying Wrasse are available in spring and summer. Look for scintillating skin and bright eyes. Ask the fishmonger to scale and clean the fish. Allow at least 400g/14oz per serving.

Cooking Most wrasse are fit only for making soup, but some larger varieties, such as ballan wrasse, can be baked whole. Make a bed of sliced onions, garlic, smoked bacon and potatoes, bake at 200°C/400°F/Gas 6 until soft, then add the wrasse, moisten with white wine and bake for 10–15 minutes.

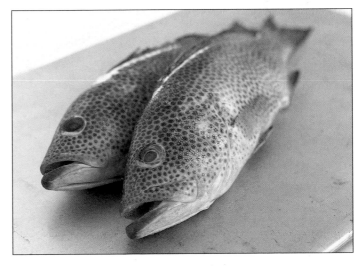

OILY FISH

Fish such as herrings, mackerel and sardines have always been popular because they are cheap and nutritious, but now they are considered the ultimate "good for you" food. In recent years they have received an excellent press, owing to their healthy properties. Not only do they contain protein and vitamins A, B and D, but the Omega-3 fatty acids in their flesh are known to reduce the risk of clogged arteries, blood clots, strokes and even cancer. People who eat fish regularly tend to live longer – the Japanese, among the world's greatest fish eaters, have one of the lowest rates of heart disease.

Oily fish are pelagic fish, which swim near the surface of the sea and live in shoals that can be quite enormous. The largest family of oil-rich fish are the *clupeiformes*: herrings and their relatives – sardines, anchovies, sprats and pilchards. Other oily fish are smooth-skinned mackerel and tuna.

Below: Herring

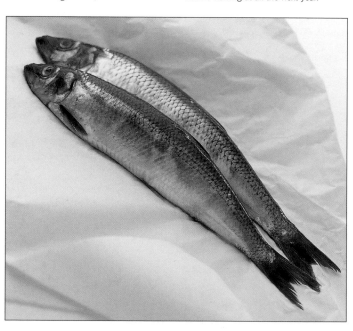

THE HERRING FAMILY

Herring *(Clupea harengus)*

Herrings belong to the same family of fish (clupeids) as sprats and pilchards. There are numerous different varieties of herring, each confined to its own area – the North Sea, Baltic, White Sea (an inlet of the Barents Sea), the coast of Norway and many colder coastal areas. Herring are prodigiously fertile fish, which is just as well, since they have been overfished for centuries and are becoming more scarce.

Herring are slender silver fish with a central dorsal fin and large scales. They seldom grow to a length of more than 35cm/14in. Their oily flesh can be cured in many ways, including smoking, salting, drying and marinating in vinegar.

Habitat Herring live in huge shoals in cold northerly waters, where they feed on plankton. They are migratory fish which come inshore to spawn. They sometimes change their habitual route for no apparent reason, so that there may be a glut in a particular area for several years, but no herring at all the next year.

Boning a whole herring

Herring must be scaled before cooking; the scales virtually fall off by themselves, so this is easy to do. Whether or not you leave the head on is a matter of choice.

1 First scale the herring, then slit the belly with a sharp knife and remove the innards.

2 Lay the fish on a chopping board, belly-side down. With the heel of your hand, press down firmly all along the backbone.

3 Turn the herring over and lift off the backbone. You will find that most of the small side bones will come away with it.

Varieties Herring are mostly known by the name of the region where they are located – North Sea, Norwegian, Baltic, for instance. Each variety has its own spawning season, which influences the eating qualities of the fish.

Buying Like all oily fish, herring must be absolutely fresh, or they will taste rancid. They are at their best before they spawn. Look for large, firm fish with slippery skins and rounded bellies containing hard or soft roes; hard roes are the female eggs, soft roes the male milt. Soft herring roes are considered a particular delicacy. By running your hands along the belly of the fish, you will be able to tell whether the roes are hard or soft.

Once they have spawned, herrings lose condition and weight and their flesh becomes rather dry. If the fishmonger cleans them for you, be sure to keep the roe. As herrings contain numerous soft bones, you might ask him to bone or fillet them for you. They can be gutted either through the belly or through the gills, leaving the roe inside.

Above: Herring fillets

Cooking The oiliness of the flesh makes herrings particularly suitable for grilling (broiling) and cooking on a barbecue. Score whole fish in several places on both sides for even cooking. Herring benefit from being served with an acidic sauce, such as gooseberry or mustard, to counteract the richness.

Whole herrings are excellent when baked with a stuffing of breadcrumbs, chopped onions and apples. They are also good wrapped in bacon and grilled (broiled), or grilled with a mustard sauce. Both whole herrings and fillets are delicious rolled in oatmeal and then pan-fried in bacon fat. Serve them with a little lemon juice squeezed over.

Herring fillets can be made into fish balls, or cooked in a sweet-and-sour sauce. They are also delicious soused in a vinegary marinade flavoured with herbs and spices.

Fillets are also traditionally made into rollmops or smoked to make kippers – these processes are explored fully in the chapters on Pickled and Smoked Fish.

Alternatives Sardines, sprats and mackerel can be cooked in the same way as herrings.

Herring roes

Soft roes have a creamy, melting texture. They can be tossed in seasoned flour, gently fried in butter and served as they are, or they can be devilled with cayenne pepper and Worcestershire sauce and served on hot toast. They also make a delicious omelette filling. Poached in stock and mashed, they can be used as a spread, in a stuffing for whole baked herrings or added to a sauce or savoury tart filling. Hard roes have a grainy texture, which people tend either to love or loathe. They can be baked or braised under the fish to add extra flavour.

Above: Soft herring roes

Cooking Whole anchovies can be grilled (broiled) or fried like sardines, or coated lightly in egg and flour and deep-fried. They make an excellent *gratin* when seasoned with olive oil and garlic, then topped with breadcrumbs and baked. Fillets can be fried with garlic and parsley, or marinated for 24 hours in a mixture of olive oil, onion, garlic, bay leaves and crushed peppercorns. Anchovy essence (extract) and anchovy paste are useful ingredients.

Escolar *(Lepidocybium flavobrunneum)*

These belong to a group of fish known collectively as Gempylidae. They have long brownish-grey bodies with a lateral line and faint pale spots, and firm, rich oily flesh. These often solitary fish can grow up to 1m/1yd.
Habitat Escolar are a pelagic, oceanic species generally found in tropical and sub-tropical waters around South America.
Other names Also called snake mackerel.
Buying Escolar is sold as fillets, almost always frozen.
Cooking The rich oiliness of this fish needs a sharp flavour to counteract its richness. Grill (broil) or griddle the fillets with tangy tomatoes, rocket (arugula) and plenty of lime or lemon juice, or treat it like mackerel.

Anchovies *(Engraulis encrasicolus)*

Above: Anchovies

These small fish seldom grow to more than 16cm/6¼in. They have steely blue backs, shimmering silver sides, and the upper jaw protrudes markedly. Most anchovies are filleted and preserved in salt or oil, but if you are lucky enough to find fresh fish, you are in for a real treat.
Habitat Anchovies are pelagic fish and are found in tightly packed shoals throughout the Mediterranean, in the Black Sea (where, pollution has depleted stocks) and the Atlantic and Pacific Oceans. Stocks off the Portuguese coast are being overfished, and those in the Bay of Biscay have all but disappeared.
Other names In French, anchovy is *anchois*, in Italian *acciuga* or *alice*, in Spanish *boquerón*.
Buying Buy fresh anchovies from well-managed fisheries. Ideally, fresh anchovies should be eaten straight from the sea. The best anchovies come from the Mediterranean and are at their peak in early summer. By the time they have been exported, however, they will have lost much of their flavour. When buying fresh anchovies, look for scintillating skins and bright, slightly bulging eyes.
Preparing You are unlikely to find a fishmonger willing to clean anchovies for you, but they are easy to prepare at home.

To gut, cut off the head and press gently along the body with your thumb to squeeze out the innards. To fillet, run your thumbnail or a stubby blunt knife along the length of the spine from head to tail on both sides and lift off the fillets.

Left: Sardines

Freezing It is worth freezing anchovies when they are plentiful. Remove the heads and clean the fish, then pack them in a box, separating the layers with sheets of clear film (plastic wrap). Cover the box with a lid and freeze. Thaw before using.

Sardines and Pilchards *(Sardinia pilchardus)*

It is a common misconception that sardines and pilchards are different fish: a pilchard is merely a larger, more mature sardine. Even the largest pilchards grow to only 20cm/8in, while sardines may be only 13–15cm/5–6in long. They are slim fish, with blue-green backs and silvery bellies. Their flesh is compact and has a delicious, oily flavour. Canned sardines and pilchards are very popular as store-cupboard (pantry) items because they are convenient and easy to prepare.

Habitat Sardines take their name from Sardinia, where they were once abundant. They are pelagic shoaling fish, and are found throughout the Mediterranean and Atlantic. Various related species are also found in other parts of the world.

Other names Sardines are easy to spot on foreign menus: they are *sardine* in French, *sardina* in Italian and Spanish, and *pilchard* or *sardine* in German.

Buying Sardines are at their best in spring and early summer. They do not travel well, so try to buy fish from local

Below: Pilchards

Above: Sprats

waters and avoid any stale-looking specimens. Small sardines have the best flavour, but larger fish are better for stuffing. Allow 3–5 sardines per serving.

Cooking Whole sardines are superb simply grilled (broiled) plain or cooked on a barbecue, which crisps the skin. They can be coated in breadcrumbs, fried and served with tomato sauce, made into fritters or stuffed with capers, salted anchovies or Parmesan and baked. They make an excellent sauce for pasta and are delicious marinated and served raw.

Alternatives Large anchovies or sprats can be used instead of small sardines.

Sprats *(Sprattus sprattus)*

These small silvery fish look very similar to sardines, but are slightly squatter. Once the sprat was an important fish, but now they are seldom sold fresh, being mostly smoked or cured.

Habitat They are abundant in the Baltic, North Sea and the Atlantic, and, since they can tolerate low salinity, are also found in fjords and estuaries.

Other names Sprats are *sprat* in French, *papalina* in Italian and *espadin* in Spanish. Smoked sprats are called *brisling* in Norway.

Cooking Sprats can be cooked in the same way as anchovies and small sardines. They are delicious when fried in oatmeal or deep-fried in batter.

Raw sprats can be marinated in vinaigrette; they are often served as part of a Scandinavian smorgasbord.

shake them in a plastic bag containing flour seasoned with salt and cayenne pepper. Deep-fry until very crisp.

"Blue" fish

Although they are not related to each other, several species of particularly oily fish are known collectively as "blue" fish. All have very smooth, taut skin with virtually undetectable scales and firm, meaty flesh. Varieties of blue fish are found in almost all temperate and tropical seas.

Mackerel *(Scomber scombrus)*

These streamlined fish are easily identified, thanks to their beautiful greenish-blue skin. They have wavy bands of black and green on their backs, while the bellies are silvery. The smooth, pale beigey-pink flesh is meaty, with a distinctive full flavour.
Habitat Mackerel are pelagic shoaling fish, often found in huge numbers in the North Atlantic, North Sea and Mediterranean. They spend the winter near the bottom of the cold North Sea, not feeding at all.

Below: Mackerel

Above: Whitebait

Whitebait

This name is given to tiny silver fish – only about 5cm/2in in length – that are caught in summer as they swim up estuaries. The name can refer to immature sprats or herrings, or to a mixture of both fish.
Other names Whitebait are *blanchaille* in French; this name is also used to describe tiny freshwater fish. The Italian name for them is *bianchetti*; the Spanish *aladroch*.
Buying Whitebait do not need to be cleaned. They are available fresh in spring and summer, and frozen all year round. Allow about 115g/4oz per person when serving them as an appetizer.
Cooking Whitebait are cooked whole, complete with heads. They are delicious deep-fried and served with brown bread and butter. Prepare them for cooking by dunking them in a bowl of milk, then

Below: Jack mackerel, which are not true mackerel, are common in New Zealand.

Other names Larger mackerel are known as *maquereau* in French; small specimens are called *lisette*. In Italian, mackerel is called *sgombro* and in Spanish it is known as *caballa*.
Buying Mackerel are delicious when extremely fresh, but not worth eating when they are past their best. They are in their prime in late spring and early summer, just before spawning. Look for firm fish with iridescent skin and clear, bright eyes. Small mackerel are better than large fish.

Below: Mackerel fillets can be cooked in the same way as herring – they are especially good lightly coated in oatmeal and pan-fried.

Larger specimens are sometimes sold filleted, and either sold fresh or smoked. Mackerel is a popular canned fish, and may be canned in either oil or tomato sauce.
Cooking Whole mackerel can be grilled (broiled), cooked on a barbecue, braised or poached in court-bouillon, white wine or cider. Slash both sides of each fish before cooking them over direct heat. Like herrings, they need a sharp sauce to counteract the richness of the flesh; classic accompaniments are gooseberry, sorrel, horseradish or mustard sauce. Fillets can be cooked in the same way as herring – coated in oatmeal and fried, or braised with onions and white wine. Raw mackerel fillets can be marinated in sweet-and-sour vinaigrette to make an appetizer.

Bluefish
(Pomatomus saltatrix)
Found in the Mediterranean and American Atlantic waters, bluefish are highly aggressive and are often fished for sport. They have shiny blue-green backs and masses of very sharp teeth. Bluefish are hugely popular in Turkey, where they are displayed in fish markets with their bright red gills turned inside out like elaborate rosettes to indicate their freshness. The flesh of bluefish is softer and more delicate than that of mackerel, but they can be cooked in the same way.

Right: Bluefish in a Turkish market with their bright red gills displayed.

Other varieties of mackerel
Chub mackerel *(Scomber japonicus colias)* are similar to Atlantic mackerel, but are also found in the Mediterranean and Black Sea. They have larger eyes and less bold markings on their backs. **Spanish mackerel** *(Scomber colias)* have spots below the lateral line. The rarer *Orcynopsis unicolor* is found near the coast of North Africa. It has silvery skin with spots of gold.
Horse mackerel *(Trachurus trachurus)* or **scad** and similar fish such as **jack mackerel** and **round robin** vaguely resemble herrings and are not, despite their name, true relatives of mackerel. They are perfectly edible, but their flesh is rather insipid and they tend to be bony. They can all be cooked in the same way as mackerel.

THE TUNA FAMILY

Tuna has been a popular food for centuries. The fish were highly prized by the Ancient Greeks, who mapped their migratory patterns in order to fish for them. A shoal of immense tuna fish travelling through the high seas is a magnificent sight, although satellite tracking has robbed the experience of some of its excitement. These beautiful, torpedo-shaped fish can grow to an enormous size (up to 700kg/1540lb). They have immensely powerful muscles and firm, dark, meaty flesh. There are many varieties of tuna, but due to centuries of overfishing, only about half a dozen varieties are available commercially.

Habitat Tuna are related to mackerel and are found in warmer seas throughout the world, as far north as the Bay of Biscay.

Other names In French, tuna is *thon*, in Italian *tonno*, in Spanish *atún*. In Japan, where it is eaten raw, it is called *maguro*.

Buying Tuna is usually sold as steaks. It is very substantial, so allow only 175g/6oz per serving. Depending on the variety, the flesh may range from pale beigey-pink to deep dark red. Do not buy steaks with heavy discolorations around the bone, or which are dull-looking and brownish all over. The flesh should be very firm and compact.

Cooking Tuna becomes greyish and dry when overcooked, so it is essential to cook it only briefly over high heat, or to stew it gently with moist ingredients like tomatoes and (bell) peppers. It has

Below: Tuna steaks

become fashionable to sear it fleetingly, leaving it almost raw in the middle; if this is not to your taste, cook the tuna for about 2 minutes on each side – no more.

The following cooking methods are suitable for most types of tuna. Steaks can be seared, grilled (broiled), baked or braised. They benefit from being marinated for about 30 minutes before cooking. Tuna marries well with Mediterranean vegetables, such as tomatoes, (bell) peppers and onions. Most varieties can be eaten raw as *sashimi*, *sushi* or *tartare*, but they must be absolutely fresh. Tuna fillets are delicious cut very thin, dusted with flour and cooked like veal *scaloppine* in butter. Grilled (broiled) tuna makes a superb addition to a classic Salade Niçoise.

Albacore *(Thunnus alalunga)*

Also known as longfin, this tuna is found in temperate and tropical seas, although only the smaller specimens venture into the North Sea. Albacore has pale, rosy flesh which resembles veal. Once known as "Carthusian veal", it could be eaten by monks when eating meat was not permitted. Albacore from the Pacific and Atlantic oceans are among the few varieties that are still being fished at sustainable levels.

Other names Albacore is also known as "white" tuna. In French it is *thon blanc* or *germon*; in Italian *alalunga* and in Spanish *atún blanco* or *albacora*.

Cooking Because its rosy-white flesh is so akin to veal, albacore is often cooked in similar ways – as escalopes (scallops) or larded with anchovy fillets and pork back fat, and braised.

False albacore *(Euthynnus alletteratus)*

This comparatively small tuna (weighing about 15kg/33lb) is found only in warmer waters, generally off the coast of Africa. It is highly sought-after in Japan, where it is used for *sashimi*.

Above: Bigeye or blackfin tuna steaks

Bigeye *(Thunnus obesus)*

This fat relative of the bluefin is found in tropical waters. It has rosy flesh and is substituted for bluefin when that superior tuna is unavailable. As a result, it has suffered from overfishing and is now endangered. It is sometimes known as blackfin tuna. Other languages continue the rather rude reference to its obesity; In French, it is *thon obèse*, in Italian, *tonno obeso* and in Spanish *patudo*.

Bluefin *(Thunnus thynnus)*

Considered by many to be the finest of all tuna, bluefin are also the largest, and can grow to an enormous size (up to 700kg/1,540lb), although the average weight is about 120kg/264lb. Bluefin have dark blue backs and silvery bellies. Their oily flesh is deep red and has a more robust flavour than albacore. Bluefin is the classic tuna for *sushi* and *sashimi*. Its popularity means that bluefin from all waters are now critically endangered, so avoid eating these.

Habitat Bluefin are found in the Bay of Biscay, the Mediterranean and tropical seas. They are very strong swimmers and a dense shoal of bluefin powering its way through the sea is an awesome sight.

Other names In Australia, the fish is known as Southern bluefin. Owing to its bright red flesh, bluefin is *thon rouge* in

Left: Bluefin tuna

French. In Italian it is merely *tonno*; in Spanish it is known as *atún*.

Buying Bluefin tuna is extremely expensive, largely because the Japanese will pay almost any price for it. It has an almost gamey flavour and is best when it has been kept for a week. Once the flesh has turned from bright red to light brown, however, it should be avoided at all costs – the tuna is past its prime. Ideally, avoid buying any bluefin tuna, even farmed or "ranched" fish, as farming relies on capture of juveniles from the wild.

Bonito *(Sarda sarda)* and Skipjack *(Katsuwonus pelamis)*

These fish fall somewhere between mackerel and tuna. There are two main types of bonito: Atlantic *(Sarda sarda)* and skipjack or oceanic. The Atlantic bonito is also found in the Mediterranean and Black Sea; skipjack is most commonly found in the Atlantic and Pacific Oceans.

Bonito are inferior to true tuna in quality and taste, with pale flesh which can sometimes be rather dry. Skipjack are usually used for canning. They are popular in Japan, where they are known as *katsuo* and are often made into dried flakes *(katsuobushi)*, which is a main ingredient of *dashi* (stock).

Other names
Skipjack have dark blue parallel lines along their bellies and are sometimes known as "striped tuna". This gives them the French name *bonite à ventre rayé* (striped belly). In Italian they are *bonita*; in Spanish, *listado*.

Frigate mackerel *(Auxis rochei)*

Despite its name, this fish is actually a tuna that is found in the Pacific and Indian Oceans. It grows to only about 50cm/20in and has red, coarse flesh. Some are small enough to cook whole.

Yellowfin *(Thunnus albacores)*

These large tuna are fished in tropical and equatorial waters. Weighing up to 250kg/550lb, they resemble albacore, but their fins are yellow. They have pale pinkish flesh and a good flavour.

Other names Confusingly, the French and Italians call yellowfin *albacore* and *tonno albacora* respectively. In Spanish, it is *rabil*.

Buying Since yellowfin tuna come from warm oceans, in Europe they are generally sold frozen as steaks. Make sure that they have not begun to thaw before you buy. Frozen yellowfin is available all year round.

Cooking Very fresh yellowfin can be eaten raw as *sashimi* or *sushi*, but is better cooked in any recipe that is suitable for tuna.

Salade Niçoise
Tuna is the essential ingredient of this substantial Provençal salad, whose other components consist of whatever is fresh and available. Although the salad can be (and often is) made with drained canned tuna, it is infinitely nicer to use fresh seared or grilled (broiled) fish. Arrange some shredded cos or romaine lettuce in a salad bowl and add the tuna, some quartered hard-boiled eggs, thickly-sliced cooked new potatoes, tomato wedges, crisply cooked green beans, some black olives and a few anchovy fillets. Just before serving, toss the salad in a little garlic-flavoured vinaigrette dressing.

Above: Bluefin tuna steaks

FLAT FISH

All flat fish start life as pelagic larvae, with an eye on each side of their head like a round fish. At this stage, they swim upright near the surface of the sea. As they mature, the fish start to swim on one side only and one eye moves over the head on to the dark-skinned side of the body. Later, they gravitate to the sea bed and feed on whatever edible creatures pass by. Because they do not have to chase their food, their flesh is always delicate and white, without too much muscle fibre. They have a simple bone structure, so even people who are nervous about bones can cope with them. With the exception of flounder, flat fish are seldom found outside European waters.

Brill (Scophthalmus rhombus)

Similar to turbot in appearance and taste, brill is regarded as the poor relation, although it has fine softish white flesh with a delicate flavour. Brill

Above: Brill

can grow to about 75cm/30in and can weigh up to 3kg/6½lb, but are often smaller. The fish have slender bodies, and there are small, smooth scales on the dark grey skin on the top. The underside is creamy or pinkish white.
Habitat Brill live on the bottom of the Atlantic, Baltic Sea and Mediterranean.
Buying Brill is considerably cheaper than turbot and available almost all year round, as whole fish or fillets. In the North Sea, much of the brill is taken as a by-catch in beam-trawl fisheries and many of these fish are immature, so do not buy brill from this area. They spawn in spring and summer;

Left: Dab

females can contain a great deal of roe just before spawning, and can lose condition after spawning so avoid buying them during these seasons. There is a high percentage of wastage in all flat fish, so you will need a 1.5kg/3–3½lb fish for four.
Cooking Brill can hold its own against robust red wine and is often cooked in a *matelote* (fish stew) or red wine sauce. Small fish (up to 2kg/4½lb) are best cooked whole; they can be baked, braised, poached, steamed, pan-fried or grilled (broiled). Whole poached brill is excellent garnished with prawns (shrimp) or other shellfish. Fillets of brill *à l'anglaise* are coated in egg and breadcrumbs and pan-fried in butter.
Other names In French, brill is *barbue*, in Italian *rombo liscio*, "smooth turbot"; its Spanish name is *rémol*.
Alternatives Any halibut, sole or turbot recipe is suitable for brill.

Dab (Limanda limanda)

There are several related species of dab, none of which has much flavour. European and American dabs are small lozenge-shaped fish, which seldom grow to more than 35cm/14in. They have brownish, rough skin and a lateral line.
Habitat Dabs are found in shallow water on the sandy bottom of the Atlantic and off the coast of New Zealand.
Other names The so-called false dabs are more elongated than their European counterparts. In America, dabs are known as sand dabs. In French, they are *limande*, in Italian *limanda* and in Spanish *limanda nordica*.
Buying Only eat dabs when they are very fresh. Make sure they have glossy skins and smell fresh. Dabs are usually sold whole, but larger fish may be filleted.
Cooking Dabs have rather soft, insipid flesh. Pan-fry them in butter or grill (broil) them. Fillets can be coated in egg and breadcrumbs and fried.

Above: Halibut

Below: Halibut Steaks

Halibut (Hippoglossus hippoglossus)

Halibut are the largest of the flat fish, sometimes growing up to 2m/6½ft and weighing well over 200kg/440lb, although they normally weigh between 3kg/6½lb and 15kg/33lb. Halibut have elegant, greenish-brown bodies, a pointed head with the eyes on the right-hand side, and pearly white undersides. The flesh is delicious with a fine, meaty texture.
Habitat Atlantic halibut live in very cold, deep waters off the coasts of Scotland, Norway, Iceland and Newfoundland, and migrate to shallower waters to spawn. The stock level in these northern waters is extremely low and fish from the Atlantic should be avoided. A warm water variety is found in the Pacific. These fish are voracious predators, which will eat almost any type of fish, and will even devour birds' eggs that roll off cliffs.
Other names Greenland halibut, a long-lived and inferior fish, is best avoided, especially as it too has suffered from overfishing. True halibut is called *flétan* in French and *halibut* in both Italian and Spanish.
Buying Choose Pacific halibut as an alternative to Atlantic or Greenland halibut. Excellent fish are available from Alaska from March to November. Whole young halibut weigh 1.5–2kg/3¼–4½lb, and one will amply serve four. Larger fish are almost always sold as steaks or fillets. Go for steaks cut from the middle and allow 175–200g/6–7oz per serving.
Cooking Young halibut can be baked, braised, poached or cooked *à la bonne femme*, with shallots, mushrooms and white wine. The flesh of large halibut can be dry, so should be braised or baked with wine or stock.
Alternatives Brill can be substituted for halibut in any recipe. Turbot or John Dory can also be used.

Flounder (Platichthys flesus)

Another large family of fish, species of flounder are found in many parts of the world, from Europe to New Zealand. The mottled greyish-brown skin has orange spots and is rough. Flounders can grow to 50cm/20in, but they usually measure only 25–30cm/10–12in.
Habitat Flounders live close to the shore and are sometimes found in estuaries. They spend their days on the sea bed, not feeding, but become active at night.
Other names Many types of flounder are found in America, where they are variously known as summer, winter and sand flounders. Other varieties have such descriptive names as arrowtooth, black, greenback and yellowbelly. In France, they are called *flet*, in Italy, *passera pianuzza*; in Spain, *platija*.
Buying Like dabs, flounders must be extremely fresh. Apply the same criteria.
Cooking As for dabs, brill or plaice.

Below: Flounder

Megrim *(Lepidorhombus whiffiagonis)*

Small yellowish-grey translucent fish with large eyes and mouths, megrim seldom grow to more than 50cm/20in in length. They have dryish, rather bland flesh and are not considered much worth eating.

Habitat Found mostly to the south of the English Channel.

Other names Nowadays often marketed as Cornish sole. Megrim is also known by the alternative names of whiff or sail-fluke. In France it is called *cardine franche*; in Italy *rombo giallo* (although you are unlikely to find it on a restaurant menu in either country). In Spain, where it is quite popular, it is called *gallo*.

Buying Megrim are either sold whole or as fillets. They need to be extremely fresh, so make sure you smell them before you buy. Allow a 350g/12oz fish or at least two fillets per serving.

Cooking Whole fish can be coated in batter or breadcrumbs and deep-fried, or poached or baked. Their flesh can sometimes be rather dry, so use plenty of liquid. Fillets are best crumbed and deep-fried. Remove the coarse skin before frying or grilling (broiling).

Alternatives Lemon sole, plaice, dab or witch (Torbay sole).

Above: Megrim

Above: Plaice

Plaice *(Pleuronectes platessa)*

These distinctive-looking fish have smooth, dark greyish-brown skin with orange spots. The underside is pearly white. The eyes are on the right-hand side; a ridge of bony knobs runs from behind them to the dorsal fin. Plaice can weigh up to 7kg/15½lb, but the average weight is 400g–1kg/ 14oz–2¼lb. They have soft, rather bland white flesh, which can sometimes lack flavour.

Habitat Plaice are found in the Atlantic and other northerly waters, and in the Mediterranean. They are bottom-feeding fish which, like flounder, are most active at night.

Other names In France, plaice are *plie* or *carrelet*; in Italy, *passera* or *pianuzza*; in Spain, *solla*.

Buying Stocks of plaice are in decline in the North Sea, so try to buy fish from the Irish Sea. Plaice must be very fresh, or the flesh tends to take on a woolly texture. These fish are available all year, whole or as fillets, but

Left: Plaice fillets

are best avoided in the summer months, when the flesh is flaccid and tasteless. In fresh plaice, the orange spots on the dark skin will be bright and distinctive. Dark-skinned plaice fillets are cheaper than white-skinned, but there is no difference in flavour. There is a lot of wastage on plaice, so you should allow a whole 350–450g/12–16oz fish per serving, or 175g/6oz fillet.

Cooking Any sole or brill recipe is suitable for plaice. Deep-fried in batter, plaice is a classic "fish and chip shop" favourite. Whole fish or fillets can be coated in egg and breadcrumbs and pan-fried. Steamed or poached plaice is highly digestible and makes good food during illness. For plaice *à la florentine*, bake a whole fish or white-skinned fillets in stock and white wine, lay it on a bed of lightly-cooked spinach, cover with a cheese sauce and grill (broil) until bubbling and browned.

Alternatives Flounder, dab, sole and brill can all be substituted for plaice.

Sole/Dover sole *(Solea solea)*

Arguably the finest fish of all, Dover sole have a firm, delicate flesh with a superb flavour. Their oval bodies are well proportioned, with greyish or lightish brown skin, sometimes spotted with black. The eyes are on the right-hand side. The nasal openings on the underside are small and widely separated, which distinguishes these sole from lesser varieties. Dover sole can weigh up to 3kg/6½lb, but the average weight is 200–600g/7oz–1lb 6oz.

The Ancient Romans adored sole and called them *solea Jovi* ("Jupiter's sandal"). The firm flesh was often preserved. During the reign of Louis XIV of France, sole was regarded as truly fit for a king, and the great chefs of the time created extravagant sole dishes. In the earlier part of the 20th century, it was the mainstay of English fish cooking.

Habitat Dover sole are found in the English Channel and the Atlantic Ocean and also in the Baltic, Mediterranean and North Seas. They come inshore to spawn in spring and summer. For the most part, they spend their days buried in the sand on the sea bed and hunt for food at night.

Other names Sand or partridge sole *(Pegusa lascaris)* are very similar in appearance to Dover sole and are sometimes sold as "Dovers", although they are smaller and inferior fish. Their distinguishing feature is a much larger nasal opening on the underside. Another species, known as "tongues", *(Dicologlossa cuneata)* are smaller still (only 7.5–10cm/3–4in in length). In France, these fish are sometimes sold as baby Dover sole, when they are known as *séteaux* (or *cétaux*) or *langues d'avocat* ("lawyers' tongues"). In French Dover sole is *sole*; in Italian, *sogliola*; in Spanish, *lenguado*.

Buying Sole are at their best three days after being caught, so if you are sure that you are buying fish straight from the sea, keep them for a couple of days before cooking. The skin should be sticky and the underside very white. Nowadays, whole sole are graded by weight;

Above: Dover sole (top) and lemon sole

Below: Turbot

Other names In America, lemon sole are known as yellowtail flounder. In France, they are *limande-sole*, in Italy *sogliola limanda*; in Spain, *mendo limón*.

Buying Lemon sole are available all year round and are sold whole or as fillets. They must be very fresh and should have a tang of the sea. Don't buy immature fish (less than 25cm/10in long) and those caught between April and August, which is the breeding season.

Cooking Lemon sole are best cooked simply; use them in any dab, plaice or Dover sole recipe.

Turbot *(Psetta maxima)*

What turbot lacks in looks, it makes up for in texture and taste. Highly prized since ancient times, it was called *le roi de carême* ("the king of Lent") in the Middle Ages. All the great chefs of the time created sumptuous recipes for turbot, marrying the fish with langoustines, truffles, lobster sauce and beef marrow. Turbot have tiny heads and large, almost circular bodies with tough warty brown skin like a toad. They can grow to 1m/40in in length and can weigh as much as 12kg/26½lb. The flesh is creamy white, with a firm, dense texture and a superb sweet flavour.

a 225g/8oz fish will serve one person. If you want to serve two, buy a fish weighing at least 675–800g/1½–1¾lb (which will yield four decent-size fillets, but could prove costly). It is best to buy a whole fish; if you ask the fishmonger to fillet it for you, keep the bones and trimmings to make fish stock. Avoid buying immature sole (less than 28cm/11in long) and fish caught between April and June, which is the breeding season.

Cooking There are many recipes for sole, but a plain lightly grilled (broiled) fish served with a drizzle of melted butter and lemon juice is hard to beat. Skin both sides before cooking. Small sole can be coated in egg and breadcrumbs and pan-fried or deep-fried; larger specimens can be poached, steamed or cooked in butter *à la meunière*. Fillets can be fried, poached in wine or served with an elaborate sauce, or given an Asian twist with soy sauce, lemon grass and ginger.

Alternatives
Nothing tastes quite like Dover sole, but lemon sole and other flat fish can be cooked in the same way.

Lemon sole *(Microstomus kitt)*

Despite the name, lemon sole is related to dab, plaice and flounder. These fish are oval in shape, with the widest part well towards the head. They have smooth reddish brown skin with irregular marbling and a straight lateral line, very small heads and bulging eyes. The flesh is soft and white, similar to plaice but slightly superior. It is a good alternative to the more expensive Dover sole.

Habitat Lemon sole are found in the North Sea and Atlantic Ocean and around the coast of New Zealand. They lead largely stationary lives on the stony or rocky sea bed and vary enormously in size depending on local conditions.

Turbot kettle
In the days of affordable luxury, a whole huge turbot might be steamed in a magnificent diamond-shaped copper turbot kettle with handles on the points and a grid for lifting out the cooked fish.

Nowadays you will find only one of these kettles in the kitchen of a stately home or a fine restaurant. Modern turbot kettles are made of stainless steel or aluminium.

Above: Chicken turbot

Habitat Turbot live on the sea bottom in the Atlantic, Mediterranean and Black Seas, and have been introduced to New Zealand waters. They can be farmed successfully, and this has improved both the quality and the size of the fish.
Other names The name is the same – *turbot* – in French, *rombo chiodato* (studded with nails) in Italian; *rodaballo* in Spanish. Small young turbot, weighing up to 2kg/4½lb, are called chicken turbot.
Buying Turbot is extremely expensive; a really large wild fish can cost several hundred pounds (dollars). Farmed fish are cheaper, but can be fatty. Turbot should have creamy white flesh; do not buy fish with a blue tinge.

It is available all year round, sold whole, as steaks and fillets. A chicken turbot weighing about 1.5kg/3–3½lb will feed four people. There is a high percentage of wastage, so if your fishmonger fillets a whole

turbot for you, ask for the bones to make a superb stock. Turbot is over-fished in the North Sea, so buy fish from other areas, and ask for line-caught fish or those caught in "dolphin-friendly" nets. Avoid turbot less than 30cm/12in long and do not buy them during their breeding season (April to August).
Cooking It is neither practical nor economical to cook a whole turbot that weighs more than about 1.5kg/3–3½lb in a domestic

Below: Witch

kitchen. To cook a chicken turbot, grill (broil) it or poach in white wine and fish stock. Traditionally, turbot was poached in milk to keep the flesh pure white, then served with hollandaise sauce. Almost any cooking method is suitable for turbot, except perhaps deep-frying, which would be a waste. Creamy sauces such as lobster, parsley and mushroom go well with plainly-cooked turbot. Chunks of poached turbot dressed with a piquant vinaigrette, make a superb salad.
Alternatives Nothing quite equals turbot, but brill, halibut, John Dory and fillets of sole make good substitutes.

Witch *(Glyptocephalus cynoglossus)*

This member of the sole family has an elongated body like a sole, with a straight lateral line on the rough, grey-brown skin. The flesh tastes rather insipid.
Other names Nowadays usually marketed as Torbay sole. Also known as witch flounder and pole flounder. In French, it is *plie grise*, in Italian *passera cinoglossa*; in Spanish *mendo*.
Buying Witch are available all year round, usually only near the coast where they are caught – mostly off the south-west coast of England. They are only worth eating when very fresh.
Cooking It is important to season Witch well before cooking. They are best grilled (broiled), but any sole recipe is suitable.

MIGRATORY FISH

Certain species of fish undertake an astonishing annual mass migration from one area to another to spawn or feed. They follow a specific route, although how they know which route to take remains a mystery. Each year salmon and sea trout migrate from the sea to spawn in the fresh water of the river; having spawned, they return to the sea, and so the pattern continues. Eels, on the other hand, travel from rivers and lakes to spawn in salt sea water, entailing a journey of thousands of miles. The whole process is truly one of nature's miracles.

EELS (Anguillidae)

There are more than twenty members of the eel family. All are slim snake-like fish with smooth slippery skin and spineless fins. The Anguillidae family are freshwater fish, but other species, such as conger, moray and snake eels, are marine fish. Eels have fatty white flesh with a rich flavour and firm texture.

Eels have been a popular food since Roman times, and were highly prized in the Middle Ages. Their mysterious life cycle gave rise to all sorts of improbable myths; one popular belief was that they were loose horsehairs which came to life when they touched the water. The less fanciful but equally amazing truth was only discovered by a Danish scientist at the end of the 19th century.

Habitat Freshwater eels are born in the Sargasso Sea. Each female lays up to 20 million eggs and both she and her male partner die immediately after the eggs have been laid and fertilized. The eggs hatch into minuscule larvae, which are carried on the ocean currents to the coasts of Europe and America, then back to the rivers where their ancestors matured. This journey takes a year for American eels and between two and three years for European eels. No one has yet fathomed how the babies know which direction to take, since they have never seen "home". When the baby elvers enter the estuaries in huge flotillas, they are tiny transparent

Above: Young eels

creatures not more than 8cm/3¼in long. As they mature, their skin colour changes to yellow, then to green and finally to silver. At this stage, the eels begin the long journey back to the Sargasso Sea, where they spawn and immediately die.

Varieties Tiny elvers are known as glass eels (*civelles* or *piballes* in French). Adult European eels (*Anguilla anguilla*) and American eels (*Anguilla rostrata*) are *anguille* in French, *anguilla* in Italian and *anguila* in Spanish. The Japanese eel (*Anguilla japonica*) and Australian eel (*Anguilla australis*) are both known as the shortfinned eel, while *Anguilla dieffenbachii* is the longfinned eel.

Buying Wild stocks of European or common eels are severely depleted and are best avoided until stocks can be replenished. Even farmed eels rely on taking juveniles from the wild, so try to only buy in moderation. You may find tiny elvers for sale in the spring – these are a great delicacy and are extremely expensive. One kilo/two pounds can consist of up to two thousand tiny elvers.

Adult eels are at their best in autumn (fall) when they have turned silver with almost black backs. Females weigh three times as much as males, so a female silver eel is highly prized. Farmed eels are available all year round. Eels should be bought alive, as they go off very quickly once dead. Ask the fishmonger to chop them into 5cm/2in lengths.

Skinning an eel

Grip the eel in a cloth and bang its head sharply on a hard surface to kill it. Put a string noose around the base of the head and hang it firmly on a sturdy hook or door handle. Slit the skin all round the head just below the noose. Pull away the top of the skin, turn it back to make a "cuff", then grip with a cloth or two pairs of pliers and pull the skin down firmly towards the tail. Cut off the head and tail. Alternatively, kill the eel and chop it into sections, leaving the skin on. Grill (broil) the pieces, skin up, turning frequently until the skin has puffed up on all sides. When cool enough to handle, peel off the skin.

Cooking Tiny elvers can be tossed in seasoned flour and deep-fried; soak them first in acidulated water to remove the mud. Eel is a versatile fish that can be fried and served with parsley sauce. It is good poached or braised in red wine. If you grill (broil) it, marinate it first, then wrap it in bacon to keep the fish moist. Eel is excellent in soups and casseroles, such as *matelote*, and the rich flesh marries well with robust Asian flavours. Two classic English eel recipes are jellied eels and eel pie with mashed potatoes and green "liquor". Eels are also delicious smoked.

Conger eel *(Conger conger)*

These marine eels can grow to an enormous size – sometimes up to 3m/9ft 9in, although the average length is 60–150cm/2–5ft. They are ferocious carnivores with long, thick scaleless bodies and very bony firm white flesh.
Habitat Conger eels are found in temperate and tropical seas, living in rocky crevices and wrecks. Many live in deep water, but some prefer to lurk in shallow inshore waters.
Other names In French, conger eel is *congre*, in Italian *grongo*, and in Spanish *congrio*.
Buying Conger has the merit of being cheap. It is available from early spring to autumn (fall) and is usually sold cut

Below: Conger eel steaks

into steaks. Ask for a middle cut from near the head end; the tail end is extremely bony. If you are offered a whole conger, ask the fishmonger to fillet it and keep the head and bones for soup or stock.
Cooking The meaty flesh of conger eel is best used for soups or hearty casseroles. Its density makes it good for terrines. Thick middle cuts can be roasted, poached or braised and served with a *salsa verde*.

Above: Fierce-looking conger eel, which is a ferocious carnivore.

Moray eel *(Muraena helena)*

These eels are even more fearsome than the conger eel. They grow to only about 2m/6ft 6in, but are extremely vicious and will not hesitate to bite. Moray eels have long, flattened bodies and thick, greenish leathery skin with a pattern of light spots and no scales. The white flesh is rather tasteless and very bony.
Habitat Most species of moray eel are found in tropical and sub-tropical waters, but some occur in the Atlantic and Mediterranean. These eels typically anchor the tail end of their bodies in rock crevices and corals and wait with their mouths agape for catching prey that comes too close.
Buying Morays are mostly fished for sport and are seldom found in fishmongers. When they are available, they are sold in chunks.
Cooking Morays are fit only for soup, and are often used in the traditional *bouillabaisse*. They can be cooked gently in cider, then the flesh removed and used in fish pies or fish cakes. The tail end is full of sharp bones. Avoid it, unless you are making stock.

Right: Atlantic salmon

THE SALMON FAMILY

Known as the "king of fish", salmon is probably the most important of all fish, prized by sportsmen and gastronomes alike. Various species are found throughout the world, but the finest by far is the Atlantic salmon. All salmon spawn in fresh water. Some species spend their lives in landlocked waters, but after two years, most salmon migrate upstream to the sea to feed before returning to spawn in the rivers where they were born. This arduous trek makes them sleek and muscular. Once they return to fresh water, they stop feeding, only starting again when they go back to the sea.

Salmon have suffered from over-fishing and environmental disturbance, and wild fish have become rare and expensive. Once, it was possible to land salmon weighing 20kg/44lb or more, but such magnificent fish have now disappeared. Fortunately, salmon can be farmed successfully, although early salmon farms produced fish with flabby, bland flesh, often riddled with sea lice, which attacked and further decimated the wild stocks. Lessons have been learned, and it is now possible to buy healthy, well-flavoured farmed salmon.

Atlantic salmon *(Salmo salar)*

These magnificent fish have silvery-blue backs, silver sides and white bellies. In comparison to their large, powerful bodies, their heads are quite small. The heads and backs are marked with tiny black crosses. Salmon's fine fatty flesh is deep pink and firm with a superb, rich flavour.
Habitat Atlantic salmon are found in all the cold northern waters of Europe and America. They are spawned in rivers, then undertake the exhausting journey back to the sea, returning to the river to spawn in their turn. When young salmon, which are 10–20cm/4–8in long, first migrate to the sea, they are called smolts. After a year or two of voracious feeding, they reach a weight of

Below: Salmon steaks

1–2kg/2¼–4½lb and make their first spawning run; these young fish are called grilse. The males develop elongated hooked jaws; this is just to help them fight the strong currents, since they do not feed during the spawning run. Some fish may spawn only once or twice in their lifetimes; others up to four times.

Salmon were a popular food in the Middle Ages, when they were braised with spices, potted or salted, or made into pies and pâtés. Once they became rarer, they were regarded as a luxury and chefs vied to marry them with extravagant ingredients such as lobster, crayfish and cream. Only recently has salmon once again become affordable.
Other names The deep, cold lakes of Canada and North America are home to landlocked salmon; these are variously known as ouananiche, lake salmon and sebago. In French, salmon are *saumon*, in Italian *salmone*; in Spanish *salmón*.
Buying Stocks of wild Atlantic salmon are so severely overfished that it is considered a threatened species, so buy only for very special occasions. Atlantic salmon is widely farmed, but make sure the fish are organic, or at least come from a reputable fishery. Ethical fishmongers will tell you which fish are wild and which are farmed. If your preference is for wild fish, buy Pacific salmon, particularly fish from Alaska. Wild salmon are sleeker, with firmer, lustrous skin and deep pink flesh. They are available from spring to late summer. Late-spawning fish which return to the sea in autumn (fall) are known as kelts; because they have not

eaten for many months, kelts are thin and in poor condition and are not worth buying. Grilse – young salmon with an average weight of 1.4kg/3lb – are cheaper than large wild fish and will provide a generous meal for two. Scottish and Irish wild salmon are the finest of all; Atlantic salmon from Greenland and Scandinavia is less highly regarded.

The quality of farmed salmon can be variable. The flesh should be firm and dark pink with creamy marbling and not too much fat, not flabby and pale or greyish. Salmon heads are surprisingly heavy, so if you buy whole salmon allow about 350–400g/12–14oz per serving. If buying steaks or cutlets, you will need only about 200g/7oz per person.

Cooking There is almost no limit to the ways in which you can prepare and cook salmon. It can be eaten raw as a salmon *tartare*, *sashimi* or in *sushi*. It can be marinated in oil, lemon juice and herbs or salted and marinated to make *gravad lax*. It can be poached, pan-fried, seared, grilled (broiled), baked or braised, or enveloped in pastry as *saumon en croûte* or *coulibiac*. Poached salmon is delicious hot or cold; a whole fish poached in *court-bouillon* makes a superb festive dish served with mayonnaise and dressed with cucumber. It is also excellent with a spicy salsa. Hot poached salmon cries out for hollandaise or rich seafood sauce or *beurre blanc*. If you do not

have a fish kettle large enough for a whole salmon, wrap the fish in foil, moisten with white wine, then bake.

Salmon fillets can be thinly sliced and flash-fried, or sandwiched together with fish or shellfish mousse or vegetable purée and baked or braised. They are delicious made into fish cakes, kedgeree, pâté and mousse. Try them potted in butter flavoured with mace, or as *rillettes*. Steaks can be cooked in red wine, poached, baked *en papillote* with white wine and herbs or grilled (broiled), pan-fried or cooked on a barbecue. Salmon is also delicious cold- or hot-smoked. It can be cured in salt and is one of the world's most popular canned fish.

Alternatives Sea trout and good-quality brown or rainbow trout can be used instead of salmon.

Pacific salmon *(Onorhynchus)*

Five species of Pacific salmon are found around the Pacific coast from California to Alaska and another is found in northern Japan. Even the largest, the Chinook or king salmon, is smaller and slimmer than its Atlantic counterpart. Other Pacific salmon include the sockeye or red

salmon, chum or dog salmon and pink salmon. Pacific salmon are shorter-lived than Atlantic salmon, but much more prolific breeders. None of the five species is as fine as Atlantic salmon and all types are frequently sold canned.

Sea trout *(Salmo trutta)*

Although they are closely related to the brown trout, sea trout differ from other species in that they migrate to the sea like salmon. They closely resemble salmon, but have smaller heads and squarer tails. Sea trout seldom grow to more than 3kg/6½lb, which makes them more manageable for cooking. They have fine, dark pink flesh, which is beautifully succulent and has a delicate flavour.

Other names Sea trout are also known as salmon trout or sewin. In French, they are *truite de mer*, in Italian *trota di mare*, and in Spanish *trucha marina*.

Buying Sea trout are always wild, but they do not cost so much as wild salmon. They are sold whole; a 2kg/½lb fish will serve 4–6 people. They should be bright and silvery with an almost golden sheen.

Cooking As for salmon.

Above: Sea trout

EXOTIC FISH

Thanks to modern transportation, unusual exotic fish from tropical seas all over the world are now available in European and North American markets. Warm water fish never have quite as good a flavour as those from colder climes, but they add variety to a fish diet and are often very colourful. Do not be alarmed at the prospect of cooking unfamiliar fish; they can be cooked in the same way as other species, and lend themselves to exotic flavourings, so you can experiment with new taste sensations.

Barracouta/Snoek *(Thyrsites atun)*

This long thin fish has smooth blue-grey skin with silver sides and belly, a flat dorsal fin running almost the length of the body and a series of spines near the tail. Barracouta can grow to 2m/6½ft long, but are generally 60–90cm/ 24–36in in length. The lower jaw protrudes, and there is a single lateral line. The dryish flesh is dark, but whitens on cooking. Barracouta have long, irregular bones. The fish are often canned, which softens the bones and makes them more palatable.
Habitat Barracouta are widely distributed in temperate regions of the southern hemisphere.
Other names In Australia and New Zealand, the name barracouta is often shortened to "couta". In South Africa, these fish are always known as snoek.
Buying Barracouta are not sold fresh in the northern hemisphere, but you may find them canned or smoked.
Cooking Barracouta can be grilled (broiled), fried or baked. They are often pickled in vinegar and spices, and marry well with Asian flavours. Smoked barracouta is absolutely delicious.

Barracuda *(Sphyraena barracuda)*

These fearsome-looking game fish have long slender bodies, forked tails and sharp teeth capable of delivering a vicious bite. There are about twenty species of barracuda. The largest is the great barracuda, which has dark

Above: Barracuda

bars and scattered black blotches on its greenish skin. This fish can grow to over 1m/3¼ft in length. Other species include the yellowtail and the small Pacific and Mexican barracudas. All have meaty, rich, oily flesh, which has the reputation of being toxic. Play safe by not eating raw fish; properly cooked, it is perfectly acceptable.
Habitat Barracuda are found in warm waters, mainly in the Pacific and Caribbean, but sometimes in warmer Atlantic seas. Young fish travel in schools, but older specimens are solitary. They are full of curiosity and will follow divers around the reefs, or even walkers along the shore, which gives them the undeserved reputation of being predatory.
Other names In French, barracuda is known as *brochet de mer* because it resembles pike. Italians call it *luccio marina* and in Spain it is *espeton*.

Below: Barramundi

Buying Small barracuda up to 3kg/6½lb are best. Ask the fishmonger to scale and fillet them. Larger fish are often sold already filleted. Barracuda is available all year round.
Cooking The rich flesh of barracuda lends itself well to Asian flavourings. It is oily, so avoid cooking with butter, cream or too much oil. Small whole barracuda can be grilled (broiled), cooked on a barbecue or baked. Fillets and steaks can be curried or marinated in spices and grilled or baked.
Alternatives Any firm-fleshed oily fish, such as tuna or bonito.

Barramundi *(Lates calcifer)*

This beautiful giant perch has an elongated silver body with a dark grey back, a curved lateral line and a protruding lower jaw. Barramundi can grow to an enormous size, often weighing more than 20kg/44lb; the record catch so far weighed 250kg/ 550lb. The best size for eating is about 10kg/22lb, although whole baby

barramundi (or "barra") are popular in Australia. The chunky white flesh has a delicious, quite delicate flavour.
Habitat Barramundi are found in Indo-Pacific waters, from Japan to the East Indies. They often swim close to the shore and are sometimes found in estuaries and brackish water.
Other names Barramundi are sometimes known as giant perch.
Buying Until recently you would have been unlikely to find barramundi outside the Antipodes and Asia. Now, however, they are being successfully farmed in the New Forest, and are available in British supermarkets and fishmongers. Small fish are sold whole and larger specimens are sold as steaks or fillets. Look for bright skin and white flesh.

Below: Flying fish

Cooking Whole fish can be baked, fried, braised, grilled (broiled) or cooked on a barbecue. Cook fillets and steaks in the same way as bream, porgy and snapper.

Flying fish (Exocoetidae)

These are the fish that gave their name to the exocet missile, due to their habit of gliding (not flying) amazing distances through the air at about 60kph/40mph. They are supported by a disproportionately large, highly-developed, wing-like, spineless pectoral fin. Flying fish begin their "flight" below the water, at high speed, bursting through the surface into the air. Only then do they expand their pectoral fins, which allow them to glide for about 30 seconds before dropping tail-first back into the water. Flying fish may look spectacular, but their flavour is less exciting than their appearance.

Habitat Various species of flying fish are found in the Caribbean, Pacific and warm Atlantic waters. They are attracted by bright lights and are sometimes lured by fishermen who hang a lamp over the side of the boat to encourage the fish to "fly" into their nets.
Other names The French call flying fish *exocet*, the Italians *pesce volante*, the Spanish *pez voador*.
Buying Flying fish are usually displayed whole so that customers can admire their exotic shape. Large fish are sometimes filleted. They do not travel well, so are best eaten near the shores where they are caught.
Cooking Whole fish or fillets can be dusted in seasoned flour and deep-fried, baked au gratin or braised with tomatoes and onions.

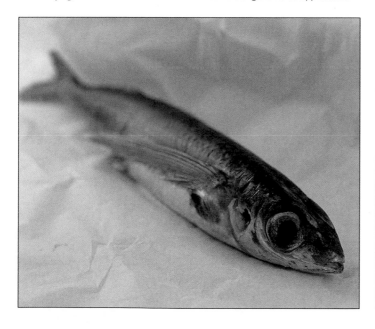

Fugu fish – delicious or deadly
Ranking high amongst the ugliest fish in the world is the puffer or fugu fish, the eating of which constitutes a kind of Japanese roulette, since the internal organs (roe, liver, kidneys etc, depending on the species) contain a toxin five hundred times more deadly than cyanide. Nonetheless, fugu are regarded as a great gastronomic treat in Japan, where chefs train for many years to learn how to prepare this potentially deadly luxury. One slip of the knife and the lethal poison may be released into the flesh, resulting in instant death to the poor unfortunate who eats it.

Happily, it is now possible to farm fugu fish that are free from toxins, so the health of the gourmet population of Japan should be more secure in future.

Left: Strawberry Grouper

Grouper *(Epinephelus)*

Groupers are members of the sea bass family. Dozens of species of these non-shoaling carnivorous fish are found in all the warm seas of the world; all have firm white flesh and make good eating. They have beautiful colouring, often with mottled skin. One of the largest is the spotted jewfish or giant grouper, which can weigh more than 300kg/660lb; even larger is the Queensland grouper, which can weigh over half a ton. Smaller species include the red, black, yellowmouth and Malabar groupers.
Habitat Warm water groupers inhabit all warm seas, from Africa to the Caribbean. Most inhabit rocky shores, but many live on deepwater reefs.
Other names In Australia, grouper is called rock or reef cod. In France, *merou*; in Italy, *cernia*; in Spain, *mero*.
Varieties There are two basic types of grouper; red and black. Red groupers have reddish-brown skin with attractive yellowish markings. Black groupers range from pale grey to very dark.
Buying Groupers are available all year round. Fish weighing up to 5kg/11lb are sold whole, or may be filleted or cut into steaks. All grouper taste very similar and are interchangeable.

Cooking Grouper can be cooked in all the same ways as sea bass. It goes well with spices and Caribbean flavourings.
Alternatives Sea bass and bream can be substituted for grouper.

Mahi mahi/Dolphinfish *(Coryphaena hippurus)*

These strange and beautiful fish have long, tapering bodies, with a high ridge of fin running down the body from the head to the forked, swallow-like tail. They are among the fastest swimmers, with a top speed of 80kph/50mph. Their skin changes colour as they swim, from green and gold to silver and grey. The average weight is about 2.5kg/5½lb, but fish have been known to grow to ten times that weight. The flesh is firm and white, with an excellent sweet flavour.
Habitat Mahi mahi are found in almost all the warm seas of the world. They are very inquisitive fish, which makes them easy to catch, since they are drawn to objects floating on the water.
Other names Mahi mahi is the Hawaiian name for these fish, which are also known as dorade or dolphinfish, though they are not related to dolphins. In French, they are called *coryphene*, in Italian *lampuga* and in Spanish *llampuga*.

Buying Available from spring through to autumn (fall), mahi mahi is sold as steaks or fillets. Do not buy frozen fish, as it is completely lacking in flavour.
Cooking The Hawaiians eat mahi mahi raw, but it is best grilled (broiled) or fried. It marries well with spicy flavours and is delicious with a piquant salsa.
Alternatives Monkfish, John Dory, cod or any firm-fleshed fish can be substituted.

Milkfish *(Chanos chanos)*

Highly prized in South-east Asia, milkfish have streamlined silver bodies with a long, forked caudal fin. Their flesh is soft and rich, but very bony. The average length is 1m/1yd. They have no teeth and feed by sucking up algae.
Habitat Milkfish are found in the Indian and Pacific oceans where they live in shoals around reefs and coastal areas. They migrate to mangrove swamps, lakes and estuaries to spawn, and are collected and raised in ponds for commercial fish farming.
Buying Milkfish are sold frozen or smoked, usually whole. If buying a whole fish, ask the fishmonger to scale and clean it for you. A 500g/1½lb fish will feed two people.

Above: Mahi mahi

Left: Parrot fish come in a huge variety of colours.

Buying Many supermarkets now stock parrot fish. Check their provenance and avoid buying those from the Caribbean in order to protect endangered coral reefs. Make sure that the colours are clear and bright. The average fish from the fishmonger's slab will feed one person; a larger 800g–1kg/1¾–2¼lb fish will serve two. Larger fish are sometimes sold filleted, or can be filleted on request.

Cooking Parrot fish can be rather bland, so spice them up with tropical flavours, such as coconut milk, garlic, chilli and lemon grass. Whole fish can be baked or braised.

Alternatives Red snapper, bream and John Dory can all be used instead of parrot fish.

Pomfret *(Stromateus* spp*)*

These small silvery fish look rather like coins. Their almost circular bodies have very pointed dorsal and anal fins and curved forked tails, not unlike those of flat fish. Scales are almost absent and the white flesh is fairly soft, with a mild flavour. Together with their close relation, the American butterfish, pomfret make good eating.

Cooking The best way to cook milkfish is in the Filipino style – boiled with plenty of chillies, onions, fresh ginger and vinegar to cut the richness. Steaks can also be grilled (broiled), but beware of the numerous fine, sharp bones. Boneless milkfish steaks are available in the Philippines; you might find them in Asian supermarkets.

Parrot fish *(Scarrus* spp*)*

Perfectly adapted to living in proximity to coral reefs, parrot fish have hard, parrot-like beaks (evolved from fused teeth) with which they nibble the coral. There are almost a hundred species of parrot fish. All have compact, brightly coloured bodies and large scales. They come in an incredible variety of vibrant hues. The largest is the rainbow parrot fish, which can grow up to 1m/3½ft, but most are only 30cm/12in long. Like many types of exotic fish, parrot fish look much better than they taste.

Habitat Parrot fish are found in tropical and sub-tropical seas. They live in large numbers around coral reefs, crushing the coral to reach the soft sea creatures inside, or scraping algae from surrounding rocks. Coral reefs in the Caribbean are now endangered, since urchins which used to eat the seaweed that grows on them have all but disappeared, and only the parrot fish are left to keep the corals clean and stop them from being smothered.

Other names In French, they are *perroquet*; in Italian *pesce pappagallo*; in Spanish *vieja*.

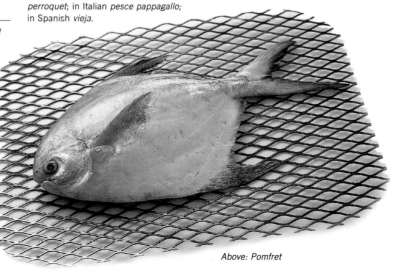

Above: Pomfret

Habitat A variety of pomfret is found in the Mediterranean, but the best-flavoured fish come from the Indian and Pacific oceans. Butterfish are found off the north-west coast of America.

Buying Pomfret are available most of the year, either fresh or frozen. Small fish weighing about 400g/14oz are sold whole and will feed one person. Fillets from small fish are rather thin, so it is best to choose a larger fish if possible and ask the fishmonger to fillet it.

Other names Pomfret from the north-west Atlantic are known as butterfish, and in America also go by the names of dollar fish, and pumpkinseed fish, owing to their shape, which in Europe is likened to that of the chestnut. In France, they are called *castagnole du Pacifique*; in Italy *pesce castagna* and in Spain *castagneta*.

Buying Pomfret are available most of the year. A small whole fish weighing about 400g/14oz will feed one person. Fillets from small pomfret are rather thin, so if possible, buy a larger fish and ask the fishmonger to fillet it for you.

Cooking Whole pomfret can be grilled (broiled), fried, baked, poached or steamed. This fish goes well with spices and Asian flavours such as coconut, lemon grass and tamarind. Beloved of Indian chefs, pomfret makes excellent curries and is often cooked in a tandoor as tikka masala. Because the fillets are thin and the flesh is soft, pomfret fillets should be cooked only briefly.

Alternatives Trout can be used instead of pomfret, as can any flat fish.

Pompano (Alectis ciliaris) and Jack (Seriola)

This large family of fish comprises more than two hundred species. All are oily fish, similar to mackerel, but with a stronger flavour. The dark flesh becomes lighter on cooking. Jacks vary enormously in size and shape, but all have forked tails and virtually scaleless iridescent skin. Among the most common jacks and pompanos are the small leatherjacket, the larger yellowtail, the amberjack and crevalle jack. The best of all for culinary purposes is the Florida pompano, which has white, meaty flesh, while the oddest-looking is the lookdown, a small glum-looking fish with a flat, thin body and a high domed forehead.

Habitat Pompano and jacks are found in warm seas worldwide. They travel in schools, around coral reefs or, like the Florida pompano, close to the shore.

Other names In Australia and New Zealand, yellowtail jack is known as kingfish. In French, jack is *carangue*; in Italian *carango*; in Spanish *caballa*.

Below: Yellowtail jack or kingfish

Pompano is *palomine* in French; *leccia stella* in Italian and *palometa blanca* in Spanish.

Buying Pompano and jack are available all year round. They are usually sold whole, but may be filleted. Outside Florida, you are likely to find only farmed pompano, but this is of excellent quality.

Cooking Jack can be cooked in the same way as mackerel. The robust flesh lends itself to spicy Asian flavours such as chilli, ginger and coriander. Pompano and jack can be stuffed with breadcrumbs or crab meat and baked, grilled (broiled) or cooked on a barbecue. They can also be cooked *en papillote*, steamed or poached in court-bouillon flavoured with Asian ingredients such as soy sauce or Thai fish sauce and fresh ginger. The Japanese use the fillets raw as *sashimi*.

Snapper (Lutjanidae)

More than 250 species of snapper are found in warm seas throughout the world. The best-known and finest to eat is the American red snapper (*Lutjanus campechanus*), which is bright red all over. The silk snapper is similar, but has a yellow tail. Other species include the pink snapper, or *opakapaka*, mutton snapper, which is usually olive green with vertical bars (but can change colour), the yellowtail snapper and the African and Indo-Pacific. All have domed heads with large mouths and big eyes set high on the head. Most snappers weigh between 1.5 and 2.5kg/3¼ and 5½lb, although mutton snappers can weigh up to 10kg/22lb, while yellowtails average only 250g/9oz. Snappers have firm, slightly flaky well-flavoured white flesh.

Above: Red and emperor snappers

Habitat Red snapper come from deep waters around Florida and Central and South America. Other varieties are found in warm waters from the Atlantic to the Caribbean and Indo-Pacific.
Other names Snapper are sometimes known as Cubera. In the Indian Ocean and Arabian Sea they are known as job or jobfish. In French, *vivaneau*; in Italian, *lutianido*; in Spanish, *pargo*.
Buying Snapper are available all year round, but mutton and Cubera stocks are seriously depleted, so avoid buying these. American or Northern red snapper are subject to overfishing; try to buy farmed red snapper. Many fish sold as red snapper are a different, inferior species; true American red snapper have red eyes. A whole fish weighing about 1kg/2¼lb will feed two people, while a 2kg/4½lb fish makes a good meal for four people.

Cooking Snapper is a versatile fish that can be baked, poached, pan-fried, grilled (broiled) and steamed. It lends itself to exotic and Caribbean flavours, such as chilli, mango and coconut.
Alternatives Grey mullet, bream, John Dory and sea bass can be substituted.

Tilapia *(Tilapia)*

Members of the enormous *Cichlids* family, tilapia have only one nostril on either side of their heads. The female is considerably smaller than the male, and scientists have now successfully bred tilapia that produce offspring that are almost exclusively male. Tilapia are freshwater fish, but can also live in salt water and are found in tropical seas. Their flesh is white and moist, with a pleasant, sweet flavour.

Habitat Tilapia are found in warm tropical waters, both fresh and salt. They are farmed all over the world.
Other names In Egypt and Israel, tilapia are sometimes marketed as St. Peter's fish (not to be confused with John Dory).
Buying Tilapia are available all year round. Small fish are sold whole, but larger fish are filleted. A small whole fish (about 350g/12oz) will serve one person; a 675g/1½lb fish serves two.
Cooking Whole tilapia can be stuffed and baked, grilled (broiled) or even cooked on a barbecue. The bland flesh benefits from robust Chinese flavourings and spices. Fillets can be coated in egg and breadcrumbs or batter and deep-fried.
Alternatives Carp, bream and zander can be used instead of tilapia.

Trevally *(Caranx lutescens)*

Trevally is a handsome fish with smooth, iridescent blue, green and silver skin, spiky fins and tail, and firm white flesh with a delicate flavour. Adult fish are about 33cm/15in long, but larger females can grow up to almost 1m/1yd.
Habitat Trevally are shoaling fish that are found in large numbers in the warmer coastal waters of New Zealand, mainly around the North Island.
Other names Known to the Maoris as araara. King George trevally is a popular and deliciously meaty variety.
Buying Trevally are sold whole or as fillets. They are almost always frozen. A whole 700g/1lb 5oz fish will serve up to four people.
Cooking Whole trevally can be baked or cooked *en papillote*. Fillets can be pan-fried or grilled and served with tomato salsa or a spicy sauce.

Above: Tilapia

CARTILAGINOUS FISH

This curious group of fish, called *chondrichthyes*, have no bones. Their skeletons are made entirely of cartilage. Many of these very ancient fish exist only as fossils, but about 500 species are still living, including edible fish such as shark, dogfish, ray and skate. Cartilaginous fish are thought to have evolved from freshwater fish which adapted to life in the sea. Unlike other fish, they have no swim bladders to control buoyancy, but in compensation have developed very large livers, whose high oil content helps the fish to float.

Almost all cartilaginous fish have long snouts and mouths set well back on the underside of the head. They have several rows of teeth, arranged one behind the other. As one row wears away, they start to use the next. They have stiff fleshy fins and no scales, but their bodies are covered with backward-facing denticles, which give them a rough texture. Once these fish die, the urea they contain turns into ammonia, imparting an unpleasant smell and taste, so it is essential that they are eaten very fresh.

THE SHARK FAMILY

The shark family is a large one, ranging in size from the small dogfish to the huge basking shark, which can weigh up to 4000kg/8800lb, and whose liver alone weighs 500–700kg/1100–1540lb. Edible sharks include porbeagle, blue shark, mako, tope and dogfish. Shark flesh is firm and slightly sweet, with a meaty texture.
Buying All species of shark are slow-growing, long-lived, and have a very low reproductive capacity. As a result, they are disappearing from the world's oceans at an alarming rate. About 100 million are killed every year, many for their fins, which the Chinese use to make the soup. Until stocks are replenished, it is best not to buy or eat any species of shark.

Shark is sold as steaks, loin or fillets. The flesh has a faint smell of ammonia, which disappears during cooking if the shark is fresh. However, after a week or so, it becomes very pungent and nothing will get rid of it.

Cooking Shark meat is a match for robust flavours and is excellent in curries. Steaks can be grilled (broiled), pan-fried or cooked on a barbecue. They can be dry, so marinate them in olive oil and lemon juice, or lard them with pork back fat before cooking.

Shark can also be braised or baked *au gratin* in a mornay sauce, makes a good addition to a fish soup or casserole and can be served cold in salads, dressed with a lemony mayonnaise. It is also ideal for home-smoking.
Alternatives Any meaty fish can be used instead of shark in recipes; try monkfish, swordfish and tuna.

Blue shark *(Prionace glauca)*

This migratory shark has exceedingly sharp teeth and is regarded as a man-eater. It has a sleek indigo-blue back, shading to bright blue on the sides and a snow white belly. It seldom grows to more than 4m/13ft in length. The very white flesh is not especially good, but the fins are used to make the Chinese favourite, shark's fin soup.

Above: Shark loin can be bought as a piece or cut into steaks. The meat can be dry, so is best marinated.

Other names In French, blue shark is *peau bleu*, in Italian *verdesca*; in Spanish *tintorera*.

Dogfish *(Scyliorhinus caniculus)*

Three species of these small members of the shark family are commonly eaten; the lesser spotted dogfish, the spur-dog or spiny dogfish *(Squalus acanthius)* and the larger, more portly nursehound *(Scylorhinus stellaris)*. The first has grey-brown skin with numerous brown spots, the second has grey skin, while the nursehound's skin is reddish. The thick rough skin is almost always removed before sale to disguise the shark-like appearance of these fish. Lesser spotted dogfish grow to about 80cm/32in, spur-dogs to 1.2m/4ft and nursehounds to 1.5m/4ft 9in; The flesh is white or pinkish with a firm texture and a good flavour. It is, of course, boneless.

Above: The lesser spotted dogfish, which is generally sold skinned but not filleted, is more commonly known as huss or even rock salmon.

Filleting dogfish
The central cartilage in dogfish is very easy to remove, and there are no small bones. It is usually sold as a whole skinned fish. To fillet, use a sharp knife with a long blade to cut down through the flesh on either side of the cartilage, using the full length of the blade and keeping it as close to the cartilage as possible. The fillets will fall away.

Habitat Different varieties of dogfish are found in cool temperate waters all around the world.

Other names Dogfish are variously known as huss, flake, rigg and even rock salmon, although this last is a complete misnomer. Spur-dogs are also known as spinebacks or spiky dogs. In French, they are *petite* or *grande roussette*, depending on their size, or, misleadingly, *saumonette* (little salmon). In Italian they are called *gattopardo* (leopard); in Spanish *pata-roxa*.

Buying Dogfish are sold skinned, often as fillets. They are cheap and available all year round. They must be very fresh, so sniff before you buy to make sure they do not smell of ammonia.

Shark à la Créole
Shark is a very popular fish in the Caribbean and the southern states of North America. This recipe reflects the mixture of the two cultures.

For 4 people you will need 4 shark steaks. First, make a marinade with the juice of 2 limes, 2 crushed garlic cloves, 2 seeded and chopped red chillies, salt and ground black pepper. Dilute the marinade with 15ml/1 tbsp water and pour into a non-metallic dish. Add the shark steaks, turn them over in the marinade so that they are coated, then cover and leave to marinate for several hours in a cool place or in the refrigerator.

When ready to cook, slice 2 red onions, 4 shallots and 4 tomatoes. Seed 2 red or green fresh chillies and chop the chillies finely. Heat 30ml/2 tbsp oil in a shallow pan, add the vegetables and chillies and cook until brown. Drain the shark steaks and lay them on top of the vegetables. Cover and cook gently for about 20 minutes, until tender. Squeeze over the juice of a lime and garnish with chopped parsley. Serve with creole rice and black-eyed beans (peas).

Cooking Dogfish has good firm flesh and can be cooked in the same ways as monkfish and skate. It is excellent in casseroles and is the perfect fish for fish and chips (french fries). It can be grilled (broiled) or cooked on a barbecue with a coating of olive oil, or cooked and flaked and used in salads.

Mako shark *(Isurus oxyrinchus)*

Part of the family of mackerel sharks, mako are swift surface swimmers with streamlined blue-grey bodies and bright white bellies, which grow to 2–3m/6½–9¾ft. They are found in sub-tropical and temperate-warm seas. Mako sharks have firm white flesh and are usually sold as loins or fillets. The flesh can be rather bland, so it will benefit from a robust marinade.

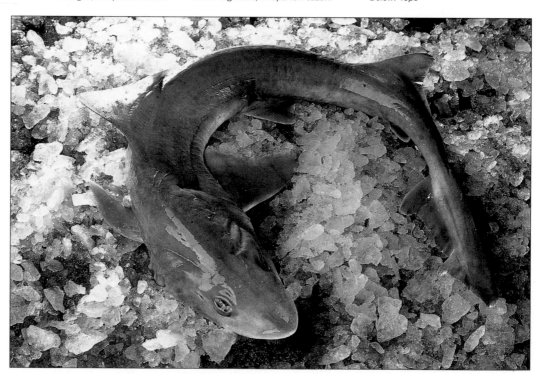

Other names In French, *taupe bleu*, in Italian *squallo mako* or *ossirina*; in Spanish *marrajo*.

Porbeagle *(Lamna nasus)*

These stocky, dark mole-grey sharks are closely related to the great white shark. They are surface swimmers, found in cold and temperate seas, but little is known about their growth or longevity. Porbeagles are widely regarded as the finest of all the sharks for eating, with firm, meaty pink flesh which is sometimes likened to veal. It is usually sold as loin or fillets.
Other names In French, porbeagle is known as *taupe* or *veau de mer*; in Italian it is *smeriglio*; in Spanish *cailón*.

Cooking Porbeagle so closely resembles veal that it can be sliced into thin escalopes (scallops), dipped in egg and breadcrumbs and then pan-fried like *scallopine alla milanese*. It can also be used in any other shark recipe.

Tope *(Galeorhinus galeus)*

These small grey sharks have pointed upward-tilting noses and serrated triangular teeth. Although edible, they do not taste particularly good and are best cut into chunks and used in mixed fish soups and casseroles.
Other names In French it is *milandre*, in Italian *cagnesca*, in Spanish *cazón*.

Above: Porbeagle, which is sometimes sold in fishmongers and markets by its French name, taupe.

Below: Tope

Ray and Skate *(Raja)*

Although they are different members of the same family, it is virtually impossible to distinguish between ray and skate on the fishmonger's slab, since only the "wings" are sold, never the whole fish. These fish have large, kite-shaped bodies with long thin tails and enlarged flattened pectoral fins (the wings). The skin is greyish-brown and smooth, knobbly or even thorny, depending on the species. Ray and skate have short snouts and large mouths on the underside with sharp slashing teeth. They can be

Below: Ray wing

differentiated by the shape of the snout; in skate, this is pointed. The largest rays can grow to 2.5m/8ft and weigh up to 100kg/220lb.

The thornback ray (*Raja clavata*) is considered to have the best flavour, but there is little to distinguish between the edible skates and rays. They have moist, meaty pinkish flesh with a fine texture and good flavour. Normally, only the wings are eaten, but the cheeks are regarded as a delicacy, as are the small medallions from the tail known as "skate knobs". The liver also makes good eating.

Habitat Rays and skates are found in cold and temperate waters. They are lazy bottom-living fish that hide on the sea bed waiting for their prey to pass by. They have evolved a way of breathing without opening their mouths. Most rays lay eggs, each enclosed in a four-horned black sac known as a "mermaid's purse".

Other names Among the edible rays and skates are the common skate (*raie* in French, *razza* in Italian; *raya* in Spanish), thornback ray or roker, rough skate and butterfly skate.

Buying All species of skate are severely endangered and should be avoided. Smaller varieties of ray (spotted, cuckoo and starry) are sustainable, so try to ensure that what you buy is a mature specimen of one of these species. Ray is available most of the year, but is best in autumn (fall) and winter. Smaller wings are sold whole; if you want a larger piece, then ask for a middle cut. The wings are covered with a clear slime, which regenerates itself even after death. To test for freshness, gently rub off the slime and make sure that it reappears. Even fresh ray smells faintly of ammonia. This is normal, and the smell will disappear during cooking.

Cooking Before cooking ray, wash it well in cold water to eliminate the ammoniac smell. If the skin is still on scrape it off after cooking. The classic ray dish is *raie au beurre noir* (with black butter). Poach the wings in water acidulated with a little vinegar or *court-bouillon* for about 10 minutes, then drain and sprinkle with capers. Brown some butter (do not let it burn and blacken) and pour it over the fish. Ray can also be grilled (broiled), deep-fried in batter or curried. Its gelatinous quality makes it good for soups and fish terrines and mousses.

Alternatives Fillets of brill, sole, John Dory or turbot can be used instead.

Skinning cooked ray

1 Lay the fish on a board. With a blunt knife, scrape off the skin from the thicker part towards the edge.

2 Discard the skin. Scrape the flesh off the cartilage in the same way.

Deep Sea and Game Fish

Deep in the world's oceans live several varieties of fish that never come close to the shore. Many have odd shapes and vibrant colours, which consumers seldom see, since the fish are filleted on board the boats that travel far out to sea to trawl the fish. Most edible deep-sea fish are found around the coasts of New Zealand, South Africa and South America. The Caribbean is home to huge game fish, such as marlin, and keen fishermen will pay vast sums for a day's sport. Little is known about the life cycles of these creatures, but it is certain that, as stocks of the more common fish decline, we shall see many more deep-sea fish appearing in the supermarkets.

Chilean sea bass/Patagonian toothfish (Dissostichus eleginoides)

Not a true sea bass, this fish is also known as Patagonian toothfish, ice fish and Antarctic sea bass. It is a slow-growing, late-maturing fish which can live for 50 years and grow to over 2m/2yd long. The white flesh has a good meaty texture and a pleasant flavour, but it does not compare to true sea bass.
Habitat Chilean sea bass inhabit the southern oceans from Antarctica to the Falkland Islands and South America, living at depths of between 300 and 3,500m (980–11,500ft).

Below: Hoki fillets are very long and thin. The flesh is pinkish white, and has a flaky texture that is similar to hake when cooked.

Buying Chilean sea bass is vulnerable to overfishing. Try to ensure that you buy fish from the environmentally sound fisheries around South Georgia. The spawning season is from June to September, so although the fillets are sold year-round, it is best to avoid buying during this period.
Cooking Cook Chilean sea bass in the same way as cod or any round white fish.

Grenadier/Rattail (family Macrouridae)

There are many species of these curious-looking shoaling fish. They may be the most abundant of all fish, although since they live at depths of between 200m/656ft and 6000m/19,700ft, it is hard to be sure. Grenadiers have large pointed heads that contain sensors to help them navigate in the ocean depths, and bodies that taper into filament-like tails. Despite their odd appearance, grenadiers are good to eat. The white flesh has a delicate, fairly moist texture.
Habitat Grenadiers are distributed throughout the world. They live at great depths, feeding on luminous creatures that they can detect even in the dark.
Buying Grenadier fillets are available all year round. You may find fresh fish, but in the northern hemisphere it is more usual to find the fish frozen.
Cooking Fillets can be deep- or pan-fried or brushed with oil and grilled (broiled). They benefit from a creamy sauce and are good baked *au gratin*.
Alternatives Cod, hake, hoki or any other fairly firm white fish can be used instead of grenadiers.

Hoki (Macruronus novaezelandiae)

Although hoki resemble grenadiers in appearance, they are actually related to hake and have the same white flesh and flaky texture. They have blue-green backs with silvery sides and bellies, and their tadpole-like bodies taper to a point. The average length of a hoki is 60cm–1m/24–39in.
Habitat Hoki occur in large numbers around the coasts of Southern Australia and New Zealand. They live at depths of 500–800m/1640–2626ft.
Other names In Australia, hoki are inaccurately called blue grenadier. In New Zealand, they are sometimes called whiptail or blue hake.
Buying Hoki is available all year round, as fillets, loins and other cuts. It is frequently used to make fish fingers (breaded fish sticks).
Cooking The delicate white flesh is suitable for most cooking methods, particularly frying. It can sometimes taste insipid, so is best served with a robust tomato-based sauce or a creamy sauce. Hoki can be cubed for kebabs and is an excellent fish for smoking.
Alternatives Hake and monkfish can be substituted for hoki.

Marlin (family Istiophoridae)

More usually fished for sport than for commerce, marlin are magnificent-looking billfish, renowned for their speed and endurance. The name billfish comes from their greatly elongated upper jaw, which forms a bill or spear. They have beautiful slender bodies with smooth iridescent skin and a high dorsal fin, which they fold down when speeding through the water.

There are several species of marlin, the best-known being blue, black (the largest marlin), white (the smallest) and striped. All can attain enormous weights of up to 300kg/660lb but the average size is 160–200kg/352–440lb. The deep pink flesh is high in fat and has a fairly firm texture with a disappointingly undistinguished flavour.
Habitat Marlin are found in warm seas throughout the world. Unusually for predators, they have no teeth, but use their bill to stun schooling fish, and

then to spear them.

Other names In French, marlin are *makaire*, in Italian *pesce lancia*, in Spanish *aguja*.

Buying Atlantic blue marlin are overfished, so avoid these and buy fish from tropical waters. Marlin are available in summer usually as loins and steaks. Try to buy cuts from smaller fish if possible. In the United States, marlin is almost always sold smoked rather than fresh.

Cooking Cook as swordfish, or cut into cubes and marinate to make ceviche.

Alternatives North Atlantic swordfish and yellowfin tuna can be substituted for marlin.

Sailfish (*Istiophorus* spp)

The sailfish resembles marlin, but looks even more spectacular. It has a beautiful streamlined body with a golden back spotted with blue, and a high, wavy blue dorsal fin which it unfurls like a sail to travel through the water at up to 96kph/60mph. Sailfish are tremendous fighters and will perform amazing aerial acrobatics when hooked.

Habitat As for marlin.

Other names Sailfish are *voilier* in French, *pesce vela* in Italian and *pez vela* in Spanish.

Buying Available in summer as loins and steaks. Buy cuts from smaller fish.

Cooking As for marlin.

Below: Marlin steaks

Orange roughy (*Hoplosthetus atlanticus*)

These ugly but delicious fish have dark orange bodies and fins, massive heads with conspicuous bony ridges and protruding lower lips. They are very slow-growing and probably the longest-lived of all fish; they begin to breed at around 30 years, and may live for up to 150 years.

Habitat For many years, orange roughy were believed to inhabit only Icelandic waters. In the 1970s, however, large numbers were found on the opposite side of the world in the deep waters around New Zealand and most of the world's stocks now come from there.

Other names In Australia roughy is sometimes known as sea perch. In French it is *hopostète orange*, in Italian *pesce specchio* (mirror fish); and in Spanish *reloj*. Also known by the unattractive name of slimehead.

Buying Orange roughy are always cleaned and filleted at sea, and are only sold as fillets, usually frozen. Because

Above: Orange roughy fillets

Above: Redfish

they are so slow-growing, they are extremely vulnerable to exploitation and stocks are endangered. Never buy fresh orange roughy in January or February, which is the breeding season. Until stocks are replenished, it is best to avoid this fish altogether.

Cooking Orange roughy holds together well when cooked, and its flavour marries well with other seafood. It can be used for soups and stews, and is good poached, pan-fried, roasted or steamed.

Alternatives Atlantic cod, pollack or any firm white fish can be used instead of orange roughy.

Redfish/Ocean perch *(Sebastes marinus)*

These beautifully-coloured red fish were once the most important deep-sea fish, with vast catches being landed every year in northern fishing ports. As new

varieties of fish have become widely available, however, their popularity has declined. Redfish can grow to about 5kg/11lb. The flesh is white and moist, with a sweet flavour.

Habitat Redfish inhabit the deep waters of the Atlantic and Arctic Oceans.

Other names Redfish are known as ocean perch or Norway haddock. In French, they are *rascasse*; in Italian, *scorfano* (ditto); in Spanish, *gallineta nórdica*.

Buying Redfish are very slow-growing fish and stocks are severely depleted. Avoid buying North Atlantic species, and go for those from the Pacific. Redfish are available all year round, sold whole or as steaks and fillets.

Cooking Redfish is suited to all cooking methods. It marries well with Mediterranean flavours and spices, and is very good baked in a creamy sauce.

Alternatives Pollack, Atlantic cod or hake can be substituted for redfish.

Blackened Redfish

A favourite recipe from New Orleans is blackened redfish, a spicy Creole dish. Fillets of redfish are thickly coated on both sides with a mixture of dried herbs and spices – crushed peppercorns and coriander seeds, cayenne pepper, paprika, dried thyme and oregano – then seared on both sides in a very hot frying pan or griddle until the spice crust is blackened and charred and the fish is cooked. The contrast between the aromatic, crunchy crust and the tender white fish is delicious.

However, this fierce cooking method produces plenty of smoke, so remember to open the kitchen window.

Above: Swordfish

Stuffed Swordfish Rolls
Swordfish steaks can be pounded lightly between two sheets of clear film (plastic wrap) and used to roll around a stuffing. Choose 1cm/½in thick steaks and pound lightly using a meat mallet or rolling pin until they are only 5mm/¼in thick.

Make a stuffing using finely grated Parmesan cheese, breadcrumbs and chopped fresh herbs bound together with an egg. Roll the swordfish steaks around the stuffing and secure with wooden cocktail sticks (toothpicks).

Place the swordfish rolls in a shallow, heavy pan and pour over about 300ml/½ pint/ 1¼ cups well-flavoured tomato sauce. Bring to the boil, then reduce the heat and simmer for 30 minutes, turning once. Remove the swordfish rolls from the sauce and discard the cocktail sticks. Return to the sauce and serve hot.

Swordfish (family Xiphiidae)

Famous as both a culinary and game fish, swordfish differs from other billfish in having neither scales nor teeth. In all other respects, it is as dramatic and graceful to look at as it powers through the water with only the curve of its dorsal fin visible above the surface. Its long "sword"

Below: Swordfish steaks

represents up to one-third of its total length and appears to be a powerful weapon, but no one is certain whether it is actually used to kill its prey, or merely to stun small fish. Swordfish can grow to an enormous size, sometimes weighing up to 600kg/1320lb. Their excellent white, meaty flesh is very low in fat and tends to dryness, so it needs careful cooking.
Habitat Swordfish are migratory fish which are widely distributed in warm, deep waters around the world. They occasionally migrate into northern European seas, but are more commonly found in the Mediterranean.

immature. By-catches include endangered marine turtles. Buy fish only from US managed waters in the North Atlantic. Fresh swordfish is available all year round, usually sold as steaks. Frozen fish is also available, but is best avoided. Because swordfish is so meaty and substantial, 150–165g/5–5½oz will provide an ample portion for one person. Try to buy thick steaks, as thinner ones are more apt to dry out during cooking.
Cooking It is essential not to let swordfish dry out during cooking, so baste it frequently with olive oil when grilling (broiling) or cooking on a barbecue and serve with a drizzle of olive oil or some herb butter. Swordfish makes excellent kebabs and can withstand a robust or spicy sauce. It is delicious marinated in a mixture of olive oil and lemon juice flavoured with garlic and fresh herbs, then seared in a very hot ridged pan.

Other names In French, swordfish is *espadon*; in Italian it is *pesce spada*; in Spanish, *pez espada*.
Buying Swordfish are vulnerable to overfishing and are often caught when

Grilled (broiled) or barbecued (grilled) swordfish are good served with a spicy, tomato and coriander (cilantro) salsa.
Alternatives Tuna can be used instead of swordfish.

Miscellaneous Fish

Right: Garfish

A few fish do not slot neatly into any obvious category. The only connection between the fish described in this chapter is that they are all exceptionally good to eat. They are a strange-looking collection, from the hideously ugly monkfish to the slimline but no more beauteous John Dory and the needle-like garfish with its unappealing phosphorescent green bones. Monkfish and John Dory are seldom sold whole, so there is an enormous amount of wastage, which sadly makes these gastronomically excellent fish extremely expensive to buy.

Garfish/Needlefish (family Belonidae)

There are more than fifty species of needlefish. Most inhabit tropical seas, but some, like the garfish, are found in cooler waters, and one species is found only in fresh water. Many people find the needle-like appearance of the garfish off-putting, despite (or perhaps because of) their vibrant silver and blue-green colouring and their long spear-like beaks.

Needlefish can grow to 2m/6½ft, but are more commonly up to 80cm/32in in length. Their bones are a phosphor-escent green even when cooked (this coloration is completely harmless), and even their flesh has a greenish tinge, although this whitens on cooking. Despite these physical disadvantages, garfish are good to eat, with firm flesh from which the backbone can easily be removed, since you can hardly miss it.
Habitat Garfish inhabit the Atlantic Ocean and Mediterranean Sea, sometimes straying into fresh water. Other needlefish are found in the

tropics, the Black Sea and the Pacific Ocean, while the Atlantic is also home to the saury, another sub-species. When they are frightened or being chased by predators, needlefish sometimes leap out of the water and launch themselves through the air like dangerous missiles. Unfortunate fishermen have been severely injured by their needle-sharp beaks.
Other names The French for garfish is *aiguille* or *orphie*, the Italian is *aguglia*, and the Spanish is *aguja*. Saury is also known as skipper, because of its habit of skipping over the water to escape from predators. Saury and needlefish are *balaou* in French; *costardello* in Italian and *paparda* in Spanish.
Buying Garfish are sold whole. If you do not want to serve the fish that way, ask the fishmonger to clean it and cut it into 5cm/2in chunks.
Cooking To cook a whole garfish, wash it thoroughly inside and out, rub the cavity with lemon juice, then curl the fish around and stick the pointed beak into the tail end so that it forms a ring. Brush with a marinade of olive oil, lemon juice, garlic and chopped parsley and grill (broil) or barbecue for about 15 minutes, basting frequently.

Chunks of garfish or saury can be coated in seasoned flour and pan-fried in butter and oil, or stewed with onions and tomatoes. They are gelatinous fish, so make excellent soups and stews or fish couscous.

John Dory (family Zeidae)

These fish were said to be sacred to Zeus, hence the Latin name of *Zeus faber*. The olive-brown bodies of these fish are so slim that they look almost like upright flat fish. Dories have extremely ugly faces and spiny dorsal fins from which long filaments trail. Their most distinguishing feature is a large black spot ringed with yellow right in the middle of their bodies; this is said to be the thumb print of St Peter. The story goes that the saint lifted a John Dory in the Sea of Galilee, leaving his thumb and finger prints on either side, and found in its mouth a gold coin, which he used to pay the unpopular tax collectors. This delightful fable is highly unlikely, since John Dory are not found in the Sea of Galilee, which is a freshwater lake. John Dory is also known as "St Peter's fish". Despite its unattractive appearance, John Dory is one of the most delicious of all fish, with firm, succulent white flesh which is on a par with turbot and Dover sole.
Habitat Dories are found in the Atlantic; those from American coastal waters are known as American dories (*Zenopsis ocellata*), while fish from the eastern Atlantic, from Britain and Norway to Africa, and from the Mediterranean are European dories (*Zeus faber*). Another species, from the southern hemisphere (*Zeus japonica*), inhabits the Indo-Pacific oceans.
Other names The name John Dory is said to come from the French *jaune doré* (golden yellow), which describes

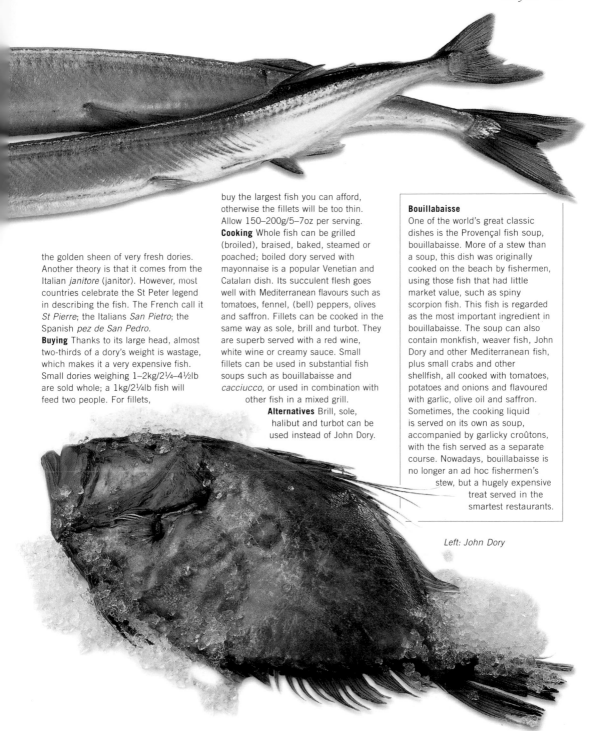

the golden sheen of very fresh dories. Another theory is that it comes from the Italian *janitore* (janitor). However, most countries celebrate the St Peter legend in describing the fish. The French call it *St Pierre*; the Italians *San Pietro*; the Spanish *pez de San Pedro*.

Buying Thanks to its large head, almost two-thirds of a dory's weight is wastage, which makes it a very expensive fish. Small dories weighing 1–2kg/2¼–4½lb are sold whole; a 1kg/2¼lb fish will feed two people. For fillets,

buy the largest fish you can afford, otherwise the fillets will be too thin. Allow 150–200g/5–7oz per serving.
Cooking Whole fish can be grilled (broiled), braised, baked, steamed or poached; boiled dory served with mayonnaise is a popular Venetian and Catalan dish. Its succulent flesh goes well with Mediterranean flavours such as tomatoes, fennel, (bell) peppers, olives and saffron. Fillets can be cooked in the same way as sole, brill and turbot. They are superb served with a red wine, white wine or creamy sauce. Small fillets can be used in substantial fish soups such as bouillabaisse and *cacciucco*, or used in combination with other fish in a mixed grill.

Alternatives Brill, sole, halibut and turbot can be used instead of John Dory.

Bouillabaisse
One of the world's great classic dishes is the Provençal fish soup, bouillabaisse. More of a stew than a soup, this dish was originally cooked on the beach by fishermen, using those fish that had little market value, such as spiny scorpion fish. This fish is regarded as the most important ingredient in bouillabaisse. The soup can also contain monkfish, weaver fish, John Dory and other Mediterranean fish, plus small crabs and other shellfish, all cooked with tomatoes, potatoes and onions and flavoured with garlic, olive oil and saffron. Sometimes, the cooking liquid is served on its own as soup, accompanied by garlicky croûtons, with the fish served as a separate course. Nowadays, bouillabaisse is no longer an ad hoc fishermen's stew, but a hugely expensive treat served in the smartest restaurants.

Left: John Dory

Monkfish/Anglerfish (*Lophius piscatorius*)

This extraordinarily ugly fish has an enormous head equipped with a "rod and lure" to catch its food; hence its alternative name of anglerfish. It has a huge mouth fringed with lethally sharp teeth and a dangling "rod" (actually the first spine of the dorsal fin) on its nose. Its comparatively small body has brown, scaleless skin. On the fishmonger's slab, the only part of a monkfish you are likely to see is the tail, since the head is almost always removed because of its extreme ugliness, disproportionate weight and the fact that only the cheeks are worth eating. The tail is quite another matter; it is one of the finest of all fish, with a superb firm texture and a delicious sweetness, rather like lobster meat. In fact, some unscrupulous caterers have been known to pass off monkfish as fresh lobster. The only bone the tail contains is the backbone, which makes it especially easy to prepare and pleasant to eat. Monkfish liver, if you can find it, is considered to be a great delicacy.

Habitat Monkfish are found in the Atlantic and Mediterranean. They lurk on the sea bottom dangling their "fishing rods" to lure passing fish. They are extremely predacious and will sometimes swim up to the surface to prey on small birds.

Varieties The best monkfish are *Lophius piscatorius* and the similar *L. budegassa*, which is highly prized in Spain. American monkfish or goosefish (*L. americanus*) is considered inferior, while New Zealand monkfish (*Kathetostoma giganteum*) is truly a poor relation.

Other names Monkfish is also known as monk or angler. In French, it is *lotte* or *baudroie*, *crapaud* or *diable de mer* ("sea toad" or "sea devil"). In Italian, it is *coda di rospo* or *rana pescatrice* ("fishing frog"); in Spanish, *rape*.

Buying Monkfish is available all year, but is best in spring and summer before spawning. It is sold as whole tails, fillets or medallions. Generally speaking, the larger the tail,

Below: Monkfish

the better the quality; avoid thin, scraggy tails. For tails with the bone in, allow about 200g/7oz per person. A 1.5kg/3¼lb tail will serve four to six people. Ask the fishmonger to skin the tail and remove the membrane.

Cooking One of the best ways to cook a whole monkfish tail is to treat it like a leg of lamb; tie it up with string, stud with slivers of garlic and thyme or rosemary leaves, anoint with olive oil and roast in a hot oven. This dish is known as *gigot de mer*. Monkfish can also be grilled (broiled), made into kebabs, pan-fried, poached and served cold with garlicky mayonnaise, or braised with Mediterranean vegetables or white wine, saffron and cream. It goes well with other seafood such as salmon, red mullet and shellfish, and is classically used in bouillabaisse and other fish soups. Thin fillets are delicious marinated in olive oil and lemon juice, then coated with flour and sautéed in butter.

Alternatives Nothing has quite the same nice firm texture as monkfish, but conger eel, John Dory or Atlantic cod can all be used instead.

Opah (*Lampris regius*)

Variously called moonfish, sunfish or mariposa, this beautiful, slim, oval fish has a steel blue back shading into a rose pink belly, with silver spots all over its body. It has glorious red fins, jaws and tail, and, unusually, is the only member of its family. It is toothless and scaleless, and can grow to an enormous size. Some specimens weigh over 200kg/440lb and measure more than 2m/6½ft, although the average weight of those caught is about 20kg/44lb. The flesh is salmon pink, with a flavour similar to tuna.

Habitat Opah are found in warm waters throughout the world, but so far only solitary specimens have been caught, and little is known about them.

Preparing monkfish tails

The tails are the best part of the monkfish. Because of their high water content, fillets should be cooked with very little liquid. They are easy to prepare.

1 Grasp the thick end of the tail firmly with one hand and peel off the skin with the other, working from the thick to the thin end.

2 Carefully pull off the thin, dark or pinkish membrane.

3 Fillet the tail by cutting through the flesh on either side of the backbone with a sharp knife (there are no small bones). The bone can be used to make stock.

Other names In French, opah is *poisson lune*, in Italian, *lampride* or *pesce rè*; in Spanish, *luna real*.

Buying Should you be lucky enough to find opah on the fishmonger's slab, ask for it to be cut into steaks or fillets.

Cooking Treat opah in the same way as salmon or tuna, taking great care not to overcook, and serve with a creamy sauce.

Alternatives Tuna or salmon.

Sablefish/Black cod *(Anoplopoma fimbria)*

These sleek, grey-skinned fish are better known as black cod. Although sablefish do resemble cod, they are not related, but are members of the Anoplopomatidae family, a group of fish confined to the North Pacific. They can live for over 100 years and grow to 1m/1yd, although most commercially caught fish measure no more than 60cm/24in and weigh 4.5kg/10lb. Highly prized by the Japanese, sablefish have pearly white flesh, velvety flakes and an exceptionally sweet, rich flavour. They are rich in beneficial oils.

Above: Monkfish tail can be filleted and then roasted like a leg of lamb in a hot oven with olive oil, herbs and garlic.

Habitat Sablefish inhabit the cold, deep waters of the north eastern Pacific Ocean from northern Mexico to the Gulf of Alaska, westwards to the Aleutian Islands and into the Bering Sea. They are highly migratory.

Other names Also known as black cod or butterfish.

Buying Fresh Alaskan and Canadian black cod is available from late February to mid-November. Frozen fish are available year-round and are sold as steaks or thick fillets. Smoked sablefish is popular in Canada and can sometimes be found in specialist shops in Britain.

Cooking Black cod baked with miso sauce has become a classic dish. It can also be braised, grilled or home-smoked.

Alternatives No other fish can match the distinctive flavour and texture of sablefish, but Atlantic cod or turbot can be used instead.

FRESHWATER FISH

Nothing can beat the taste of a freshwater fish, caught, cleaned and cooked within a couple of hours of being pulled from the lake or river, especially if you have caught it yourself. The flesh of freshwater fish is fragile, so generally speaking, they are only really good to eat when they are absolutely fresh. Sadly, many of the world's rivers and lakes are so polluted that supplies of good, untainted fish are low, so many of the freshwater fish we buy are farmed. A major problem with all freshwater fish is that they often contain numerous small, very fine bones, which many people find off-putting. Apart from trout and zander, you will find few of the fish in this chapter on the fishmonger's slab; most are eaten by the anglers who catch them for sport. If you are lucky enough to be given a freshly caught fish, you will relish the experience.

Barbel *(Barbus)*

These "bearded" fish (the Latin name means "beard") live in fast-flowing rivers. They have brown backs, yellowish sides and white bellies. Barbel have rather tasteless flesh and are extremely bony, so they are not regarded as prime river fish. They are popular in the Loire and Burgundy regions of France, where they are typically poached or braised with a red wine sauce.
Cooking Barbel need strong flavours to enhance their intrinsic blandness. Small young fish can be grilled (broiled) and

served with a well-seasoned butter; larger fish (up to 1.75kg/4–4½lb) are best used in a stew, such as *matelote*.

Bream *(Abramis brama)*

The appearance of bream, with their flat oval greenish-brown bodies covered with gold scales, is more attractive than their taste. The bony flesh is soft and bland, and can sometimes taste muddy, since bream live in the silt near the bottom of pools and slow-flowing rivers. Despite this, bream was an extremely popular fish in the Middle Ages. It was caught in fishponds around the country and used in numerous recipes.

Above: Red carp

Cooking Bream is best used in braised dishes and stews. It should be soaked in acidulated water for several hours before being cooked to eliminate the taste of silt.

Carp *(Cyprinus carpio)*

Carp are members of the minnow family, which contains more than 1500 different species. They are among the hardiest of all fish and can live for hundreds of years. Although they can grow to over 35kg/77lb, most of the carp caught weigh only about 2kg/4½lb; anything larger than this and the keen angler is in seventh heaven. There are three main varieties of carp; the very scaly common carp; the scaleless leather carp and the mirror carp,

Above: Bream

Right: Carp

Carp roe

This roe has a delicate texture and flavour and is much sought after in France, where it is poached and served in pastry cases or ramekins, or made into fritters, omelettes and soufflés. A classic dish is *tourte de laitances* (soft roe or milt), which combines puréed carp and pike with soft carp roes; the mixture is then baked in a puff pastry tart.

---

which has only a few large irregularly spaced scales that can easily be removed with a fingernail. All carp are handsome fish with compact, meaty flesh that varies in taste according to how the fish is cooked.

Originally natives of Asia, carp were highly prized by Chinese emperors as ornamental pets and as food; they frequently featured on festive banquets. Travellers along the Silk Routes brought them to Europe, where they proliferated in unpolluted fresh water and became a staple food of Eastern European Jews who lived far from the sea, but could cultivate carp in ponds. The tongues were regarded as a delicacy. Carp are still immensely popular in Chinese cuisine; the lips are considered the finest part, and they command high prices in restaurants.

Habitat In their natural state, carp like living in muddy and polluted waters, which they seem to prefer to clean streams and lakes. Nowadays, they are extensively farmed

in clean ponds. In the wild, they are considered the most difficult of all freshwater fish to catch; despite being toothless, they are powerful fighters, and can demolish fishing tackle.

Other names In French, carp is *carpe*, in Italian and Spanish, *carpa*.

Buying Most commercially available carp are farmed and weigh 1–2kg/ 2¼–4½lb. A 2kg/4½lb fish will amply serve four. Look for a plump fish, preferably containing roe or milt, which is considered a delicacy. You may find live carp for sale; if so, ask the fishmonger to prepare the fish, gutting it and removing the bitter gall bladder from the base of the throat. If you buy a common carp, ask the supplier to scale it for you.

Preparing If you have to scale carp yourself, pour boiling water over the fish to loosen the scales before scraping them off.

Cooking Carp is a very versatile fish, which can be delicious if prepared with interesting flavourings. It can be filled with fish mousse or stuffing and baked, and is also excellent braised, opened out

and grilled (broiled) or deep-fried, or poached in a sweet-and-sour sauce. A traditional German or Polish Christmas Eve dish is carp cooked in beer or white wine. Carp marries well with Asian flavours such as ginger, soy sauce and rice wine, and makes a good addition to fish stews and soups that have been well flavoured with plenty of tomatoes and garlic.

Carp can be cooked *au bleu*, as described in the chapter on Buying and Preparing Fish, or stewed with red wine and mushrooms to make a *meurette*. A classic dish is *carpe à la Juive*, a sweet-and-sour cold dish made with whole or thickly-sliced carp braised with onions, garlic, vinegar, raisins and almonds. When cooked, the whole fish (or a fish sliced and reformed into the original shape), is left to go cold in the sauce, which solidifies into a flavoursome jelly.

Alternatives Catfish, perch and zander can be substituted for carp.

Catfish *(Ictalurus* spp*)*

These fish take their name from the long whiskery barbels which help them to locate their prey in the muddy waters where they live. There are dozens of species, ranging from tiny fish to gigantic specimens weighing several hundredweight. Catfish are extremely hardy and can live out of

Above: Catfish

water for a considerable time. These fish are found all over the world, but the best fish for eating are the American species known as bullheads, which have firm, meaty, rather fatty white flesh and very few bones.

Habitat Catfish are bottom-living fish that feed on live and dead prey. They inhabit muddy waters throughout the world and are successfully farmed in the United States and Canada.

Other names In French, catfish is *silure*; in Italian *pesce gatto*; in Spanish *siluro*.

Buying Catfish is sold skinned and usually filleted. Its chunky flesh is filling, so 175g/6oz is ample for one person. Sniff the fish before you buy to make sure that it smells fresh and sweet. Avoid fillets from very large fish, which can be rather coarse.

Cooking The classic southern American cooking method for catfish is to coat it in cornmeal, deep-fry it and serve with tartare sauce. It can also be grilled (broiled) or pan-fried in butter, baked, or cooked like eel, whose flesh it resembles. The tough skin must be removed before cooking. Catfish makes a good addition to fish soups and stews with hearty flavourings such as garlic and tomatoes, or Caribbean spices.

Alternatives Any trout or perch recipe is also suitable for catfish.

Char *(Salvelinus alpinus)*

These trout-like fish are members of the salmon family. They have attractive silvery-green sides dotted with pale spots, and rose-pink bellies. The white flesh is firm and succulent, with a delicate flavour. Sadly, these fish, which once inhabited cold lake waters in large numbers, are becoming increasingly rare in the wild. They can, however, be farmed successfully. The most common varieties are Arctic char, char, brook trout and lake trout. All can be distinguished from trout by their smaller scales and rounder bodies.

Habitat Arctic char are found in cold-water lakes in the United States, Canada, Britain and Iceland. Other species inhabit the lakes of northern France and the Swiss Alps. Brook and lake trout (which are actually char) live

Potted Char

When char proliferated in the Lake District in England in the 18th and 19th centuries, potted char became a popular delicacy. It was often sold in white china pots that were decorated with painted fish.

1 To make potted char, flake some leftover cooked fish, removing all skin and bones.

2 Weigh the boned fish. Melt an equal quantity of butter in a pan. Flavour the butter with nutmeg or mace and salt and pepper. Pour the butter over the flaked fish.

3 Put the prepared fish into ramekins. Cover with clear film (plastic wrap) and chill until the mixture is firm.

4 Seal with a thin layer of clarified butter and cover again; it will keep in the refrigerator for a week. Salmon, trout, whitefish and grayling can be prepared in the same way.

in the lakes of North America; Dolly Varden is found from western North America to the Asian coast.

Other names Char is *omble chevalier* in French, *salmerino* in Italian, and *salvelino* in Spanish.

Buying You may be lucky enough to find wild char in summer and early autumn (fall). Farmed Arctic char from Iceland and America are available all year round. Small fish are sold whole; larger char may be cut into steaks.

Cooking Char can be cooked in the same ways as trout. It can be poached, baked, braised, fried, grilled (broiled) or cooked on a barbecue.

Grayling *(Thymallus arcticus)*

A relative of trout, grayling is an attractive silvery fish with a small mouth and a long, high dorsal fin spotted with gold. These small fish (rarely weighing more than 1.2kg/2½lb) have firm white flesh with a delicate trout-like flavour; they are said to smell of thyme when first caught, but their scent and flavour is fleeting, so they should be eaten within hours of being caught.

Habitat Grayling are found in lakes from Europe to North America and the northern coasts of Asia, but as these become more polluted, their numbers are declining.

Other names In France, grayling is called *ombre*; in Italy *temolo*; in Spain *salvelino* or *timalo*.

Cooking Grayling must be scaled before cooking. Pour boiling water over the fish and scrape off the scales with a blunt knife. These fish are excellent brushed with melted butter and grilled (broiled) or pan-fried, preferably on the shore where they were caught. To enhance the faint aroma of thyme, put a few fresh thyme leaves inside the fish. They can also be baked and potted like char.

Gudgeon *(Gobio gobio)*

Small fish with large heads and thick lips, gudgeon have delicious, delicate flesh. They live at the bottom of lakes and rivers all over Europe and, freshly caught and crisply fried, gudgeon were once a common sight in cafés on riverbanks in France.

Other names Gudgeon are *goujon* in French, a name that has come to have a much wider application. Nowadays, deep-fried strips of any white fish are known as *goujons*.

Cooking Gudgeon must be gutted and wiped clean before cooking. Coat them in flour or very light batter and deep-fry until very crisp and golden. Sprinkle with salt and serve with lemon wedges.

Roach *(Rutilis rutilis)*

These members of the minnow family have greenish-grey skin and golden eyes. They can weigh as much as 1.75kg/4–4½lb. Their white flesh is firm and has quite a good delicate flavour. Their greenish roe (which turns red on cooking) is excellent to eat. Roach are not the easiest fish to eat, because they contain so many bones. Use tweezers to remove as many bones as possible before cooking.

Habitat Roach inhabit sluggish waters in Europe and North America. Unusually for members of the minnow family, they are also sometimes found in brackish coastal waters.

Other names In French, roach is *gardon*, in Italian *triotto*, in Spanish *bermejuela*.

Cooking Small roach can be fried with other tiny fish to make a *friture*. If you can cope with the bones, larger fish can be grilled (broiled) or pan-fried, or baked in white wine.

Pike-Perch/Zander *(Stizostedion lucioperca)*

Zander (sometimes spelt sander) look like a cross between perch and pike, but have a much more delicate and appealing flavour than the latter. They have greenish-grey backs with dark bands, and hard, spiny dorsal fins and

Above: Roach

gills. Zander can grow quite large, sometimes weighing up to about 5kg/11lb, and fillets from fish this size are delicious and meaty. American pike-perch are known as walleye. Zander can be farmed successfully, and are cooked in the same way as perch.

Perch *(Perca fluviatilis)*

These beautiful fish have greenish gold skins and coral fins. Their humped backs have a spiky dorsal fin, which makes them difficult to handle. Perch are highly prized for their firm, delicate white flesh and are considered to be one of the finest freshwater fish. They grow slowly and can reach a weight of 3kg/6½lb, but the average weight is only about 500g/1¼lb.

Above: Zander

Habitat Perch are found in sluggish streams, ponds and lakes throughout Europe and North America, and as far north as Siberia.

Other names The American yellow perch is very similar to the common variety and is often simply called "perch". In French, perch is *perche*; in Italian *pesce persico* ("Persian fish"); in Spanish, *perca*.

Cooking Unless perch are scaled the moment they are caught, this is a near impossible task. The only solution is to plunge the fish into boiling acidulated water for a few moments, then peel off the entire skin. Small perch can be pan-fried or deep-fried in oil. Fillets can be pan-fried and served with a buttery sauce such as hollandaise, a herbed béarnaise or *beurre blanc*. Larger fish can be baked, poached or grilled (broiled), or stuffed with seasoned breadcrumbs and braised in wine.

Pike *(Esox lucius)*

Described by Izaac Walton in *The Compleat Angler* as the tyrants of fresh water, pike are indeed fearsome creatures, with their elongated upturned noses and jaws equipped with hundreds of sharp teeth. Pike can grow to an enormous size, sometimes up to 1.5m/5ft. The larger the fish, the better the sport for anglers, but fish this size are not good to eat, as the flesh is dry and tough; the best size for eating is 1–2kg/2¼–4½lb. Pike have soft white flesh that is full of lethally sharp bones. Despite this, they are highly regarded in France. During the spawning season, pike roes can become toxic, so they should never be eaten.

In the Middle Ages, pike were highly prized in France and were cultivated in the fish ponds of the Louvre for the delectation of the king. Monks also farmed the fish to enjoy on meatless

Above: Pike are large, fearsome-looking freshwater fish.

days. The voracious appetites of these fish earned them the nickname *grands loups d'eau* ("great water wolves").

Habitat Pike lurk in the streams and ponds of Eastern Europe, Britain and France. They are solitary, aggressive predators who like nothing better than to eat a duckling or water rat. Their close relations, muskellunge and pickerel, are found in the United States and Canada. Fish from fast-flowing streams taste better than those that are fished from ponds.

Other names The large American pike, muskellunge (a corruption of the French for "long mask", *masque allongé*) is also known as musky. In France, pike is called *brochet* (pickerel is *brocheton*); in Italy, *luccio (luccio giovane)*; in Spanish *lucio (lucio joven)*.

Pike Quenelles

The most famous recipe involving pike is *quenelles de brochet*, featherlight oval fish dumplings poached in water or fish stock. To make enough for four people, you need 450g/1lb skinned pike fillets, 4 egg whites, 475ml/16fl oz/2 cups chilled double (heavy) cream, salt, white pepper and nutmeg.

1 Purée the fish until smooth, adding the egg whites one at a time until completely amalgamated. Chill.

2 Whip the cream until stiff, then fold it into the fish mousse. Season and chill for at least an hour.

3 To cook, bring a pan of water or fish stock to a bare simmer. Shape the fish mousse into ovals using two tablespoons dipped in hot water and drop them into the trembling (not boiling) liquid, a few at a time.

4 Poach for about 10 minutes, until the quenelles are cooked through, but still creamy in the centre. Lift the cooked quenelles out of the water with a slotted spoon and drain on kitchen paper.

5 The quenelles are delicious served with a creamy sauce. Alternatively, cover them with a rich béchamel and bake *au gratin*.

Buying Pike are at their best in autumn (fall) and early winter. The best fish to buy are small whole fish weighing 1.2–1.7kg/2½–4½lb, which will feed four to six people. Large pike are sold cut into steaks; these can be tough.

Cooking Scale pike before cooking. Pour over a little boiling water – not too much, as the natural slime on the fish keeps it tender. Whole fish can be stuffed and baked or braised. Small pike are good cooked *au bleu*, or poached in a *court-bouillon* and served with *beurre blanc*. Pike is also traditionally cooked *à la Juive*, like carp. Sorrel, horseradish and similar sharp-flavoured ingredients make excellent accompaniments. Fillets and steaks are best marinated for several hours before cooking to offset any dryness. They can then be pan-fried, braised or baked with white wine and served with a creamy shellfish sauce. They can be made into mousses, terrines and fish cakes.

Shad *(Alosa)*

The largest member of the herring family, shad is a migratory fish which spawns in fresh water. It resembles a fat silvery-green herring and can weigh up to 5kg/11lb. The three main species of shad are the allis, thwaite and American. They resemble fat silvery-green herrings. Although the white flesh has a fine, rich flavour, it is full of fine bones, which make eating the fish rather difficult. The best part of the shad is the large-grained roe, which has the wonderfully crunchy texture of caviar and is said by some to have aphrodisiac qualities.

Habitat Allis and thwaite shad are caught in the Loire and Garonne rivers in France during the spawning season. American shad is found all along the coast from Canada to Florida. During the 19th century, American shad were introduced to the Pacific and are now fished from Alaska to southern California. Pollution and overfishing for its highly-prized roe have decimated the numbers of shad in this region.

Other names In French, shad is *alose*, in Italian *alosa*, in Spanish *sábalo*.

Buying Shad are at their best in spring when they are full of roe. They are usually sold whole. A 1.5kg/3–3½lb fish will amply serve four. Ask the fishmonger to clean and scale the fish and persuade him, if you can, to bone it for you. Make sure you keep the roe, which is also good to eat.

Cooking Once the fish is cooked, make a series of incisions about 10cm/4in apart along its length and pull out as many bones as possible with your fingers. Whole shad can be stuffed with fish mousse (whiting is traditionally used), spinach or sorrel and baked, or poached and served on a bed of sorrel with *beurre blanc*. Fillets and steaks are good grilled (broiled), deep-fried or pan-fried and served with tomato sauce; check for small bones before serving. Shad roes are delicious briefly poached, then creamed with butter, cooked finely chopped shallots, cream, egg yolks and lemon juice. Serve them on toast as a rich appetizer or savoury, or use them to garnish a cooked shad.

Sturgeon (family Acipenseridae)

You have only to see a sturgeon to know that it is a "living fossil", part of a family of fish which were abundant in prehistoric times. The bodies of these long thin fish are armour-plated with several rows of bony scales that extend along their length. They have long, shovel-shaped snouts, with four whiskery barbels that are used for detecting food. Sturgeons are noted for their longevity, sometimes living more than 150 years, growing to a length of 9m/29½ft and weighing up to 1400kg/3080lb. There are about two dozen species of sturgeon, among them European, Beluga, Sevruga, Oscietra and the sterlet, which is found in Russian rivers. They have firm white flesh with a rich texture. Sturgeon can, however, be dry and somewhat indigestible. The fish is often sold smoked, but its real glory is its roe (caviar), the ultimate luxury food (see Dried and Salted Fish). In Russia, the bone marrow (*vésiga*) of the fish is dried and used in the classic recipe, *coulibiac*.
Habitat Sturgeon are migratory fish that live in the sea but swim into rivers to spawn. Once common in Europe and America, they are now found mainly in rivers that feed the Black and Caspian Seas. They are successfully farmed in France and California.

Below: Sturgeon steaks

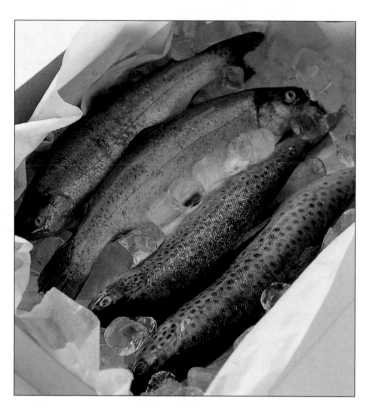

Above: Brown and rainbow trout

Other names In French, sturgeon is called *esturgeon*, in Italian it is *storione*, and in Spanish, *esturión*.
Buying Because they are slow-maturing, wild sturgeon are vulnerable to over-exploitation. Avoid buying fish from the wild and instead go for farmed sturgeon, which is available all year round. It is sold as steaks or large cuts.
Cooking Sturgeon needs careful cooking to make it palatable, and should be marinated or barded with canned anchovy fillets to keep it moist. Its texture is similar to veal, and it is often cooked in the same ways, as breaded fillets or braised steaks. It can be poached in white wine (or, for a touch of luxury, champagne), or baked in a creamy sauce with onions. In Russia, sturgeon is traditionally poached with vegetables and served hot with tomato sauce, or cold with a piquant garnish of mushrooms, langoustines, horseradish, lemon, gherkins and olives. It can also be home-smoked very successfully.

Tench (*Tinca tinca*)

This fat-bodied relative of the minnow has a coppery-green body covered with small scales and a thick coating of slime. Tench are hardy, fighting fish, which make great sport for anglers. They live in sluggish streams and have a tendency to taste muddy, but they make a good addition to a fish stew. They can also be baked or fried, and should be served with a robustly flavoured sauce to enliven the rather bland flesh. They must be scaled and thoroughly cleaned before cooking; scalding them with boiling water helps to remove the scales.

Trout (family Salmonidae)

The best-known of all freshwater fish, trout are popular with gourmets and fishermen alike. The two main species are brown trout *(Salmo trutta)* and rainbow trout *(Salmo gairdneri)*. Rainbow trout are probably the more familiar since they are extensively farmed and are available everywhere. They have silvery-green bodies with dark spots and a pinkish band along the sides. Wild fish have moist white flesh with a sweet flavour; farmed rainbow trout are often fed on a special diet to give the flesh a pink tinge, which is considered to be more appealing.

Brown trout come from cold mountain streams and lakes. They have coppery-brown skin dotted with red or orange and brown spots. Their flesh is a delicate pink and their flavour exquisite, but sadly they are seldom found in stores; to enjoy a fresh brown trout, you should befriend an angler.

Golden trout and coral trout are both farmed hybrid trout, with beautiful, vibrantly coloured skin. Their pinkish flesh is more like that of rainbow trout and tastes very similar.

Habitat Rainbow trout are native to America, but have been introduced to many other parts of the world. Brown trout are natives of Europe and have been introduced to America. Golden trout are not found naturally in the wild, but are increasingly farmed for their attractive coloration.

Other names In French, trout is *truite*, in Italian *trota*; in Spanish *trucha*.

Buying Trout are available all year round, usually farmed. Unlike many other fish, they are quite robust and freeze well, so frozen trout are perfectly acceptable. For fresh trout, look for a good coating of slime, bright clear eyes and red gills. Trout are almost always sold whole with the head on. They are very inexpensive, and you should allow one fish per person, unless they are very large.

Cooking Trout are arguably the most versatile of all fish and can be cooked in myriad ways. They are easy to eat, as the flesh falls away from the bone once cooked. The best way to cook a freshly-caught trout is *à la meunière*; dust it with flour, fry in clarified butter until golden brown, and season with lemon juice and parsley. Live trout can be cooked *au bleu*. Other cooking methods include poaching in *court-bouillon*, baking, braising, frying, grilling (broiling) and cooking on a barbecue. Trout marry well with many flavours, such as bacon, onions, garlic and mushrooms.

Left: Coral trout

In Normandy, they are often baked *en papillote* with apples, cider and cream. They are also excellent for home-smoking and make delicious mousses and terrines. A classic, if clichéd, recipe is trout with almonds (hazelnuts make good alternatives). If you find roes in your trout, these can be puréed, mixed with seasoned breadcrumbs and used as a stuffing for the fish.

Alternatives Almost any freshwater fish can be used instead of trout.

Whitefish (family Salmonidae)

Members of the salmon family, whitefish are silvery white in colour. They resemble trout, but have larger scales and smaller mouths. They live in cold, clear lochs and lakes in northern Europe and America. In Britain they are sometimes called vendace or powan. They have a pleasant texture and flavour, somewhere between trout and grayling, but not so fine as either.

Left: Golden trout are spectacular in appearance.

DRIED AND SALTED FISH

Since prehistoric times, the dehydrating effects of sun and wind have been used as a means of preserving fish almost indefinitely. Even today, in remote communities, long ropes strung with split and salted fish hung out to dry like washing are a common sight. Any fish can be dried in this way – cod, haddock, herring, mackerel and even freshwater fish such as eel, pike, salmon and sturgeon.

Dried/Salt cod and Stockfish

The most common commercially available dried fish is cod and its relatives (haddock, ling and pollack). When dried, these look – and feel – like old shoe leather, but once reconstituted in water, the flesh softens and tastes delicious when cooked. Depending on its country of origin, dried cod is known as *baccalà* (Italy), *bacalhau* (Portugal) and stockfish (Scandinavia, northern Europe, the Caribbean and Africa). Stockfish differs from other types of dried cod in that it is not salted before being dried. Whatever the type, dried cod must be soaked for many hours in fresh, cold water – sometimes for up to a couple of weeks – before it becomes palatable. Stockfish needs to be beaten with a rolling pin to tenderize it, and you may find you need a saw to cut it. The world is divided between those who believe that the result is worth all this

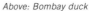

effort and those who detest salt cod in all its forms. The Portuguese boast that they have a different recipe for every day of the year. The Scandinavians and the northern Italians love salt cod, too, while the French pound it into a rich creamy mousse, *brandade de morue*, with lashings of olive oil and garlic.
Buying Depending on where you buy it, dried and salt cod may be split down the backbone or sold whole. Thick middle cuts are better than end cuts. Salt cod will keep for months if stored in a dry place.

Below: Salt cod

Above: Bombay duck

Preparing Salt cod needs less soaking than stockfish, but it still needs to be left to soften in a bowl of cold water for at least 24 hours, changing the water every 8–12 hours. Taste the fish before cooking to check that it is not too salty; if it is, continue to soak it.
Cooking Dried and salt cod can be poached or baked. Never cook it in boiling water, as it tends to toughen. It is a classic ingredient of Provençal *allioli*, a salad consisting of vegetables and hard-boiled eggs served with garlic mayonnaise. In Spain and Portugal, salt cod is cooked with tomatoes, (bell) peppers, olives, onions and garlic. It goes well with potatoes and split peas in a stew, or on top of a mound of mashed potatoes. Salt cod makes wonderful fish cakes, fritters and mousses.

Bombay duck

Quite why this dried form of a small transparent fish from the Indian sub-continent should be called Bombay duck, no one knows for sure; it is possibly a corruption of the Bombay name for the fish, *bommaloe macchli*. Bombay duck is often served as an appetizer or used as a garnish for curries and rice dishes. Uncooked Bombay duck has an unpleasantly pungent smell which fades a little when it is grilled (broiled), but is intensified

Above: Mojama

reconstitutes into a gelatinous, viscous mass with a texture resembling calf's foot jelly. It is highly nutritious and eaten as a tonic, but should be avoided at all costs, since the process of acquiring fins can be immensely cruel; quite frequently the fins are cut off living sharks and the mutilated bodies are thrown back into the sea.

SALTED FISH ROE

The best-known and most expensive salted fish roe is caviar, the eggs of the sturgeon. Other salted roes include grey mullet, cod, lumpfish and salmon. In Sweden, bleak roe is compressed into a form of caviar paste called *løjrom* or *kaviar*, which has a pretty orangey-pink colour. It tastes rather sweet, and is definitely an acquired taste.

Caviar

Made from sturgeon roe lightly cured with salt and borax, caviar is the most expensive food in the world. It has a unique texture, and the tiny eggs burst on the roof of the mouth to release a salty liquid with an elusive, incomparable flavour. The three main types of caviar take their names from the species of sturgeon from which the eggs come. The rarest is beluga, which comes from the largest fish; one beluga can contain over 50kg/110lb of roe. The dark grey eggs are quite large and well separated. Oscietra is golden brown, with smaller grains and an oily texture, which many prefer to beluga. Sevruga is the cheapest caviar. It comes from the smallest and most prolific fish and has small pale greenish-grey grains with a markedly salty flavour.

Shark's fin

Dried shark's fin is highly prized in China, where it is served at banquets, either braised or as the central ingredient in an extremely expensive soup. The fins from the many species of sharks that inhabit the Indo-Pacific oceans are sun-dried and preserved in lime. In its dried state, shark's fin looks like a very bushy beard, but after long soaking it

Below, clockwise from bottom left: sevruga, oscietra and beluga caviar

Above: Shark's fin

when it is deep-fried. When grilling (broiling), keep the heat low. It is ready when it is crisp and it curls at the edges. When cold, serve with drinks or crumble over curries or rice.

Mojama

Popular in Spain, Sicily and other countries with an Arabic influence, *mojama*, *mosciame* or *missama* is made from fillets of tuna that are salted, then dried in the sun for about three weeks. It is eaten as a snack with a glass of chilled fino sherry, or served on slices of baguette that have been rubbed with garlic and drizzled with olive oil.

Arguably the best caviar of all comes from Iran; the finest is marketed as "Imperial caviar" and each can contains only the eggs from a single fish. The best caviar is "harvested" from fish that are just about to spawn; the eggs are very pale and full of flavour.

Each type of caviar is graded. The finest, malassol, is slightly salted. Second grade caviar is saltier and may be made from a mixture of roes. Inferior quality sevruga roe is pressed into a solid mass (pressed caviar), which squashes the eggs. It has a strong, salty taste and can be oily. It is fine for cooking and has the advantage of being cheaper. The best caviar is always fresh; pasteurization will ensure that it keeps longer, but the quality will be compromised.

Despite its high price, caviar is so sought-after that the world's population of sturgeon is endangered almost to the point of extinction, due to overfishing, poaching and pollution. Sturgeon were once common in European rivers, but are now found almost exclusively in the Caspian Sea. Recently, however, the fish have been farmed successfully in France, so there may be some hope for the future of caviar.

Buying Thanks to overfishing, habitat loss and pollution, sturgeon from the Caspian sea, which produces most of the world's caviar, are severely endangered. Avoid buying Russian caviar, particularly beluga (not too difficult, bearing in mind the stratospheric price) and choose farmed caviar from Italy, France or America. Never buy caviar that seems suspiciously cheap; it may not have been cured properly, or may have been made with damaged eggs. There is a huge illicit trade in second-rate caviar, which can taste unacceptably oily or salty. At worst, it might even poison you. You get what you pay for, so buy the best you can afford from a reputable dealer. Caviar should be kept in the refrigerator at 0–3°C/32–37°F; any warmer and it will become too oily. Once you have opened a can or jar of caviar, eat the contents within a week.

Above: Black and red lumpfish roe

Serving Caviar should be served chilled, preferably on a bed of crushed ice. Never serve or eat it with a silver spoon, as this will react with the caviar and give it a metallic taste. A proper caviar spoon is made of bone, but a plastic one would do at a pinch. Traditionally, caviar is served with *blinis* and sour cream. Chopped hard-boiled (hard-cooked) egg and onions make it go further. It is also delicious with toast and unsalted (sweet) butter. Some people believe that a squeeze of lemon enhances the flavour; others that it spoils the taste. Allow about 25g/1oz caviar per person as a first course. Or use a few grains as a garnish.

Lumpfish roe

Sometimes known as "mock" or Danish caviar, this is the roe of the arctic lumpfish, which is as unpleasant as its name. The tiny eggs are dyed black or orange-red and look pretty as a garnish for canapés. They can be eaten with sour cream and blinis, but bear no resemblance to real caviar. Lumpfish roe is sold in glass jars.

Grey mullet roe/Bottarga/Tarama

Dried grey mullet roe is a great delicacy and is very nutritious. The orange roe is salted, then dried and pressed. It is usually packed in a sausage shape inside a thin skin, which should be removed before the roe is used. Wrapped in clear film (plastic wrap), it will keep for several months. Grey mullet roe is the traditional ingredient of taramasalata, although smoked cod's roe is often used instead. In Mediterranean countries it is also known as bottarga or *poutargue*. Bottarga is delicious finely grated over steaming hot pasta. Ready-grated bottarga is available from good Italian delis.

Salmon caviar/Keta

This is made from orange-pink salmon roe. The eggs are larger than sturgeon caviar and have a pleasant, mild flavour and an excellent texture. They make an attractive garnish for fish pâtés and mousses, or can be eaten with sour cream and blinis. The name *keta* comes from the Russian for chum salmon. Salmon caviar is sold in jars. Trout caviar is also available.

Above: Grey mullet roe or bottarga

Right: Trout caviar

Far right: Salmon caviar, which is also known as keta.

PICKLED FISH

Pickling in vinegar or brine is another effective way of preserving fish. It is particularly well suited to oily fish such as herrings and eels.

Baltic/Bismarck herring

The herrings are split like kippers (smoked herrings) and marinated in white wine vinegar and spices. The fillets are layered with onion rings and carrot rounds for 24 hours. These are delicious with sour cream.

Boquerones

Delicious white anchovy fillets from Spain and Portugal are marinated in garlic, salt and vinegar, and have a

Below: Maatjes herring

Above: Baltic or bismarck herring

fresh, piquant taste that is quite different from salty canned or bottled anchovies. They can be eaten straight from the tray or fried as a delicious garnish for a fish dish.

Maatjes herring

Fat young female herrings (the name means "maiden" or "virgin" in Dutch) are lightly cured in salt, sugar, spices and saltpetre, which turns the flesh brownish-pink. In Holland and Belgium they are eaten with chopped raw onion. The Scandinavian equivalent is *matjes*. These have a stronger flavour and are generally eaten with sour cream and chopped hard-boiled egg.

Pickled herring

Herring fillets are marinated in vinegar and spices, then coated in a sour cream sauce.

Soused herring and Bratheringe

These marinated herrings are deliciously addictive and simple to prepare at home. In the German version, *bratheringe*, herring fillets are lightly floured and fried until golden, then steeped in a boiled marinade of vinegar, pickling spice and herbs. Soused herring are not fried first.

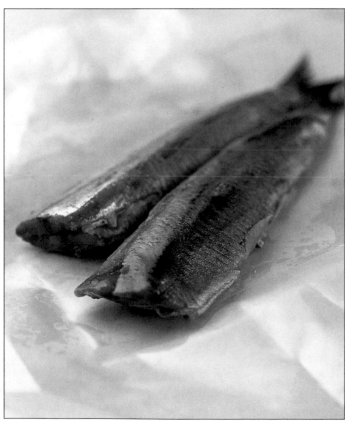

Rollmop Herrings

Like *ceviche*, rollmops are not cooked by heat, but by the action of vinegar. For four servings, halve 8 herring fillets lengthways and soak them for several hours in heavily salted water. Make a marinade by mixing about 600ml/ 1 pint/2½ cups vinegar with 2 bay leaves, 2.5ml/½ tsp coarsely crushed white peppercorns, 15ml/ 1 tbsp pickling spice and 1 sliced sweet onion in a pan. Bring to the boil, then leave until cold. Drain and dry the herring fillets. Slice a second sweet onion finely. Roll each herring fillet around a little sliced onion and some of the peppercorns and spices. Secure with a cocktail stick (toothpick) and pack tightly into a preserving jar. Pour over the marinade and leave for at least five days before eating.

Below: Rollmop herrings

Rollmops

These consist of herring fillets rolled up, skin side out, around whole peppercorns and pickling spice, and secured with wooden cocktail sticks (toothpicks). The rolls are marinated in white wine vinegar with onion slices and, sometimes, gherkins. Serve rollmops with rye bread and butter, or a cucumber salad with a sour cream and dill dressing.

Gravad lax/Gravlax

A wonderfully succulent Swedish speciality, *gravad lax* has achieved great popularity. It is fresh raw salmon fillet cured with dill, sugar, salt and coarse peppercorns. *Gravad lax* is widely available, often packed with a sachet of dill-flavoured mustard sauce, which makes the perfect accompaniment.

Jellied eels

Market stalls in Britain selling this traditional Cockney dish are becoming increasingly rare, but jellied eels are available frozen and in cans. Jellied eels are made by boiling pieces of eel in a

Below: Gravad lax

Below: Jellied eels

marinade of white wine vinegar and herbs, then leaving them in the liquid with masses of chopped parsley until the mixture sets to a light jelly. Serve with thick slices of bread and butter.

Home-cured Gravad Lax

Although almost every supermarket sells ready-cured *gravad lax*, it is very easy to prepare at home. For eight people, you will need 1–1.2kg/2¼–2½lb absolutely fresh middle-cut salmon, boned and cut lengthways into two fillets. For the curing mix, mix together 30ml/ 2 tbsp coarse sea salt, 30ml/2 tbsp caster (superfine) sugar, 15–30ml/ 1–2 tbsp coarsely crushed peppercorns (black or white) and a good handful of fresh dill, chopped. Lay one salmon fillet skin side down in a non-metallic dish. Cover with a generous layer of the curing mix. Lay the second fillet on top, skin side up, and sprinkle on the remaining curing mix. Cover with clear film (plastic wrap). Place a wooden board slightly larger than the fish on top and weight down with heavy cans or weights. Leave in the refrigerator for at least 72 hours, turning the salmon every 12 hours and basting it with the juices that have oozed out. To serve, slice the *gravad lax* on the diagonal, a little thicker than you would for smoked salmon. Serve with a mustard and dill sauce.

CANNED FISH

This is a very useful staple ingredient. While it never has the subtle texture and flavour of fresh fish, canned fish can be excellent in its own right and is invaluable for salads and sandwiches.

Anchovies

Fillets of this fish are canned in oil (olive oil is best) in small oblong cans or bottled in jars. The salty fillets are a staple ingredient of *salade niçoise* and *tapenade* (olive and anchovy paste), and are used as a topping for pizzas and *crostini*. They can be mashed into butter as a topping for grilled (broiled) fish, or chopped and mixed into tomato sauces. Anchovies enhance the flavour of many non-fish dishes (roast lamb, for example) without making them taste fishy. Once opened, anchovies perish quickly, so try to use the whole can or jar at once. Any leftovers should be submerged in oil and kept for only a day or two. As an alternative to canned anchovies, try salted anchovies, which are packed in barrels with masses of salt and cured for several months. Rinse well before using.

Pilchards

These fish are large, older sardines. They lack the subtle flavour of their younger siblings, so are usually canned in tomato sauce.

Salmon

Canned salmon is quite different in flavour and texture from fresh fish, but is useful to have in the pantry. It is richer in calcium than fresh salmon,

because the bones are softened during the canning process and can easily be eaten. Canned salmon was once the mainstay of sandwiches, salads, fish cakes and fish pies, but it has been overshadowed by inexpensive farmed fresh salmon. Canned salmon is available in several grades, from the cheapest pink chum salmon to the best-quality wild red Alaskan fish, which has a better flavour and texture. Canned salmon is good for making mousses, soufflés and fish cakes.

Sardines

Above: Canned anchovies

Left: Sardines in olive oil, which were the first fish to be canned.

These were the first fish to be canned; in 1834, a canning factory opened in Brittany to process the sardines that abounded on the Breton coast. For years, tiny Breton sardines were the best, but these fish have all but disappeared, and most sardines canned in France now come from North Africa. Large numbers of sardines are also canned in Spain and Portugal. The finest sardines are fried in olive oil before canning, a time-consuming process that makes them expensive. Most sardines are beheaded and gutted before being packed raw, complete with backbones, in groundnut (peanut) or olive oil. Inferior or damaged fish are packed in tomato or mustard

sauce. Sardines in olive oil are the best; the more expensive varieties are left to mature for at least a year before being sold to soften the bones and mature the flavour. The best way to enjoy them is to serve them whole on hot toast. They can also be mashed with lemon juice and cayenne pepper to make a pâté, stuffed into hard-boiled eggs or made into fresh or toasted sandwiches.

Tuna

In recent years, canned tuna has received a bad press because dolphins were often caught in the tuna nets and slaughtered unnecessarily. Nowadays, tuna canners have become more ecologically aware and most tuna is line-caught. The best canned tuna is the pale albacore, which is usually canned in one solid piece. Cheaper varieties such as skipjack and yellowfin are often sold as chunks or flaky broken pieces. Tuna comes packed in olive oil (the best), vegetable oil or brine, which is healthier and lighter.

Canned tuna is versatile and can be served with pasta, used in sandwiches and salads, or made into a pâté or fish loaf. It is used in the classic Italian dish *vitello tonnato* – loin of veal coated in a thick tuna-flavoured mayonnaise.

Above: Canned tuna

SMOKED FISH

Another ancient and traditional way of preserving fish is smoking. Today it is used less for preserving and more for imparting a unique flavour. There are two methods of smoking fish, cold and hot smoking, which give very different results. For both methods, the fish must first be salted in dry salt or brine. They are then smoked over different types of wood, which impart their distinctive flavour to the fish. Every smokery produces fish with a different texture and taste; it is a matter of individual choice which appeals to you.

COLD-SMOKED FISH

A high degree of skill is required when cold smoking to get the flavour and texture right. It is done at a temperature of 30–35°C/86–95°F, which cures but does not cook the fish. Some cold-smoked fish such as salmon, halibut and trout are eaten raw; others such as kippers (smoked herrings) and haddock are usually cooked, although they can be marinated and eaten as they are.

Smoked salmon

The best-loved of all smoked fish, smoked salmon is made by brining the fish, then dry curing it in sugar with flavourings such as molasses or whisky, and smoking it over wood chips (usually oak). Different wood chips give different flavours; some Scottish and Irish salmon is smoked over a fire made from old whisky barrels, which impart the flavour of the spirit. Depending on the strength of the cure, the type of wood used and the smoking time, smoked

Below: Smoked halibut

Above: Smoked salmon

salmon can vary in colour from very pale pink to deep brownish-red. The best smoked salmon has a fairly mild flavour and a moist, succulent texture.
Buying Smoked salmon is usually sold ready-sliced, with the slices separated by sheets of transparent paper. Whole sides are sliced, and the slices are reassembled to restore the original shape of the fillet. Avoid buying sliced fish that is not layered with paper, as the slices stick together. The thinner the salmon is sliced the better; thickly-sliced fish can be coarse. Whole sides are sometimes sold unsliced; these are cheaper, but you need an extremely sharp flexible knife and a degree of skill to slice the fish yourself. The most expensive smoked salmon is made from wild fish, but good-quality farmed fish give excellent results, and it can be difficult to distinguish between the two.

Freshly sliced smoked salmon is best, but vacuum packs are better value and perfectly acceptable when purchased from a reliable supplier. Frozen smoked salmon is also available and can be used at a pinch. Smoked salmon trimmings are much cheaper than slices and are perfect for mousses, pâtés and omelettes. In Jewish delicatessens, you will find *lox*, a heavily-cured salmon with a deep reddish-gold colour.

Serving Top-quality smoked salmon should be eaten just as it is, served with thinly sliced brown bread and butter. Cheaper salmon can be served in traditional Jewish style, with cream cheese as a topping for bagels (add some thin rings of raw onion, if you like), or in sandwiches. Smoked salmon makes a delicious salad. Scraps can be stirred into omelettes, quiches or flans, mixed into pasta, puréed to make mousses, or mashed into hard-boiled egg yolks and piled back into the whites. If you are slicing smoked salmon yourself, slice thinly across the grain, working from head to tail. You will need a very sharp, flexible knife with a long blade.

Cold-smoked trout

A cheaper alternative to smoked salmon is cold-smoked trout, which looks like salmon, but has a more delicate flavour. It can be eaten in the same way as smoked salmon, with thinly sliced brown bread and butter.

Smoked halibut

Sold thinly sliced like smoked salmon, smoked halibut has translucent white flesh and a very delicate flavour. It makes an excellent addition to a plate of assorted smoked fish, or can be used like smoked haddock. The flavour can be enhanced with a mild, creamy horseradish sauce.

Above: Finnan haddock

Smoked sturgeon

This smoked fish has pale pinkish flesh with a rich flavour and a succulent texture. Like smoked salmon, it should be thinly sliced across the grain. As it is a luxury fish, it should be treated like the very best smoked salmon and served in the same way. Eat it with thinly-sliced brown bread and butter.

Below: Smoked sturgeon

Above: Smoked haddock fillets

Smoked haddock

There are various forms of smoked haddock, from fluorescent dyed yellow fillets to pale naturally cured fillets and finnan haddock or "haddie", which are split and look like pale golden kippers (smoked herrings). It is now known that the artificial dyes used to colour smoked haddock can be carcinogenic; dyed fillets are also often artificially flavoured with chemicals which simulate the effect of smoking, so avoid these and enjoy natural pale beige fillets.

Finnan haddock or "haddie"

These distinctively pale, whole split haddock (with the bone left in) are named after the Scottish village of Findon where the special smoking process originated. The process gives the fish a beautiful pale corn colour and a subtle smoked flavour. Finnan haddock

can be used in any smoked haddock recipe, but must be boned and skinned after cooking. They are delicious served topped with a poached egg.

Glasgow pales

Similar to finnan haddock, Glasgow pales are lightly brined and smoked, resulting in a very delicate flavour.
Buying Avoid buying dyed smoked haddock whose only, dubious merit is that it adds colour to fish pies and similar dishes. Undyed smoked fillets are fine for such dishes, but for plain grilled (broiled) or poached haddock, you cannot beat finnan haddock.
Cooking Smoked haddock is succulent and delicious. It is usually eaten hot, but fillets can be thinly sliced and marinated (a splash of whisky works wonders) and eaten raw as an appetizer. Smoked haddock can be grilled (like kippers) or poached in milk or water. Serve it with butter or topped with a poached egg, or *à la florentine* on a bed of creamed spinach. A classic Scottish dish is ham 'n' haddie, in which finnan haddock is fried in ham fat and topped with fried ham.

Smoked haddock is used in another Scottish dish, cullen skink, a substantial chowder. It makes excellent mousse or pâté, and also features in kedgeree and omelette Arnold Bennett, a sumptuous omelette oozing with cheese, cream and smoked haddock.

Smoked herrings

Kippers

These are made by briefly brining split herrings, then hanging them up in pairs and smoking over oak fires for 4–18 hours. Dye is often added to the brine, resulting in deep reddish-brown kippers, but the best (notably Manx and Loch Fyne kippers) are undyed. Kippers can be unpopular because they have so many bones, but these are easy to deal with once you know how.
Buying Look for the plumpest kippers you can find; lean kippers can be dry. As a rule of thumb, the darker the fish, the poorer the quality. Always buy undyed kippers if possible. Frozen boil-in-the bag kipper fillets are convenient,

boneless and odour-free, but they have a flabby texture and insipid taste, and are really hardly worth eating.
Cooking Many people are nervous about cooking kippers because of the smell. To avoid any unpleasant odour, put them head-down into a tall jug (pitcher), pour over boiling water and leave to stand for 10 minutes, by which time the kippers will be cooked. If you serve kippers often, keep a jug (pitcher) especially for cooking them. They can also be microwaved and are good grilled (broiled) or shallow fried in butter. They make a delicious breakfast dish topped with a poached egg. Poached kippers make excellent mousse and pâté. Raw kippers can be marinated and served as an appetizer.

Bloaters

Herrings that are left ungutted before being briefly salted, then smoked for 12 hours, are called bloaters. The guts impart a slightly gamey flavour and the enzymes they contain cause the herring

Below: Bloaters

Boning cooked kippers

1 Lay the kipper on a plate, skin-side up. Run a knife point around the edge to lift up the skin.

2 Run the knife point down the backbone and eat the flesh that lies on top of the fine bones.

to become bloated during smoking. Because they are not gutted, bloaters do not keep as well as other smoked herring and should be eaten within a few days. Always gut them before serving. Despite their unattractive name, they are quite pleasing to look at, with silvery skin and moist flesh.
Other varieties *Harengs saurs* are a speciality of Boulogne; they are even more bloated than English bloaters. The most bloated of all are the Swedish *surströmming*. Like *harengs saurs*, they are traditionally eaten with potatoes.
Cooking Bloaters can be eaten as they are in salads and sandwiches. They can also be mashed into a paste with lemon juice and cayenne pepper or grilled and served with butter. To skin bloaters, pour over boiling water and leave for 2 minutes, then peel off the skin.

Above: Smoked eel fillets

HOT-SMOKED FISH

Fish that are cured or hot-smoked at a temperature of 80–85°C/176–185°F, which simultaneously cooks and cures them, need no further cooking. Trout, mackerel, eel and herrings can all be hot-smoked. Recently it has become fashionable to hot-smoke salmon, producing a very different flavour and texture from that of salmon that has been cold-smoked.

Arbroath smokies

These hot-smoked haddock have been beheaded and gutted but left whole. They have deep golden skin and soft pale gold flesh with a more delicate

Below: Smoked eel

flavour than cold-smoked haddock. In their native Scotland, they are a favourite breakfast or supper dish. Smokies are sold whole, so ask the fishmonger to split them open for you. Grill (broil) gently and serve with plenty of butter. When mashed with butter and lemon juice, Arbroath smokies make a delicious pâté.

Below: Arbroath smokies are always sold in pairs, tied with string.

Smoked eel

This fish has a very rich, dense texture and can only be eaten in small quantities. The skin, which is easily removed, is black and shiny, and the flesh has a pinkish tinge. The eel can be served on its own as an hors d'oeuvre, with horseradish or mustard sauce to cut the richness, or made into a salad or pâté. It is particularly delicious served on a bed of celeriac *rémoulade* (grated celeriac in a mustard-flavoured mayonnaise). Smoked eel also makes a good addition to a platter of mixed smoked fish.

When buying smoked eel, check that the skin is shiny and has not dried out. For an ample serving for one, you will need about 90g/3½oz.

Brisling, Sild and Sprats

Not to everyone's taste, these small, hot-smoked herring with rich oily flesh are usually skinned and filleted and served cold as an appetizer with brown bread and butter. They can also be brushed with melted butter and lightly grilled (broiled), served hot with toast.

Below: Hot-smoked sprats

Above: Smoked trout fillets

birch with the addition of a little peat for a smokier flavour. Smoked trout is usually sold as skinned fillets, but you may occasionally find them whole, with the head on. Skin them like smoked mackerel. Smoked trout is delicious served on its own with dill or horseradish sauce. It can be made into mousses or pâté and is also good in salads, omelettes and flans. Allow one fillet per person as an appetizer; two as a main course.

Buckling

These are large, fat ungutted herrings with a rich flavour. They are best eaten cold with bread and butter, but can be mashed into a paste or grilled (broiled) and served with scrambled eggs.

Smoked mackerel

This has a rich flavour and a succulent velvety-smooth texture. The fillets are sold loose or pre-packed. They are sometimes coated in a thick layer of crushed peppercorns. Smoked mackerel can be eaten cold in a salad, or with horseradish sauce and lemon. It makes an excellent pâté and can be flaked and added to an omelette or quiche. Try it instead of smoked haddock in a kedgeree. Allow one fillet

Above: Buckling

per person. To skin smoked mackerel, lay the fish on a board, skin side up. Starting at the tail end, peel back the skin towards the head. Pull away any fins together with their bones.

Smoked trout

Among the finest of all hot-smoked fish, trout should be plump and moist, with a beautiful golden-pink colour. The flesh has a delicate flavour and is less rich than smoked herring or mackerel. The best smoked trout is first brined, then gutted and smoked over

Below: Smoked sea trout

Above: Smoked mackerel fillets

Below: Smoked mackerel

FISH SAUCES AND PASTES

For centuries, people have produced fish sauces made by fermenting whole fish or various parts, including the entrails, into a savoury, salty liquid to flavour and enhance fish dishes. The Romans' favourite condiment was *garum*, a pungent, evil-smelling sauce obtained by soaking pieces of oily fish and their guts in brine flavoured with herbs. Similar sauces exist today, notably in the Far East. The area around Nice also boasts *pissalat*, a sauce made from fermented anchovies. Don't be confused by the term "sauce"; these are flavourings or condiments, not to be served on their own.

packing small fish such as anchovies in brine in barrels and leaving them to ferment in the hot sun for several months. Curiously, the resulting sauce does not taste of fish; it is more like a very intense soy sauce. It can be added to any savoury dishes, or mixed with flavourings such as garlic, lime juice and chilli to make a dipping sauce, or can be used to add flavour to salad dressings. The colour of fish sauce should be a clear amber; if it is dark brown it will taste too fishy.

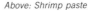

Above: Shrimp paste

Anchovy essence (paste)

Salted anchovies are processed into a thick, rich pinkish-brown sauce with an intensely salty flavour. A few drops will enhance the flavour of almost any savoury dish, but anchovy essence (paste) must be used sparingly, or it will overpower the other ingredients.

Thai fish sauce/Nam pla

Almost unheard of in the West a few years ago, *nam pla* is now an essential ingredient in every adventurous cook's pantry. It is a staple ingredient in all Far Eastern cooking; in Vietnam, it is called *nuoc cham*. The pungent, salty brown liquid is produced by

Right, from left: Thai fish sauce Worcestershire sauce and anchovy essence

Shrimp paste

A speciality of Malaysia and Indonesia, shrimp paste is made from salted, fermented shrimp. This powerful smelling paste, called *blachan, terasi* or *belacan*, is sold in blocks and is mixed with other ingredients to make a flavouring for stir-fries, soups and other savoury dishes.

Worcestershire sauce

Anyone who has tasted this spicy sauce may be surprised to learn that it contains anchovies. Originally produced in India, the precise ingredients of Worcestershire sauce remain a closely-guarded secret, but they include malt and spirit vinegar, molasses, tamarind, garlic, onions and spices as well as anchovies.

Worcestershire sauce gives a lift to any savoury dish and can be used sparingly to enliven a marinade for fish or meat. It is also essential for making a Bloody Mary cocktail. The "original and genuine" Worcestershire sauce made by Lea and Perrins is superior to all its imitators.

CRUSTACEANS

All crustaceans belong to the enormous family of decapods, ten-limbed creatures that are believed to be descendants of invertebrates that lived on the earth over 200 million and possibly up to 390 million years ago. One can only marvel at the imagination of the first person who thought of eating a crustacean. These curious-looking creatures with their hard carapaces and spidery limbs hardly look like the most attractive of foods, but the sweet flesh concealed within the shell is delicious.

CRABS AND LOBSTERS

CRABS

There are dozens of varieties of crab, ranging from hefty common crabs that will make a meal for several people, to tiny shore crabs that are good only for making soup. They are great wanderers, travelling hundreds of miles in a year from feeding to spawning grounds. As a result, crabs are often caught in baited pots sited on the sea bed far from the shore. As their bodies grow, crabs outgrow their shells and shed them while they grow a new carapace. At first the new shells are soft. These "soft-shell" crabs are a delicacy and can be eaten shell and all. Female crabs are known as hens. They have sweeter flesh than the males, but are smaller and their claws contain less flesh.

Below: Blue crabs

Above: Common or brown crab

Right: Soft-shell crabs

Other names In French, crab is *crabe*, *tourteau* (common edible crab) or *araignée* (spider crab). In Italian, *granchio* or *granseola*; in Spanish: *cangrejo* or *centolla*.

Blue crab *(Callinectes sapidus)*

These crabs have steely-grey bodies and bright, electric blue legs and claws. They are found in American waters and are prized for their white meat.

Soft-shell crabs are blue crabs that have shed their hard carapaces, leaving them deliciously tender, with sweet creamy flesh. They are extremely delicate and do not keep or travel well, so they are generally sold frozen, although you may find fresh soft-shell crabs in the United States in the summer months.

Common edible crab/Brown crab *(Cancer pagarus)*

The bodies of these large brownish-red crabs can measure well over 20cm/8in. They have big, powerful claws that can deliver an extremely nasty nip, but they contain plenty of tasty meat. Common edible crabs are found on Atlantic coasts and parts of the Mediterranean. **Cooking** These are the perfect crabs for boiling to serve cold with mayonnaise. The claws contain plenty of firm meat. After cooking, this can be removed from

Below: Spider crab

Spider crab *(Maia squinado)*

These alarming-looking crabs have spiny shells and long slender legs, which give them the appearance of enormous reddish-pink spiders; hence their alternative name of "sea spider". Those found along the Atlantic coasts measure about 20cm/8in across, but the giant species, found in the waters around Japan, measures up to 40cm/16in, with a claw span of almost 3m/9¾ft – a truly terrifying sight for arachnophobes.

the shell in one piece, marinated in a dressing containing Worcestershire sauce and Tabasco and served as a cocktail snack. The claw meat is also delicious deep-fried. The liver and roe of these crabs are also delicious.

Dungeness/California crab *(Cancer magister)*

These trapezium-shaped crabs are found all along the Pacific coast, from Mexico to Alaska. They are very similar to common edible crabs and can be cooked in exactly the same way.

King crab *(Paralithodes camtschiatica)*

Looking like gigantic spiny spiders, king crabs are hideous to behold, but very good to eat. Their very size is awe-inspiring; a mature male king crab can weigh up to 12kg/26½lb and measure 1m/39in across. Their triangular bodies are bright red, with a pale creamy underside. Every part tastes good, from the body meat to that from the narrow claws and long, dangly legs.
Buying Only male king crabs are sold; they are much larger and meatier than the females. Cooked legs are available frozen, and king crab meat is frequently canned. Unlike most crab meat, canned king crab is of excellent quality and highly prized. The best comes from Alaska, Japan and Russia, where it is sold as Kamchatka crab.

Snow crab *(Chionoetes* spp*)*

Also known as queen crabs, these crabs from the north Pacific have roundish pinkish-brown bodies and exceptionally long legs. The delicious, sweet flesh is difficult to remove from the body, but the claw meat is more accessible. Snow crab meat is usually sold frozen or canned.

Stone crab (family Lithodidae)

Similar in appearance to king crabs, stone crabs live at great depths. They have a superb flavour, but are usually sold frozen or canned rather than fresh.

Below: King crab claws

Above. Swimming crabs

Swimming crab (family Portunidae)

The main distinguishing feature of these crabs is their extra pair of legs, shaped rather like paddles. Among the many species of swimming crabs are mud or mangrove, shore and velvet crabs. Shore crabs are eaten in Italy in their soft-shelled state; they also make delicious soup. Mud crabs, with their excellent claw meat, are popular in Australia and South-east Asia.

Cooking Crab can be cooked in a multitude of ways. The sweet, succulent meat is rich and filling, so it needs a light touch when cooking; refreshing flavours suit it better than creamy sauces. Picking it out of the shell is hard work, but the result is well worth the effort. Recipes for crab meat include devilled crab (where the meat is removed from the shell and cooked with mustard, horseradish, spices and breadcrumbs); crab mornay, in which the meat is combined with a Gruyère cheese sauce enriched with sherry and mushrooms, and potted crab. The flesh marries well with clean Asian flavours such as lime juice, coriander (cilantro) and chilli; combined with these, it makes the perfect summer salad. Crab meat is perfect for fish cakes such as Maryland or Thai crab cakes. It also makes excellent soup; a classic Scottish dish is *partan bree*, a creamy crab soup made with fish stock, milk and rice.

In the shell, crab can be boiled and served with mayonnaise, steamed with aromatics or baked with ginger and spring onions (scallions).

Soft-shell crabs are usually lightly coated in flour and deep-fried. A Venetian speciality is *molecchie fritte;* the crabs are soaked in beaten egg before being fried. In China, soft-shell crabs are served with a garnish of chilli or ginger. They can also be sautéed in butter and sprinkled with toasted almonds, or brushed with melted butter and lemon juice, then tossed lightly in flour before grilling (broiling).

Crawfish *(Palinurus vulgaris)*

Crawfish are similar to lobsters, except that they have spiny shells and no claws. They are variously known as spiny lobsters, rock lobsters, langouste and crayfish (but must not be confused with freshwater crayfish). Crawfish are found on the rocky sea bed in many parts of the world. The colour of their shells varies according to where they come from: Atlantic crawfish are dark reddish-brown; those from the Florida coast are brown with pale spots; warm-water varieties can be pink or bluish-green. All turn pink or red when cooked. Crawfish have dense, very white flesh, similar to that of lobster, but with a milder flavour. Those from the Atlantic are the finest and sweetest. Crawfish from warmer waters can tend to be a little coarse.

Other names In France, crawfish are called *langouste*; in Italy they are *aragosta*; in Spain *langosta*.

Buying Crawfish are generally sold cooked. Females have the better flavour, so look for the egg sac underneath the thorax. Because there is no claw meat, allow one 450g/1lb crawfish per person. Florida crawfish are often sold frozen as "lobster" tails.

Cooking Cook as lobster. Crawfish benefit from spicy seasonings and are excellent in Asian recipes.

Crayfish *(Astacus astacus)* **and yabby** *(Cherax)*

Crayfish are miniature freshwater lobsters, which grow to a maximum length of 10cm/4in. The exception is a species found in Tasmania, which can weigh up to 6kg/13lb. Crayfish have a superb flavour and, whatever their colour when alive, turn a glorious deep scarlet when cooked. Over three hundred species are found in well-oxygenated streams throughout Europe, America and Australia, although most of the European species have been wiped out, largely through pollution and disease. Crayfish can be farmed successfully; unfortunately, the most prolific variety are the voracious American signal crayfish; these are prone to a killer disease, which they pass on to wild native crayfish, resulting in near-extinction.

Other names The most commonly available crayfish are the European, the red-claw, the American signal, the red Louisiana swamp, the greenish Turkish crayfish, the Australian yabby and the large marron, which is a deep purplish-grey colour. In France, crayfish are called *écrevisse*; in Italy, *gambero di fiume*; in Spain, *cangrejo de rio*.

Buying Fresh crayfish should be bought alive. There is a lot of wastage, so allow 8–12 crayfish per serving. Keep the shells to make stock, soup or sauces. Frozen crayfish are also available. These are fine for made-up dishes, but are not worth eating on their own.
Cooking Crayfish feature in many luxurious dishes, including bisque (a rich creamy soup), sauces and mousses. They are superb poached in a court-bouillon for about 5 minutes and served cold with mayonnaise or hot with lemony melted butter. Only the tail and claw meat is eaten; the head is often used as a garnish. The cleaned heads and shells can be used to make a shellfish stock or soup.

Below: Crayfish are tiny freshwater lobsters; there are hundreds of species.

Langoustines/Dublin Bay prawns/Scampi
(Nephrops norvegicus)

Smaller relatives of lobsters, langoustines have smooth-shelled narrow bodies with long thin, knobbly claws. They are salmon pink in colour. The largest can measure up to 23cm/ 9in, but the average length is about 12cm/4½in. Langoustines were originally found in Norway, hence their Latin name, and they are still sometimes known as Norway lobsters. Nowadays, they are caught all along the Atlantic coast, in the Adriatic and western Mediterranean. The colder the water in which langoustines live, the better the flavour.
Other names The French know them as *langoustine*; the Italians call them *scampo*, while in Spain they are called *cigala* or *langostina*.

Shelling cooked crayfish

1 Hold the crayfish between your finger and thumb and gently twist off the tail.

2 Hold the tail shell between your thumb and index finger, twist and pull off the flat end; the thread-like intestinal tract will come away. Peel the tail.

3 Hold the head and thorax in one hand. Use the other index finger to prise off the whole underside, including the gills and innards, and discard these.

4 Finally, gently twist off the claws from the head.

Left: These freshwater crustaceans, called cherabin in Australia and black tiger or African prawns elsewhere, are sometimes confused with crayfish and scampi, because, unlike all other prawns, they have a pair of extremely long, thin claws.

delicate and delicious. They must be cooked very briefly. Roast in oil and garlic in a hot oven for 3–5 minutes; split them and grill (broil) or cook on a barbecue for about 2 minutes on each side; or poach in a court-bouillon and serve hot with melted butter. Remember that most langoustines on sale are already cooked, so subject them to as little heat as possible. Langoustines are delicious served cold with mayonnaise. They make a wonderful addition to a *plateau de fruits de mer*. Langoustine tails can be baked *au gratin* in a creamy sauce with mushrooms and Gruyère cheese or served Scottish-style in a whisky-flavoured sauce. They can also be deep-fried and served with lemon wedges, but take care not to overcook them.

Buying Langoustines deteriorate very rapidly once caught, so are often cooked and frozen at sea. Live langoustines are therefore something of a rarity in British fish markets, although you will often find them in mainland Europe. If you are lucky enough to find live langoustines, and can be certain of cooking them soon after purchase, they will be an excellent buy. It is important to check that they are still moving; if they have died, they will have an unpleasant woolly texture. Unlike other crustaceans, langoustines do not change colour when cooked, so make sure you know what you are buying. Langoustines are graded by size; larger specimens are better value, as they contain more meat. They are also available frozen, often as scampi tails. If they have been shelled, allow about 115g/4oz per person; you will need twice this quantity if the langoustines are in the shell.
Cooking Most people must have encountered tasteless, badly

cooked scampi at some time in their lives. When langoustines are properly cooked, however, their flavour is

Above:
Langoustines,
which are also known as Dublin Bay prawns and scampi.

Left: Canadian lobsters are air-freighted live to Europe.

If you buy a live lobster, make sure that the pincers are secured with a stout elastic band.

Other names In French, lobster is called *homard*; in Italian, it is *astice* and in Spanish, *bogavante*.

Canadian/American lobster *(Homarus americanus)*

The hardiest species of lobster, these are found in large numbers in the waters around Canada and the North American Atlantic. They resemble the European lobster, but are greener in colour, and the claws are slightly rounder and fleshier. Although they make excellent eating, their flavour does not quite match up to that of the European species. The best-known American lobster is the Maine lobster. Canadian and Maine lobsters are air-freighted live to Europe to meet the demand for these crustaceans. Even taking into account the freight costs, they are considerably cheaper than their European counterparts.

Below: Maine lobster resembles the European lobster, but is less expensive.

LOBSTER

These are the ultimate luxury seafood. Their uniquely firm, sweet flesh has a delicious flavour and many people regard them as the finest crustaceans of all. The best lobsters live in cold waters, scavenging for food on the rocky sea bed. Like crabs, they "moult" every couple of years, casting off their outgrown shells. Their colour varies according to their habitat, from steely blue to greenish-brown to reddish-purple; all turn brick red when cooked. Lobsters grow very slowly, only reaching maturity at six years old, by which time they are about 18cm/7in long. If you are lucky enough to find a 1kg/2¼lb lobster, it will be about ten years old. This explains why lobsters are in such short supply.

Lobsters must be bought live or freshly boiled. The powerful pincers, which the creature uses for catching and crushing its prey, can be dangerous.

European lobster *(Homarus gammarus)*

These lobsters, which come from England, Scotland, Ireland, Norway and Brittany, are regarded as having the finest flavour of all. They have distinctive blue-black colouring, and are sometimes speckled with bright blue. European lobsters are becoming increasingly rare and expensive. If they are caught in reasonable numbers during the summer months, they are often held in vivariums, massive holding tanks built into the sea.

Unfortunately, lobsters do not eat in captivity, so although the vivariums make sure that they are available

Right: The Balmain bug is a warm-water variety of squat lobster from Australia that has sweet, delicious flesh.

Below: The European lobster, which is becoming rare – and very expensive – is considered the best lobster of all.

throughout the year, the quality deteriorates as the season progresses; by early spring, they tend to be thin and undernourished.

Slipper/Squat lobster *(Scyllarus arctus)*

There are over fifty species of these warm-water lobsters. They have wide, flattened bodies and spindly clawed legs. The best known squat lobsters are the Australian "bugs", and the best known of these are the Balmain and Moreton Bay bugs. The comparatively small tails contain deliciously sweet flesh. Squat lobsters are seldom sold in Europe, but can occasionally be found in France, where they are known as *cigales* (grasshoppers). Italians call them *cicala di mare* and in Spain they are called *cigarra*.

Cooking lobster

All types of lobster are best cooked very simply to allow the delicate flavour to speak for itself. They can be boiled in salted water or court-bouillon and served hot with melted butter or cold with mayonnaise, grilled (broiled) or fried in the shell with oil and butter. A plain boiled lobster can be the crowning glory of a *plateau de fruits de mer*.

Classical French cookery has a plethora of rich lobster recipes that reflect the luxurious quality of these crustaceans. These dishes, which are usually served with rice to offset the richness, include Lobster Cardinale, with mushrooms and truffles in a velvety sauce; Lobster Newburg, with a cognac and sherry-flavoured cream sauce; Lobster Bretonne, with prawns (shrimp) and mushrooms in a white wine sauce, and the world-famous Lobster Thermidor, with its unctuous brandy and mustard-flavoured sauce. More modern recipes combine lobster with Asian flavours such as ginger and star anise, but these spices should be used in moderation.

Lobster is superb with fresh pasta. Use it as a filling for ravioli or toss it into tagliolini with lemon juice and butter. Cold boiled lobster can be diced and made into a lobster cocktail or added to a salad. When cooking lobster, keep the shells to use in a shellfish stock or soup.

Preparing a cooked lobster

You'll need a large, heavy knife or cleaver and a lobster pick to remove the meat from the legs.

1 Hold the body of the lobster firmly in one hand and twist off the claws one at a time.

2 Hold the lobster the right way up on a chopping board. Insert a large sharp knife at right angles to the seam between the body and head and press down firmly to split the body and tail lengthways.

3 Turn the lobster round to face the other way and cut firmly through the head. Separate the lobster into two halves and discard the stomach sac.

4 Twist off the legs and then flatten them lightly with the back of the knife. Use a lobster pick to remove the flesh.

5 To remove the meat from the claws, first break up the claws into sections. Hold the larger section of the claw, curved side down, in one hand and sharply pull off the smaller pincer. Twist off the lower section of the claw at the joint.

6 Gently crack the claw shell with a mallet or the end of a rolling pin and remove the flesh.

7 The lobster can be grilled (broiled) in the shell with butter, or the flesh can be diced and used in sauces.

PRAWNS AND SHRIMP

Prawns are the world's most popular
crustaceans and are eaten in huge
quantities around the globe.
Thousands of species of
prawns and shrimp are
found in all of the world's
oceans and also in fresh
water. Technically, there
is no difference
between shrimp and
prawns; the names
merely indicate size.
In the fish trade,
prawns measuring
less than about
5cm/2in are known as
shrimp, except in
America, where all
prawns are known
as shrimp. Most
prawns have
narrow, tapering bodies,
curled over at the tail,
and long antennae. As is
the case with other crustaceans,
prawns that come from colder waters
have a better flavour than those from
warm waters.

Above: Pink shrimp

COLD-WATER PRAWNS

Common prawn/Pink shrimp *(Palaemon serratus)*

These translucent, brownish prawns can
grow up to 10cm/4in in length. They are
found in deep waters in the Atlantic
Ocean and Mediterranean Sea, but
related species are found throughout
the world. The French and Italians
consider these prawns the best of all;

Below: Mediterranean prawns

they have an exceptionally good flavour
and turn a glorious red when cooked.
As a result, they command enormously
high prices.
Other names Common prawns are also
known as sword shrimp or Algerian
shrimp. In France, they are called
crevette rose or *bouquet*; in Italy,
they are *gamberello*; in Spain, *camarón*
or *quisquilla*.

Deep-sea prawn *(Pandalus borealis)*

Sometimes sold as large shrimp, these
cold-water prawns live at great depths
in the North Sea. Hermaphrodite, they
all begin life as males, but become
female halfway through their lifespan.
Deep-sea prawns have translucent
pink bodies, which turn pale
salmon-pink on cooking. They
have a delicate, juicy flavour and
are almost always sold cooked.
Other names In France, these
prawns are *crevette*; Italians know
them as *gambero*; while in Spain they
are *camarón*.

Peeling and deveining prawns

1 Hold the prawn in the middle and
pull off the head and legs. Peel off
the shell, leaving on the end of the
tail if you prefer.

2 To devein, use a small sharp
knife to make a shallow incision
down the centre of the curved back
of the prawn. Use the knife tip to
remove the black vein (intestinal
tract) and discard it.

Mediterranean prawn *(Aristeus antennatus)*

These large prawns can measure up to
10cm/4in. The colour varies – the
heads can be anything from blood-red
to deep coral – but once cooked, they
turn a brilliant red. The flesh is
delicious and very succulent.
Mediterranean prawns are sold cooked
and should be served simply as they
are, with good-quality mayonnaise and
fresh French bread. Allow 3–4 each as
an appetizer.
Other names Also known as blue or
red shrimp, Mediterranean prawns are
called *crevette rouge* in France; they
are called *gambero rosso* in Italy and
carabinero in Spain.

Common/Brown shrimp *(Crangon crangon)*

These small shrimp have translucent grey bodies and measure only about 5cm/2in. They live in soft sand in shallow waters, emerging at night in darker camouflage to hunt for their prey. When cooked, they turn brownish-grey. Their small size makes them difficult to peel, but they can be eaten whole and their flavour is incomparable, with a wonderful tang of the sea. They are used to make potted shrimp.
Other names The French call these shrimp *crevette grise* or *boucaud*; the Italians know them as *gamberetto grigio*; the Spanish call them *quisquilla*.

Left: Brown shrimp

Below: Tiger prawns

Butterflied prawns
Prawns look very attractive when they are butterflied.

1 The easiest way of doing this is to deepen the incision made to remove the vein, cutting almost but not quite through to the belly.

2 The prawn is then opened out flat. If the prawns are large, make the incision through the belly to give a more pronounced shape.

WARM-WATER PRAWNS

Gulf shrimp *(Hymenopenaeus robustus)*

Warm-water prawns from the Gulf of Mexico, these are usually bright red, but may sometimes be greyish-pink. Gulf shrimp can grow up to 40g/1½oz in weight, and have succulent flesh.

Kuruma/Japanese prawn *(Penaeus japonicus)*

These large prawns can grow to a length of 23cm/9in. They have yellowish tails flecked with black. Kuruma are found throughout the Indo-Pacific region and in the Red Sea.

Tiger/King prawn/Jumbo shrimp *(Penaeus monodon)*

These huge prawns are found throughout the Indo-Pacific. They can grow up to 33cm/13in in length and are ideal for barbecuing. When raw, they are a translucent greenish-grey. Although their flavour is not as good as

Below: Gulf shrimp

that of cold-water prawns, they have succulent, firm flesh. In Europe, they are seldom sold fresh, but they freeze well and are available peeled or in the shell. Peeled tiger prawns usually have the end of the tail left on so that they can be eaten with the fingers.
Buying Wild tiger prawns are trawled and by-catch often includes endangered turtles. Only buy farmed tiger prawns.
Cooking The cardinal rule with any prawns or shrimp is not to overcook them. Ready-cooked prawns should preferably be eaten without further cooking. Serve them simply, with lemon and brown bread and butter, or in a prawn cocktail or salad. If you must cook them, use them in a dish such as pasta where they need only be heated through. They add extra flavour and texture to other fish dishes, such as fish pies, terrines and flans, and combine well with other shellfish. Small prawns or shrimp make an excellent filling for omelettes, vol-au-vents or tartlets.

Raw prawns can be boiled briefly in salt water or court-bouillon and are delicious grilled (broiled), cooked briefly on a barbecue or deep-fried in batter. With squid and fish, deep-fried prawns are an essential ingredient of an Italian *fritto misto*.

GASTROPODS

Also known as univalves, gastropods are single-shelled creatures belonging to the snail family. Most marine gastropods have the familiar snail shape, with a single spiral shell, but some look more like bivalves and others have no shell at all. All gastropods have a single, large foot which they extend and contract to crawl along at a "snail's pace". Edible gastropods vary in size from tiny winkles to conches measuring up to 30cm/12in. All can be delicious if properly cooked.

Abalone/Ormer/Sea ear

You could be forgiven for thinking that abalone (Haliotis tuberculata) were bivalves, since their ear-shaped shells give them the appearance of large mussels. Like all gastropods, they have a large, muscled foot that they use to cling to rocks and cliffs. This immensely strong foot can withstand strains up to four thousand times the weight of the abalone, which makes it very difficult to prise them from the rocks, and helps to explain why they are so expensive. Another reason for their cost is that they feed exclusively on seaweed; as their habitat becomes polluted, they die, so they are becoming increasingly rare. In some countries abalone have become a protected species. They are highly prized not only for their flesh, but also for their beautiful shells. These are

lined with iridescent mother-of-pearl. There are over a hundred species of abalone living in warm waters throughout the world. Most can grow to about 20cm/8in in length, but the shell of the red abalone (Haliotis rufescens), found in the American Pacific, grows up to 30cm/12in. Their firm flesh, which must be tenderized before it can be eaten, has a subtle flavour of iodine.

Other names In the Channel Islands, one of the few places in Europe where abalone are still found, they are known as ormers. In South Africa, they are known as perlemoen or Venus' ear. The French call them ormeau or oreilles de St Pierre; the Italians, orecchia marina; the Spanish, oreja de mar.

Buying In Europe, there is a closed season for abalone, and they are limited to only a few days in early spring. You are more likely to find fresh abalone in America, Australia and the Far East. These are often sold sliced and tenderized ready for cooking. Abalone is also available canned, frozen and dried.

Preparing and Cooking Before cooking, the intestinal sac and dark membrane and skirt must be removed. To remove the white flesh, run a sharp knife between it and the shell. Abalone flesh

Below: Abalone are large shellfish, which can grow to 30cm/12in in length.

Above: Limpets

must be beaten vigorously with a wooden mallet to tenderize it. In Japan, it is then sliced thinly and eaten raw as sashimi. If it is cooked, the technique is the same as that for squid – it must either be cooked very briefly, or given long, slow cooking. Thin slices can be sautéed quickly in hot butter, or cut into strips and deep-fried in batter or egg and breadcrumbs. In China, abalone is braised with dried mushrooms; in France, it is stewed slowly with dry white wine and shallots. In the Channel Islands, ormers are traditionally casseroled with bacon and potatoes. Abalone makes an excellent chowder.

Conch (Strombus gigas)

Pronounced "konk", conch is a large relative of the whelk. It has a distinctive spiral shell. As with all such gastropods, the opening is protected by a hard operculum, or "trap door" which must be removed for access to the flesh inside. Conch are native to Florida, the Pacific coast and the Caribbean. The shells are sought after as ornaments and musical instruments. The pinkish flesh is tasty and chewy, and must be beaten to tenderize it before eating.

Buying In their native countries, conches are available all year round. The best are young specimens, known as "thin-lipped" conches; older conches are described as "thick-lipped". They are generally sold out of the shell.

Cooking After tenderizing, conch meat can be marinated and eaten raw, or cooked in a chowder. Some conches can cause stomach upsets; the risk of this occurring can be reduced if the conch is boiled in two changes of water.

Above: Whelks

Cooking and picking winkles and whelks

1 Bring a large pan of well-salted water to the boil. Drop in the winkles or whelks and simmer for about 5 minutes for winkles; 10 minutes for whelks. Drain.

2 If the operculum is still covering the opening of the shell, remove it with a cocktail stick or pin. Insert the cocktail stick or pin into the shell and pull out the flesh.

Limpets *(Patella vulgata)*

These gastropods have conical shells. They are found throughout the world, clinging tightly to rocks. When the tide goes out, they nestle into holes in the sand, emerging at night to crawl in a 1m/39in circle around their hole in search of food. Limpets have quite a good flavour, but the small amount of flesh they contain can be very tough. It takes a great deal of effort to prise them off the rocks, so only the larger varieties, which yield more flesh, are eaten. Limpets are not available commercially so you will have to harvest them yourself.
Cooking Wash the limpets and boil them in sea water or heavily-salted water for 5–7 minutes, or cook the flesh in fish and shellfish dishes or soups.

Whelks *(Buccinum undatum)*

Smaller relatives of the conch, whelks have pretty spiral shells measuring up to 10cm/4in. They have rubbery, pinkish flesh with a good flavour, largely due to their diet. Whelks bore through the shell of other shellfish to eat their flesh.
Other names There are many varieties of whelk, including the common, the dog, the spiral and the knobbled or giant American whelk, which can grow to 20cm/8in in length. In French, they are variously known as *bulot*, *buccin* and *escargot de mer* (sea snail); in Italian, *buccina*; in Spanish, as *bocina* or *caracola*.
Buying Whelks should be bought alive; check that the operculum is tightly closed. They are sometimes sold ready-boiled and removed from the shell, but these can be rather dry. You will also find whelks pickled in vinegar, or ready-cooked and bottled in brine.
Cooking The best way to cook whelks is to boil them in sea water or heavily-salted water for about 5 minutes. Use a cocktail stick (toothpick) to prise the flesh out of the shell. The flesh of large whelks can be sautéed after boiling, or deep-fried in batter. It can be used instead of clams in a chowder, or added to cooked shellfish dishes or salads.

Winkles/Periwinkles *(Littorina littorea)*

These tiny marine snails have thick greenish-brown or black shells, each with a pointed end. Most grow no larger than 4cm/1½in and contain a morsel of chewy flesh.
Other names In France, they are *bigourneau* or *littorine*; in Italy, *chiocciola di mare*; in Spain, *bigaro*.
Buying Fresh winkles should be bought alive; check that the operculum is tightly closed. They are also available cooked and bottled in vinegar.
Cooking Like whelks, winkles need only brief cooking. Serve as an appetizer with vinegar or mayonnaise, or as part of a shellfish platter.

Left: Winkles

MOLLUSCS

The mollusc family is divided into bivalves such as mussels and oysters, which have a hinged external shell, and gastropods such as whelks and winkles, which have a single external shell. Cephalopods (squid, cuttlefish and octopus) are yet another group; unlike gastropods and bivalves, they have internal shells.

BIVALVES

CLAMS

There are hundreds of species of clam, ranging from the aptly-named giant clam which can grow to a length of 1.3m/4¼ft, to tiny pebble-like Venus and littleneck clams measuring barely 5cm/2in. Americans are passionate about clams and eat them in all sizes and forms. Their enthusiasm has spread to Europe, where clams are now extensively farmed. Large species, such as the fully mature American quahog (pronounced co-hog), have very thick warty shells; small varieties have smooth shells marked with fine circular striations. Clams have a fine, sweet flavour and firm texture, and are delicious cooked or raw.

Below: Palourde or carpetshell clams have tender flesh that can be eaten raw.

Cherrystone/Littleneck clam *(Mercenaria mercenaria)*

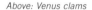

These small clams have an attractive brown and white patterned shell. They are actually quahogs, the popular name deriving from their size. The smallest are the baby littlenecks, with 4–5cm/1½–2in shells. The slightly larger cherrystones (about 7.5cm/3in), named after Cherrystone Creek in Virginia, are about five years old. Both are often served raw on the half shell; cooked,

Above: Venus clams

they make wonderful pasta sauces. Larger quahogs, which are unsuitable for eating raw, are known as steamer clams. They have quite a strong flavour and are often used for making clam chowder or pasta sauces.

Other names The French call them *palourde*; the Italians, *vongola dura*; the Spanish, *almeja* or *clame*.

Geoduck clam *(Panopea generosa)*

These enormous clams are the largest of all American Pacific shellfish and can weigh up to 4kg/8¾lb. Half this weight is made up of two long siphons, which can be extended to more than 1.3m/4¼ft to take in and expel water. Unlike the soft-shell clam, the geoduck cannot retract these siphons into the shell, and they are often sold separately. Geoducks can bury themselves up to 1.2m/4ft deep in sand, and it takes two people to prise them out. The siphons and flesh are sliced before cooking.

Palourde/Carpetshell clam *(Venerupis decussata)*

These small (4–7.5cm/1½–3in) clams have grooved brown shells with a yellow lattice pattern. The flesh is exceptionally tender, so they can be eaten raw, but are also good grilled (broiled).

Other names In French they are *palourde*; in Italian, *vongola verace*; in Spanish, *almeja fina.*

Praire/Warty Venus clam *(Venus verrucosa)*

The unattractively named warty Venus is a smallish clam measuring 2.5–7.5cm/ 1–3in. The thick shell has concentric stripes, some of which end in warty protuberances. These clams are widely distributed on sandy coasts, from Africa to Europe. They are often eaten raw on the half shell, but are also excellent cooked. The Italians dignify them with the name of "sea truffles".

Below: Cherrystone clams

Other names
Sometimes known as baby clams, the word *praire* comes from the French, who also call these molluscs *coque rayé.* In Italy they are *verrucosa* or *tartufo di mare*; in Spain *almeja vieja.*

Razorshell/Razor clam *(Solen marginatus)*

Resembling an old-fashioned cut-throat razor, these clams have tubular shells that are striped gold and brown. Razorshells are often served raw, but can be cooked like any other clam. Their flesh tastes delicious. They can often be found on sandy beaches at low tide, but as they can burrow into the sand at great speed to conceal themselves, you will need to act fast if you want to catch them.
Other names Razorshells are sometimes known as jack-knife clams. The French call them *couteau*; the Italians, *cannolicchio* or *cappa lunga*; their Spanish name is *navaja* or *longuerión.*

Soft-shell/Long-neck clam *(family Myidae)*

The shells of these wide oval clams gape slightly at the posterior end, giving them their nickname of "gapers". They burrow deep into sand and silt, so have a long tube that acts as a siphon for taking in and expelling water. This siphon can be eaten raw, or made into chowder or creamed dishes. Soft-shell clams are often used in clambakes.
Other names In French they are *mye*; in Italian, *vongola molle*; in Spanish, *almeja de rio.*
Cooking Small clams and razorshells can be eaten raw, steamed or cooked in soups and sauces. Larger clams can be stuffed and baked or grilled (broiled) like mussels, cut into strips and deep-fried in batter or breadcrumbs, or stewed with white wine or onions and tomatoes. Steamed clams can be added to salads or sauces or used as a garnish. Never throw away the juices which clams contain; these are extremely nutritious and delicious, and can be used for drinks such as *clamata*, shellfish stock or soup.

Below: Razor clams are often served raw.

Clambakes
A favourite American pastime is the clambake, a beach picnic in which soft-shell or hard-shell clams are steamed over seaweed laid on hot rocks. A pit is dug in the sand, rocks are placed inside and heated, then draped with wet seaweed. The clams are steamed over the seaweed, along with corn, sweet potatoes and, sometimes, lobsters or soft-shell crabs. The process of digging the pit and cooking the clams takes at least 4 hours, so a clambake can provide a whole day's entertainment.

Cockles

Although traditionally thought of as a typically British food, varieties of cockle *(Cardium edule)* are found all over the world. Their two equal heart-shaped shells are 2.5–4cm/1–1½in long and have 26 defined ribs. Inside lies a morsel of delicate flesh and its coral.
Other names In America, cockles are sometimes known as heart clams. In France, they are *coque*; in Italy, *cuore*; in Spain, *berberecho.*
Buying Fresh cockles are sold by volume; 1 pint weighs about 450g/1lb. Those with paler flesh are said to taste better than those with dark flesh.

Above: Cockles

The colour of the shell is an indication of the colour of the flesh, so choose cockles with pale shells. Shelled cockles are available frozen and bottled in brine or vinegar.

Cooking Cockles are full of sand, so must be soaked in salted cold water for several hours before eating. They can be eaten raw or boiled and served with vinegar and brown bread and butter. They are excellent steamed, stewed with tomatoes and onions or made into soup. Cockles can be added to risotto, pasta and other seafood dishes or served cold as an hors d'oeuvre or salad.

Below: Large New Zealand greenshell or green-lipped mussels.

Right: Ever-popular, black-shelled mussels

Dog cockle
(Glycymeridae)

With their large, flat striated shells, dog cockles resemble scallops. There are four known species of these tropical and warm-water bivalves – the true dog cockle, the bittersweet cockle, the violet bittersweet and the giant bittersweet. All are perfectly good to eat, but have a coarser texture and flavour than true cockles. They can be cooked in the same way as cockles and mussels.
Other names In French they are *amande*; in Italian, *pié d'asino* (ass's foot); in Spanish, *almendra de mar*.

Mussels *(Mytilus edulis)*

Once regarded as the poor relation of the shellfish family, mussels are now very popular, but still comparatively cheap. These succulent bivalves, with their elongated blue-black shells, have been eaten since earliest times. Unlike most other bivalves, they do not use a muscly foot to anchor themselves to rocks and poles, but with a byssus or "beard", a wiry substance produced by a gland at the base of the foot. Clumps of mussels grow wild on sea shores throughout the world and are great fun to harvest. It is essential that the waters they come from are unpolluted. Their sweet, tender flesh is nutritious and versatile. Nowadays, most commercial mussels are farmed.

There are many varieties of mussel. The best and most succulent are the blue or European mussels from cold British waters, which can grow to a length of 10cm/4in, although the average size is nearer 5cm/2in. They are large, with sweet-flavoured flesh which in the female is a beautiful orange; males have paler, cream-coloured flesh. The largest of all are the New Zealand greenshell or green-lipped mussels *(Perna canaliculus)*, which have a distinctive green lip around the internal border of the shell. These can grow to over 23cm/9in and are very meaty and substantial. They are ideal for stuffing, but their flavour is not so good as that of blue mussels.
Other names In French it is *moule*; in Italian, *cozza*; in Spanish, *mejillón*.
Buying Most mussels are farmed and are usually cleaned. They are available all year round and are cheap, so buy more than you think you will need to allow for wastage; 1kg/2¼lb will provide a generous meal for two people. Shelled mussels are available frozen, smoked and bottled in brine or vinegar.

Cooking Mussels are enormously versatile. They can be eaten raw or steamed very simply as in *moules marinière*. They are also good steamed with Mediterranean or Asian flavours. Large mussels can be stuffed and baked or grilled (broiled) with flavoured butter, bacon or pesto. They can be wrapped in bacon, threaded on to skewers and grilled; cooked in cream, wine or cider; deep-fried; or used in omelettes, soufflés, hot or cold soups, curries, pasta sauces, rice dishes such as paella, or shellfish salads. The national dish of Belgium is *moules frites*, crisply fried mussels with French fries, served with a glass of beer. For an unusual and piquant hors d'oeuvre, serve cold steamed mussels *à la ravigote*, with a vinaigrette flavoured with chopped hard-boiled egg, fresh herbs and gherkins.

OYSTERS

One of life's great luxuries, oysters evoke passionate feelings – people tend either to love or loathe them. Their unique, salty, iodized flavour and slippery texture may not appeal to all,

Below: Native oysters are the finest and most expensive of all oysters.

but their reputation as an aphrodisiac (Casanova was said to eat at least fifty every day) has contributed to their popularity, and they are prized all over the world. It was not always so; for centuries, oysters were regarded as food for the poor. Apprentices revolted at having to eat them every day of the week. As they became scarce, however, their popularity increased.

Over 100 different varieties of oyster live in the temperate and warm waters of the world. All have thick, irregular, greyish shells, one flat, the other hollow. The highly nutritious flesh is pinkish-grey with a darker mantle and a slippery texture. Their reproductive life is highly unusual. Some are hermaphrodite; others change sex from male to female in alternate years.

Oysters have been eaten for thousands of years. They were enjoyed by the Celts and Ancient Greeks, but it was the Romans who first discovered the secret of oyster cultivation. By the 19th century, European oyster beds had been so comprehensively over-fished and stocks were so low that Napoleon III ordered that shipments of oysters be brought from abroad. It is as well that he did; in 1868, a ship carrying quantities of Portuguese oysters was

forced to take shelter from a storm in the Gironde estuary. Fearing that his cargo of oysters was going bad, the captain flung them overboard. They bred prolifically, rapidly replenishing the native stocks, and managed to survive a catastrophic epidemic in 1921, which wiped out the native oysters. In 1967, however, they too were decimated by the deadly bonamia virus. Oyster cultivation on a massive scale was the only answer; nowadays, oysters are commercially produced throughout the industrialized world.

Oyster cultivation

Centuries of over-fishing and disease have decimated the world's natural stocks of oysters, a sad state of affairs which has been somewhat alleviated by oyster farming. Oysters have been farmed since Roman times, but cultivation has now become a highly lucrative business, despite being labour-intensive and very slow. Oysters need constant cosseting from the moment of hatching. A single oyster produces up to a hundred million eggs every breeding season, of which only ten oysters will survive long enough to end up on your plate. It takes at least three years to produce an oyster of marketable size; natives take up to seven years and the giant "royals" take ten years to mature. The minuscule spats must first be caught and encouraged to settle on lime-soaked tiles or slates.

After about nine months, they are transferred to oyster parks, where they are enclosed in wire grilles and carefully nurtured while they feed on plankton. After being left to grow for two or three years, they are placed in nets and fattened for about a year in shallow beds or *claires*. The final stage of the lengthy process involves placing them in clean beds for several days under stringent hygiene conditions to expel any impurities. Small wonder that they are so expensive.

Portuguese cupped oysters are cultivated on a large scale, they are known as *fines de claires* after the fattening beds where they are farmed. Fatter, tastier (and, of course, more expensive) specimens are called *spéciales claires.*

Sydney rock oyster *(Crassostrea commercialis)*

This sex-changing cupped oyster is extremely fertile and is farmed in huge numbers on the coast of New South Wales. It grows quickly and has a good flavour, but has the disadvantage of being difficult to open.

Buying The age-old rule that oysters should not be bought when there is no "r" in the month still holds good in the northern hemisphere, not because they are poisonous as was once supposed, but because their flesh becomes unpleasantly soft and milky during the summer breeding season from May to August. Smoked oysters are available and you may also find frozen oysters.

Cooking Oysters are best eaten raw with just a squeeze of lemon or a dash of Tabasco. If you prefer to cook them, do so very briefly. They are good poached or steamed and served with a *beurre blanc* or champagne sauce; stuffed and grilled (broiled); deep-fried in cornmeal batter; or as a luxurious addition to steak and kidney pie.

Left: Portuguese cupped oysters

Eastern/Atlantic oyster *(Crassostrea virginica)*

With rounded shells like those of the native oyster, these actually belong to the Portuguese oyster family and have a similar texture and flavour. In America, they are named after their place of origin; the best known is the Blue Point.

Native oyster *(Ostrea edulis)*

Considered the finest of all oysters, Natives are slow-growers, taking three years to reach their full size of 5–12cm/2–4½in. Their round shells vary in colour from greyish-green to beige, depending on their habitat, and they have a wonderful flavour. Native oysters are named after their place of origin. Among the best known are the French Belon, the English Whitstable, Colchester and Helford, the Irish Galway and the Belgian Ostendes. Native oysters are the most expensive of all oysters.

Other names The French call them *huître plate* or *belon*, to the Italians they are *ostrica*, while in Spain, they are called *ostra plana*.

Pacific/Gigas oyster *(Crassostrea gigas)*

These large cupped bivalves with their craggy elongated shells are the most widely farmed oysters in the world. They are resistant to disease and can grow to 15cm/6in in the space of four years, which makes them comparatively economical to produce. Their texture is not so fine as that of native oysters, but their large size makes them more suitable for cooking than other oysters.

Other names The Pacific oyster is also known as the rock or Japanese oyster. In French, it is *creuse* (hollow); in Italian, *ostrica*; in Spanish *ostión*.

Portuguese cupped oyster *(Crassostrea angulata)*

These scaly greyish-brown oysters are considered finer than gigas, but not so good as natives. Their flesh is rather coarse and they are declining in popularity. In France, where

SCALLOPS

Surely the most attractive of all shellfish, scallops (*Peeten maximus*) have two fan-shaped shells, one flat and the other curved, with grooves radiating out from the hinge to the outside edge. They are found on sandy seabeds in many parts of the world from Iceland to Japan. Unlike many bivalves, they do not burrow into the sand, but "swim" above the sea bed by opening and closing their shells, which gives them the appearance of leaping through the water. There are about three hundred species of scallop throughout the world, with shells ranging in colour from beige to brown, salmon pink, yellow and orange. The most common species is the common or great scallop, whose reddish-brown shell grows to a diameter of 5–6cm/2–2½in. Scallop shells contain a nugget of sweet, firm white flesh joined to the vibrant orange crescent-shaped roe or "coral", which is a delicacy in its own right.

Scallops are deeply symbolic and have long been associated with beauty. According to the legend depicted by Botticelli in one of his most famous paintings, the goddess Venus was born from a scallop shell; her Greek counterpart, Aphrodite, rode across the sea in a scallop shell pulled by six sea horses. Thanks to a miracle involving St James, scallop shells became the symbol of Christianity and the emblem of medieval pilgrims visiting the shrine at Santiago de Compostela in Spain.

Other names Sometimes known as "pilgrim shells", scallops are *coquille St Jacques* in French, *pettine* in Italian; *viera* in Spanish.

Buying Scallops are available almost all year round, but are best in winter when the roes are full and firm. The finest are individually hand-caught by divers; needless to say, they are also the most expensive. If you buy scallops in the shell, keep the shells to use as serving dishes for all sorts of fish recipes. Allow 4–5 large scallops per person as a main course, three times this number if they are small. Scallops are also available

Above: Queen scallops

shelled, which saves the effort of cleaning them. Always try to buy scallops with their delicious coral, although this is not always possible. Avoid frozen scallops, which have little or no taste.

Cooking The beard and all dark coloured parts of the scallop must be removed before they are cooked and eaten. If the scallops are large, slice the white flesh in half horizontally. Scallops require very little cooking and can be thinly sliced and eaten raw with a squeeze of lemon and a drizzle of olive oil. They need only the briefest of cooking to preserve their uniquely firm yet tender texture. Scallops can be poached for a couple of minutes in court-bouillon and served warm or cold in a salad with a tomato and basil vinaigrette or mayonnaise.

Whole scallops in the shell can be baked; seal the shells with a flour and water paste to trap the juices. They are equally delicious wrapped in bacon and grilled (broiled); pan-fried for about 30 seconds on each side; coated in egg and breadcrumbs and deep-fried; stir-fried with colourful vegetables or steamed with ginger and soy sauce. They make wonderful pâtés and mousses. A classic dish is *coquilles St Jacques*, in which poached scallops and corals are sliced, returned to the half shell and coated with Mornay (cheese) sauce, then grilled (broiled) or baked until browned. A border of mashed potato is often piped around the edge of the shell.

Queen scallop *(Chlamys opercularis)*

These miniature scallops measure only about 3cm/1¼in across. Their cream-coloured shells are marked with attractive brown ridges and contain a small nugget of white flesh and a tiny pointed coral. Queen scallops are considerably cheaper than larger scallops, but have the same sweet flavour. They are often sold out of the shell; allow at least a dozen per person. "Queenies" as they are sometimes known, are commercially farmed. They are popular in Asia and are widely used in Chinese cooking.

Above: King scallops

CEPHALOPODS

Despite their appearance, cephalopods, which include cuttlefish, octopus and squid, are molluscs and are more closely related to snails than to fish. They are highly developed creatures with three-dimensional vision, memory and the ability to swim at high speeds. They can also change colour according to the environment. Their name derives from the Greek for "head with feet", which sums up their appearance very accurately. The bulbous head contains the mouth, which has two jaws, rather like a parrot's beak. This is surrounded by tentacles covered with suckers, which are used for crawling and for seizing their prey. The sack-shaped body contains a mantle cavity which houses the stomach, gills and sex organs. Although they developed from snail-like creatures, cephalopods no longer have an external shell; instead, most have an internal calcareous shell made from spongy material which they can inflate to make themselves buoyant. The most familiar of these is the cuttlebone, from the cuttlefish. Cuttlebones often wash up on beaches, and are used by bird-owners to provide calcium for budgerigars. In Roman times, ladies ground up cuttlebones and used the powder on their faces and to clean their teeth and their jewellery.

Most cephalopods also contain an ink sac which emits a blackish fluid designed to repel predators and provide a "smokescreen" for the creature when it is under attack. This fluid, or ink, is delicious and can be used for cooking.

Below: Baby cuttlefish

Right: Cuttlefish

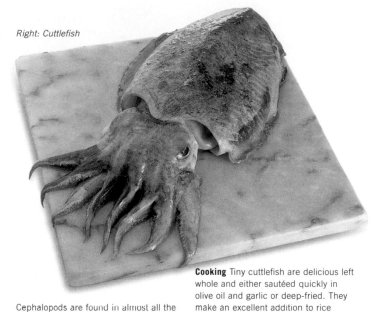

Cephalopods are found in almost all the world's oceans. Unlike many sea creatures, they have not yet suffered from overfishing and are still a sustainable food source.

Cuttlefish

The common cuttlefish *(Sepia officinalis)* has a flattened oval head with brownish camouflage stripes on the back and light coloration on the underside. It has eight stubby tentacles and two long tentacles for catching its prey. These are kept rolled up and hidden in openings near its mouth. Cuttlefish are comparatively small, with bodies measuring 25–30cm/10–12in. When unfurled, the catching tentacles double its length. As is the case with all cephalopods, the smaller the cuttlefish, the more tender the flesh. The smallest species is the Mediterranean little or dwarf cuttlefish *(sepiola)*, which grows to only 3–6cm/1¼–2½in. They are delicious, but time-consuming to prepare, as the tiny cuttlebones must be removed before cooking.

Other names The common cuttlefish is *seiche* in French, *seppia* in Italian, *sepia* in Spanish. Dwarf cuttlefish are *supion* or *chipiron* in French, *seppiolina* in Italian, and *chipirón* in Spanish.

Cooking Tiny cuttlefish are delicious left whole and either sautéed quickly in olive oil and garlic or deep-fried. They make an excellent addition to rice dishes. Larger specimens can be cooked like squid. A classic Spanish dish is *sepia en su tinta*, cuttlefish cooked in its own ink.

Octopus *(Octopus vulgaris)*

Unlike cuttlefish and squid, the octopus has no internal shell, nor does it possess catching tentacles or fins. Octopuses spend their lives lurking in clefts in the rocks on the sea bed, blocking the entrance to their secret holes with shellfish and stones. Their eight equal-size tentacles each have two rows of suckers and can grow to a length of 5m/16¼ft. The larger an octopus grows, the tougher it becomes, so smaller specimens make the best eating. Octopus ink is contained in the liver and has a much stronger flavour than cuttlefish or squid ink.

Other names Octopus is *poulpe* or *pieuvre* in French; *polpo* in Italian; *pulpo* in Spanish.

Buying It is usually sold ready-prepared and frozen, although you may find whole fresh octopus in Mediterranean fish markets. Look for specimens with two rows of suckers on the tentacles; those with only a single row are curled octopus, which are inferior.

Right: Baby octopus

Cooking Octopus needs long, slow cooking. Before including it in a recipe, it is a good idea to blanch or marinate it. If the octopus has not been prepared already, cut off the tentacles and press out the beak from the head. Discard the head, turn the body inside out and discard the entrails. Rinse it thoroughly, then pound the body and tentacles with a mallet to tenderize them before cutting them into strips. Simmer the octopus in stock or salted water for at least 1 hour, until tender. Octopus can also be stewed with Mediterranean vegetables or robust red wine, or stuffed and baked slowly. Small specimens can be cut into rings and sautéed gently in olive oil. Octopus is best served warm as a salad, dressed with a simple olive oil and lemon vinaigrette. Whole octopus can be casseroled slowly in its own juices and ink, but be aware that the ink has a strong flavour which is not to everyone's taste. The Japanese are very fond of octopus and use the boiled tentacles for sushi.

Squid *(Loliginidae)*

These have elongated heads and slender, torpedo-shaped bodies, which end in a kite-shaped fin. Their internal shell is a transparent quill, which looks like a piece of clear acetate. They have ten tentacles, two of which are very long. Squid range from tiny creatures only 7.5cm/3in long to the giant squid which weighs several tons and can grow to a length of 17m/55¼ft. The most common squid is the calamary or long-finned squid *(Loligo vulgaris)*, which is found throughout Europe. It

has smooth, sandy-red spotted skin and weighs up to 2kg/4½lb. The so-called flying squid does not actually fly, but propels itself out of the water and glides through the air like a guided missile. Squid has firm, lean, white flesh that can be tender and delicious when properly cooked.

Other names In French squid is *encornet* or *calmar*; in Italian it is *calamaro*; in Spanish *calamar* or *puntilla*.

Buying Whole squid are sold fresh or frozen and are available all year round. Make sure they contain their ink sac. Some fish-mongers and supermarkets also sell squid ink separately. Squid is also available ready-cleaned, which is very labour-saving. Whole tentacles and rings are available frozen, sometimes as part of a mixed *fruits de mer*. You can also buy ready-battered squid rings for deep-frying, but these are best avoided. Allow about 200g/7oz squid per person.

Cooking The cardinal rule with squid is to cook it either very briefly or for a long time; anything in between and it

Above: Squid

becomes tough and rubbery. The bodies can be stuffed and baked in tomato sauce, or braised with onions and tomatoes. Squid rings can be coated in batter and deep-fried, or boiled briefly and used for a salad. Tiny squid are delicious chargrilled, sautéed, or coated with egg and breadcrumbs and deep-fried. Squid can be added to pasta sauces and rice dishes such as paella. It goes well with such apparently unlikely ingredients as chorizo sausage and black pudding (blood sausage). Squid is often used in Asian recipes and lends itself to flavourings such as ginger, chilli and lime. The ink can be used to colour and flavour home-made pasta and risotto.

Above: Octopus

OTHER EDIBLE SEA CREATURES

The sea is full of weird and wonderful creatures whose strange appearance belies their delicious taste. They may be soft and gelatinous like jellyfish, warty like sea cucumbers or menacingly spiny like sea urchins, but somewhere in the world, they will be regarded as a great delicacy.

Above: Dried jellyfish

Jellyfish *(Scyphoza)*

Jellyfish can strike terror into the hearts of those who have been stung by them. These strange, transparent creatures, with their dangling tentacles, look like open parachutes. They inhabit every ocean of the world, but are eaten almost exclusively in Asia, where they are dried and used to add texture and flavour to many seafood dishes.
Buying and using You will find dried jellyfish in any Asian food store, together with jellyfish preserved in brine. Both types must be soaked in several changes of water before use. In China, slices of dried jellyfish are scalded in boiling water until they curl up, then drained and served in a dressing of soy sauce, sesame oil and rice vinegar. They are also added to shellfish or chicken stir-fries. In Japan, crisply fried strips of jellyfish are served with vinegar, and are sometimes combined with sea urchins.

Sea cucumber (Holothurioidea)

These rather enigmatic, warty, cucumber-shaped creatures rejoice in the alternative name of sea slugs. Despite their strange appearance they are considered a great delicacy in Japan and China, where they are reputed to be an aphrodisiac. The plethora of prickles along one side are actually feet, which enable them to crawl along the sea bed. Sea cucumber is known in Asia as *trepang* or *balatin*. In Japan, it is sliced and eaten raw as sashimi. Sea cucumber is available dried, but requires many hours of soaking to make it palatable. It is used in soup and in several complicated recipes which take so long to prepare that one feels it must have charms that are not immediately apparent to Western perception.

Sea squirt (Ascidiacea)

There are over a thousand species of sea squirts, small invertebrates whose bodies are enclosed in thick leathery

Above: Sea cucumber

"tunics". They have two orifices or spouts through which they siphon water in and squirt it out, and attach themselves to the sea bed or rocks and crevices. They are found in the Mediterranean, where they are a popular if esoteric food, particularly in Spain and the south of France, where the local name, violet, refers to the sea squirt's resemblance to a large purple fig. Enthusiasts eat them by splitting them in half, then scooping out the soft yellow part inside and eating it raw, despite the strong aroma of iodine. Sea squirts can accumulate

Right: Sea squirt

Right: Prickly sea urchins

Opening sea urchins

1 Wearing rubber gloves, hold the sea urchin in the palm of your hand and carefully cut around the soft tissue on the underside, using a special knife or a pair of sharp, pointed scissors.

2 Lift off the top of the sea urchin and remove the mouth and innards, which are inedible. Keep the juices to flavour shellfish sauces, egg dishes or soup.

3 Use a teaspoon to scoop out the bright orange coral.

toxins, so should never be eaten if they come from polluted waters.
Other names In French, sea squirt is *violet* or *figue de mer;* in Italian, *ovo di mare.*

Sea urchin (Echinoidea)

One of the most unpleasant experiences a swimmer can have is to tread on the long, poisonous spines of a sea urchin. To lovers of seafood, however, eating these marine creatures is one of life's great gastronomic pleasures. There are over eight hundred species of sea urchin, found all over the world, but only a few are edible. The most common European variety is the *Paracentrotus lividus*, a greenish or purplish-black hemispherical creature which measures about 7.5cm/3in across, and whose shell is covered with long spines, rather like those of a hedgehog. The females are slightly larger than the males and are said to taste better. Only the orange or yellow ovaries or gonads (known as the coral) are eaten; these have a pungent taste reminiscent of iodine.
Other names In French, sea urchins are variously known as *oursin, châtaigne de mer* (sea chestnut) and *hérisson de mer* (sea hedgehog); in Italian, they are *riccio di mare;* in Spanish *erizo de mar.*
Buying Overfishing has made sea urchins rare and expensive. The best

are the purple or green urchins with long spines; short-spined, whitish species have an extremely strong flavour and are best used in cooked dishes. Look for urchins with firm spines and a tightly closed mouth (on the underside). If you find a source of fresh sea urchins, they can be kept in the refrigerator for up to three days.
Preparing The best implement for opening sea urchins is a purpose-made *coupe oursin.* Failing this, use very sharp scissors. Wearing gloves, cut into the soft tissue around the mouth and lift off the top to reveal the coral. Alternatively, slice off the top like a boiled egg.
Cooking Sea urchins can be eaten raw or used to flavour sauces, pasta, omelettes and scrambled eggs. They make wonderful soup, which can be served in small portions in the shell and eaten with a teaspoon. The shells can also be used as containers for other seafood such as langoustines in a sea urchin sauce.

FISH AND SHELLFISH RECIPES

Fish and shellfish are both nutritious and enticing, and when properly cooked, can be among the most delicious foods imaginable. Every fish and shellfish has its own unique flavour, offering something for all tastes. In this collection of inspirational recipes there is a host of stunning contemporary creations as well as time-honoured classic dishes. With the increasingly wide range of fish and shellfish available in fishmongers and supermarkets, you can allow yourself the pleasure of experimenting and enjoying these wonderful dishes.

SOUPS

*From light, spicy broths to hearty one-pot meals, fish and shellfish soups
are a delight. Chilled Cucumber and Prawn Soup is perfect for
summer eating, while Scallop and Jerusalem Artichoke Soup and
substantial Bouillabaisse make wonderful winter warmers along with
Clam Chowder from New England. For real luxury,
treat yourself and your guests to creamy Lobster Bisque, or travel to
Asia with spicy Malaysian Prawn Laksa and the
wonderfully fragrant Thai Fish Broth.*

CHILLED CUCUMBER AND PRAWN SOUP

IF YOU'VE NEVER SERVED A CHILLED SOUP BEFORE, THIS IS THE ONE TO TRY. DELICIOUS, ATTRACTIVE AND LIGHT, IT'S THE PERFECT WAY TO CELEBRATE SUMMER.

2 Stir in the milk, bring almost to boiling point, then lower the heat and simmer for 5 minutes. Tip the soup into a blender or food processor and process until very smooth. Season to taste.

3 Pour the soup into a large bowl and leave to cool. When cool, stir in the prawns, chopped herbs and cream. Cover, transfer to the refrigerator and chill for at least 2 hours.

4 To serve, ladle the soup into four individual bowls and top each portion with a spoonful of crème fraîche, if using, and place a prawn over the edge of each dish. Sprinkle a little extra chopped dill over each bowl of soup and tuck two or three chives under the prawns on the edge of the bowls to garnish. Serve immediately.

SERVES FOUR

INGREDIENTS
25g/1oz/2 tbsp butter
2 shallots, finely chopped
2 garlic cloves, crushed
1 cucumber, peeled, seeded and diced
300ml/½ pint/1¼ cups milk
225g/8oz/2 cups cooked peeled prawns (shrimp)
15ml/1 tbsp each finely chopped fresh mint, dill, chives and chervil
300ml/½ pint/1¼ cups whipping cream
salt and ground white pepper
For the garnish
30ml/2 tbsp crème fraîche (optional)
4 large, cooked prawns (shrimp), peeled with tail intact
fresh dill and chives

1 Melt the butter in a pan and cook the shallots and garlic over a low heat until soft but not coloured. Add the cucumber and cook gently, stirring frequently, until tender.

COOK'S TIP
If you prefer hot soup, reheat it gently until hot but not boiling. Do not boil, or the delicate flavour will be spoilt.

VARIATION
If you like, you can use other cooked shellfish in place of the peeled prawns (shrimp) – try fresh, frozen or canned crab meat, or cooked, flaked salmon.

Energy 439kcal/1817kJ; Protein 18.9g; Carbohydrate 7.5g, of which sugars 7.1g; Fat 37.2g, of which saturates 23.1g; Cholesterol 255mg; Calcium 212mg; Fibre 0.5g; Sodium 245mg.

SCALLOP AND JERUSALEM ARTICHOKE SOUP

THE SUBTLE SWEETNESS OF SCALLOPS COMBINES WELL WITH THE FLAVOUR OF JERUSALEM ARTICHOKES IN THIS ATTRACTIVE GOLDEN SOUP. FOR AN EVEN MORE COLOURFUL VERSION, SUBSTITUTE PUMPKIN FOR THE ARTICHOKES AND USE EXTRA STOCK INSTEAD OF THE MILK.

SERVES SIX

INGREDIENTS

1kg/2¼lb Jerusalem artichokes
juice of ½ lemon
115g/4oz/½ cup butter
1 onion, finely chopped
600ml/1 pint/2½ cups fish stock
300ml/½ pint/1¼ cups milk
generous pinch of saffron threads
6 large or 12 small scallops, with
   their corals
150ml/¼ pint/⅔ cup
   whipping cream
salt and ground white pepper
45ml/3 tbsp flaked (sliced) almonds
   and 15ml/1 tbsp finely chopped
   fresh chervil, to garnish

1 Working quickly, scrub and peel the Jerusalem artichokes, cut them into 2cm/¾in chunks and drop them into a bowl of cold water, which has been acidulated with the lemon juice. This will prevent the artichokes from turning brown.

2 Melt half the butter in a pan, add the onion and cook over a low heat until softened. Drain the artichokes and add them to the pan. Cook gently for 5 minutes, stirring frequently. Pour in the stock and milk, add the saffron and bring to the boil. Lower the heat and simmer until the artichokes are tender but not mushy.

3 Meanwhile, carefully separate the scallop corals from the white flesh. Prick the corals and slice each scallop in half horizontally. Heat half the remaining butter in a frying pan, add the scallops and corals and cook very briefly (for about 1 minute) on each side. Dice the scallops and corals, keeping them separate, and set them aside until needed.

4 When the artichokes are cooked, tip the contents of the pan into a blender or food processor. Add half the white scallop meat and process until very smooth. Return the soup to the clean pan, season with salt and white pepper and keep hot over a low heat while you prepare the garnish.

5 Heat the remaining butter in a frying pan, add the almonds and toss over a medium heat until golden brown. Add the diced corals and cook for about 30 seconds. Stir the cream into the soup and add the remaining diced white scallop meat. Ladle the soup into individual bowls and garnish each serving with the almonds, scallop corals and a sprinkling of chervil.

Energy 408kcal/1691kJ; Protein 12.8g; Carbohydrate 18.8g, of which sugars 16.4g; Fat 31.9g, of which saturates 17.5g; Cholesterol 86mg; Calcium 150mg; Fibre 4.7g; Sodium 247mg.

MATELOTE

TRADITIONALLY THIS FISHERMEN'S CHUNKY SOUP INCLUDES CONGER EEL, BUT ANY FIRM FISH CAN BE USED. IF YOU CAN FIND IT, DO INCLUDE AT LEAST SOME EEL, AND USE A ROBUST DRY WHITE OR RED WINE FOR EXTRA FLAVOUR.

SERVES SIX

INGREDIENTS

1kg/2¼ lb mixed fish, including
   450g/1lb conger eel if possible
50g/2oz/¼ cup butter
1 onion, thickly sliced
2 celery sticks, thickly sliced
2 carrots, thickly sliced
1 bottle dry white or red wine
1 fresh bouquet garni containing
   parsley, bay leaf and chervil
2 cloves
6 black peppercorns
beurre manié for thickening, see
   Cook's Tip
salt and cayenne pepper
For the garnish
25g/1oz/2 tbsp butter
12 baby (pearl) onions, peeled
12 button (white) mushrooms
chopped flat leaf parsley

1 Cut all the fish into thick slices, removing any obvious bones. Melt the butter in a large pan, put in the fish and sliced vegetables and stir over a medium heat until lightly browned. Pour in the wine and enough cold water to cover. Add the bouquet garni and spices and season. Bring to the boil, lower the heat and simmer gently for 20–30 minutes, until the fish is tender, skimming the surface occasionally.

2 Meanwhile, prepare the garnish. Heat the butter in a deep frying pan and sauté the baby onions until golden and tender. Add the mushrooms and cook until golden. Season and keep hot.

3 Strain the soup through a large strainer into a clean pan. Discard the herbs and spices in the strainer, then divide the fish among deep soup plates (you can skin the fish if you wish, but this is not essential) and keep hot.

4 Reheat the soup until it boils. Lower the heat and whisk in the *beurre manié*, little by little, until the soup thickens. Season it and pour over the fish. Garnish each portion with the golden baby onions and mushrooms and sprinkle with chopped parsley.

COOK'S TIP

To make the *beurre manié* for thickening, mix 15g/½oz/1 tbsp softened butter with 15ml/1 tbsp plain (all-purpose) flour. Add to the boiling soup a pinch at a time, whisking constantly.

Energy 323kcal/1346kJ; Protein 31.4g; Carbohydrate 2.3g, of which sugars 1.9g; Fat 11.6g, of which saturates 6.7g; Cholesterol 103mg; Calcium 35mg; Fibre 0.8g; Sodium 192mg.

FISH SOUP WITH ROUILLE

MAKING THIS SOUP IS SIMPLICITY ITSELF, YET THE FLAVOUR SUGGESTS IT IS THE PRODUCT OF PAINSTAKING PREPARATION AND COOKING.

SERVES SIX

INGREDIENTS

1kg/2¼lb mixed fish
30ml/2 tbsp olive oil
1 onion, chopped
1 carrot, chopped
1 leek, chopped
2 large ripe tomatoes, chopped
1 red (bell) pepper, seeded
  and chopped
2 garlic cloves, peeled
150g/5oz/⅔ cup tomato purée (paste)
1 large fresh bouquet garni,
  containing 3 parsley sprigs, 3 celery
  sticks and 3 bay leaves
300ml/½ pint/1¼ cups white wine
salt and ground black pepper
For the rouille
2 garlic cloves, coarsely chopped
5ml/1 tsp coarse salt
1 thick slice of white bread, crust
  removed, soaked in water and
  squeezed dry
1 fresh red chilli, seeded and
  coarsely chopped
45ml/3 tbsp olive oil
salt and cayenne pepper
For the garnish
12 slices of baguette, toasted in
  the oven
50g/2oz/½ cup finely grated
  Gruyère cheese

1 Cut the fish into 7.5cm/3in chunks, removing any obvious bones. Heat the oil in a large pan, then add the fish and chopped vegetables. Stir until these begin to colour.

2 Add all the other soup ingredients, then pour in just enough cold water to cover the mixture. Season well and bring to just below boiling point, then lower the heat to a bare simmer, cover and cook for 1 hour.

3 Meanwhile, make the rouille. Put the garlic and coarse salt in a mortar and crush to a paste with a pestle. Add the soaked bread and chilli and pound until smooth, or process in a food processor. Whisk in the olive oil, a drop at a time, to make a smooth, shiny sauce that resembles mayonnaise. Season with salt and add a pinch of cayenne if you like a fiery taste. Set the rouille aside.

4 Lift out and discard the bouquet garni from the soup. Process the soup in batches in a food processor, then strain through a fine strainer placed over a clean pan, pushing the solids through with the back of a ladle.

5 Reheat the soup without letting it boil. Check the seasoning and ladle into individual bowls. Top each serving with two slices of toasted baguette, a spoonful of rouille and some grated Gruyère.

COOK'S TIP
Any firm fish can be used for this recipe. If you use whole fish, include the heads, which enhance the flavour of the soup.

Energy 554kcal/2334kJ; Protein 42.7g; Carbohydrate 56.8g, of which sugars 11.4g; Fat 15.2g, of which saturates 3.7g; Cholesterol 85mg; Calcium 210mg; Fibre 4.7g; Sodium 748mg.

LOBSTER BISQUE

BISQUE IS A LUXURIOUS, VELVETY SOUP, WHICH CAN BE MADE WITH ANY CRUSTACEANS.

SERVES SIX

INGREDIENTS
500g/1¼lb fresh lobster
75g/3oz/6 tbsp butter
1 onion, chopped
1 carrot, diced
1 celery stick, diced
45ml/3 tbsp brandy, plus extra for
    serving (optional)
250ml/8fl oz/1 cup dry white wine
1 litre/1¾ pints/4 cups fish stock
15ml/1 tbsp tomato purée (paste)
75g/3oz/scant ½ cup long grain rice
1 fresh bouquet garni
150ml/¼ pint/⅔ cup double (heavy)
    cream, plus extra to garnish
salt, ground white pepper and
    cayenne pepper

1 Cut the lobster into pieces. Melt half the butter in a large pan, add the vegetables and cook over a low heat until soft. Add the lobster and stir until the shell on each piece turns red.

2 Pour over the brandy and set it alight. When the flames die down, add the wine and boil until reduced by half. Pour in the fish stock and simmer for 2–3 minutes. Remove the lobster.

3 Stir in the tomato purée and rice, add the bouquet garni and cook until the rice is tender. Meanwhile, remove the lobster meat from the shell and return the shells to the pan. Dice the lobster meat and set it aside.

COOK'S TIP
It is best to buy a live lobster, chilling it in the freezer until it is comatose and then killing it just before cooking. If you can't face this procedure, use a cooked lobster; take care not to over-cook the flesh. Stir for only 30–60 seconds.

4 When the rice is cooked, discard all the larger pieces of shell. Tip the mixture into a blender or food processor and process to a purée. Press the purée through a fine strainer placed over the clean pan. Stir the mixture, then heat until almost boiling. Season with salt, pepper and cayenne, then lower the heat and stir in the cream. Dice the remaining butter and whisk it into the bisque. Add the diced lobster meat and serve immediately. If you like, pour a small spoonful of brandy into each soup bowl and swirl in a little extra cream.

Energy 406kcal/1684kJ; Protein 20.3g; Carbohydrate 13.7g, of which sugars 3.1g; Fat 25.2g, of which saturates 15g; Cholesterol 153mg; Calcium 84mg; Fibre 0.7g; Sodium 365mg.

BOUILLABAISSE

AUTHENTIC BOUILLABAISSE COMES FROM THE SOUTH OF FRANCE AND INCLUDES RASCASSE (SCORPION FISH) AS AN ESSENTIAL INGREDIENT. IT IS, HOWEVER, PERFECTLY POSSIBLE TO MAKE THIS WONDERFUL MAIN-COURSE SOUP WITHOUT IT. USE AS LARGE A VARIETY OF FISH AS YOU CAN.

SERVES FOUR

INGREDIENTS
   45ml/3 tbsp olive oil
   2 onions, chopped
   2 leeks, white parts only, chopped
   4 garlic cloves, chopped
   450g/1lb ripe tomatoes, peeled
     and chopped
   3 litres/5 pints/12 cups boiling fish
     stock or water
   15ml/1 tbsp tomato purée (paste)
   large pinch of saffron threads
   1 fresh bouquet garni, containing
     2 thyme sprigs, 2 bay leaves and
     2 fennel sprigs
   3kg/6½lb mixed fish, cleaned and
     cut into large chunks
   4 potatoes, peeled and thickly sliced
   salt, pepper and cayenne pepper
   a bowl of rouille (see Fish Soup) and
     a bowl of aioli (see Provençal Aioli
     with Salt Cod), to serve
For the garnish
   16 slices of French bread, toasted
     and rubbed with garlic
   30ml/2 tbsp chopped fresh parsley

2 Simmer the soup for 5–8 minutes, removing each type of fish as it becomes cooked. Continue to cook until the potatoes are very tender. Season well with salt, pepper and cayenne.

3 Divide the fish and potatoes among individual soup plates. Strain the soup and ladle it over the fish. Garnish with toasted French bread and parsley. Serve with rouille and aioli.

1 Heat the oil in a large pan. Add the onions, leeks, garlic and tomatoes. Cook until slightly softened. Stir in the stock or water, tomato purée and saffron. Add the bouquet garni and boil until the oil is amalgamated. Lower the heat; add the fish and potatoes.

COOK'S TIP
Suitable fish for Bouillabaisse include rascasse, conger eel, monkfish, red gurnard and John Dory.

Energy 322kcal/1344kJ; Protein 46.8g; Carbohydrate 3.2g, of which sugars 2.8g; Fat 13.1g, of which saturates 1.9g; Cholesterol 115mg; Calcium 38mg; Fibre 1.3g; Sodium 163mg.

CLAM CHOWDER

IF FRESH CLAMS ARE HARD TO FIND, USE FROZEN OR CANNED CLAMS FOR THIS CLASSIC RECIPE FROM NEW ENGLAND. LARGE CLAMS SHOULD BE CUT INTO CHUNKY PIECES. RESERVE A FEW CLAMS IN THEIR SHELLS FOR GARNISH, IF YOU LIKE. TRADITIONALLY, THE SOUP IS SERVED WITH SAVOURY SALTINE CRACKERS. YOU SHOULD BE ABLE TO FIND THESE IN ANY GOOD DELICATESSEN.

SERVES FOUR

INGREDIENTS
100g/3¾oz salt pork or thinly sliced
   unsmoked bacon, diced
1 large onion, chopped
2 potatoes, peeled and cut into
   1cm/½in cubes
1 bay leaf
1 fresh thyme sprig
300ml/½ pint/1¼ cups milk
400g/14oz cooked clams, cooking
   liquid reserved
150ml/¼ pint/⅔ cup double
   (heavy) cream
salt, ground white pepper and
   cayenne pepper
finely chopped fresh parsley, to garnish

1 Put the salt pork or unsmoked bacon in a pan, and heat gently, stirring frequently, until the fat runs and the meat is starting to brown. Add the chopped onion and cook over a low heat for about 5 minutes, until softened but not browned.

2 Add the cubed potatoes, the bay leaf and thyme sprig, stir well to coat with fat, then pour in the milk and reserved clam liquid and bring to the boil. Lower the heat and simmer for about 10 minutes, until the potatoes are tender but still firm. Lift out the bay leaf and thyme sprig and discard.

3 Remove the shells from most of the clams. Add all the clams to the pan and season to taste with salt, pepper and cayenne. Simmer gently for a further 5 minutes, then stir in the cream. Heat until the soup is very hot, but do not let it boil. Pour into a warm tureen, garnish with the chopped parsley and serve the soup immediately.

CHINESE CRAB AND CORN SOUP

FROZEN WHITE CRAB MEAT WORKS AS WELL AS FRESH IN THIS DELICATELY FLAVOURED SOUP.

SERVES FOUR

INGREDIENTS
600ml/1 pint/2½ cups fish or
   chicken stock
2.5cm/1in piece fresh root ginger,
   peeled and very finely sliced
400g/14oz can creamed corn
150g/5oz cooked white crab meat
15ml/1 tbsp arrowroot or
   cornflour (cornstarch)
15ml/1 tbsp rice wine or dry sherry
15–30ml/1–2 tbsp light soy sauce
1 egg white
salt and ground white pepper
shredded spring onions (scallions),
   to garnish

COOK'S TIP
This soup is sometimes made with whole kernel corn, but creamed corn gives a better and more authentic texture. If you can't find it in a can, use thawed frozen creamed corn instead; the result will be just as good.

1 Put the stock and ginger in a large pan and bring to the boil over a medium heat. Stir in the creamed corn and bring back to the boil.

2 Switch off the heat and add the crab meat. Put the arrowroot or cornflour in a cup and stir in the rice wine or sherry to make a smooth paste; stir this into the soup. Cook over a low heat for about 3 minutes until the soup has thickened and is slightly glutinous in consistency. Add light soy sauce, salt and white pepper to taste.

3 In a bowl, whisk the egg white to a stiff foam. Gradually fold it into the soup. Ladle the soup into heated bowls, garnish each portion with spring onions and serve immediately.

VARIATION
To make prawn (shrimp) and corn soup, substitute 150g/5oz/1¼ cups cooked peeled prawns for the crab meat. Chop the prawns coarsely and add to the soup at the beginning of step 2.

Top: Energy 374kcal/1557kJ; Protein 23.9g; Carbohydrate 11.3g, of which sugars 5.3g; Fat 26.3g, of which saturates 15.1g; Cholesterol 136mg; Calcium 189mg; Fibre 0.5g; Sodium 1629mg.
Bottom: Energy 201kcal/852kJ; Protein 11.3g; Carbohydrate 33.8g, of which sugars 9.9g; Fat 3.2g, of which saturates 0.5g; Cholesterol 27mg; Calcium 17mg; Fibre 1.4g; Sodium 695mg.

THAI FISH BROTH

LEMON GRASS, CHILLIES AND GALANGAL ARE AMONG THE FLAVOURINGS USED IN THIS FRAGRANT SOUP.

SERVES TWO TO THREE

INGREDIENTS

1 litre/1¾ pints/4 cups fish stock
4 lemon grass stalks
3 limes
2 small fresh hot red chillies, seeded
 and thinly sliced
2cm/¾in piece fresh galangal,
 peeled and thinly sliced
6 coriander (cilantro) stalks,
 with leaves
2 kaffir lime leaves, coarsely
 chopped (optional)
350g/12oz monkfish fillet, skinned
 and cut into 2.5cm/1in pieces
15ml/1 tbsp rice vinegar
45ml/3 tbsp Thai fish sauce
30ml/2 tbsp chopped coriander
 (cilantro) leaves, to garnish

1 Pour the stock into a pan and bring it to the boil. Meanwhile, slice the bulb end of the lemon grass stalks diagonally into pieces about 3mm/⅛in thick. Peel off four wide strips of lime rind with a vegetable peeler, taking care to avoid the white pith underneath which would make the soup bitter. Squeeze the limes and reserve the juice.

2 Add the sliced lemon grass, lime rind, chillies, galangal and coriander stalks to the stock, with the kaffir lime leaves, if using. Simmer for 1–2 minutes.

VARIATIONS
Prawns (shrimp), scallops, squid or sole can be substituted for the monkfish. If you use kaffir lime leaves, you will need the juice of only 2 limes.

3 Add the monkfish, rice vinegar and fish sauce, with half the reserved lime juice. Simmer for about 3 minutes, until the fish is just cooked. Lift out and discard the coriander stalks, taste the broth and add more lime juice if necessary; the soup should taste quite sour. Sprinkle with the coriander leaves and serve very hot.

Energy 124kcal/529kJ; Protein 28.2g; Carbohydrate 0.7g, of which sugars 0.6g; Fat 1g, of which saturates 0.2g; Cholesterol 25mg; Calcium 64mg; Fibre 1.3g; Sodium 40mg.

MALAYSIAN PRAWN LAKSA

THIS SPICY PRAWN AND NOODLE SOUP TASTES JUST AS GOOD WHEN MADE WITH FRESH CRAB MEAT OR ANY FLAKED COOKED FISH. IF YOU ARE SHORT OF TIME OR CAN'T FIND ALL THE SPICY PASTE INGREDIENTS, BUY READY-MADE LAKSA PASTE, WHICH IS AVAILABLE FROM ASIAN STORES.

SERVES TWO TO THREE

INGREDIENTS
115g/4oz rice vermicelli or stir-fry
   rice noodles
15ml/1 tbsp vegetable or
   groundnut (peanut) oil
600ml/1 pint/2½ cups fish stock
400ml/14fl oz/1⅔ cups thin
   coconut milk
30ml/2 tbsp Thai fish sauce
½ lime
16–24 cooked peeled prawns (shrimp)
salt and cayenne pepper
60ml/4 tbsp chopped fresh coriander
   (cilantro) sprigs and leaves,
   to garnish
For the spicy paste
2 lemon grass stalks, finely chopped
2 fresh red chillies, seeded
   and chopped
2.5cm/1in piece fresh root ginger,
   peeled and sliced
2.5ml/½ tsp dried shrimp paste
2 garlic cloves, chopped
2.5ml/½ tsp ground turmeric
30ml/2 tbsp tamarind paste

1 Cook the rice vermicelli or noodles in a large pan of salted, boiling water according to the instructions on the packet. Tip into a large strainer or colander, then rinse under cold water and drain. Keep warm.

2 To make the spicy paste, place all the prepared ingredients in a mortar and pound with a pestle. Alternatively, put the ingredients in a food processor and process until a smooth paste is formed.

3 Heat the vegetable or groundnut oil in a large, heavy pan, add the spicy paste and cook over a medium heat, stirring constantly, for a few moments to release all the flavours, but be careful not to let it burn.

4 Add the fish stock and coconut milk and bring to the boil. Stir in the fish sauce, then simmer for 5 minutes. Season with salt and cayenne, adding a squeeze of lime. Add the prawns and heat through for a few seconds.

5 Divide the noodles among two or three soup plates. Pour over the soup, making sure that each portion includes an equal number of prawns. Garnish with coriander and serve piping hot.

Energy 436kcal/1830kJ; Protein 36.9g; Carbohydrate 55.2g, of which sugars 10.1g; Fat 7.6g, of which saturates 1.2g; Cholesterol 341mg; Calcium 239mg; Fibre 0.8g; Sodium 562mg.

APPETIZERS

Fish and shellfish make the perfect light start to any meal, whatever the main course.

Titillate your taste buds with refreshing Ceviche or that old favourite, Prawn Cocktail.

Classic Oysters Rockefeller, and Gratin of Mussels with Pesto are as succulent as they are

sophisticated, while deliciously crisp Devilled Whitebait

provide piquancy and crunch. If you prefer fish to shellfish, Red Mullet

Dolmades make an unusual appetizer.

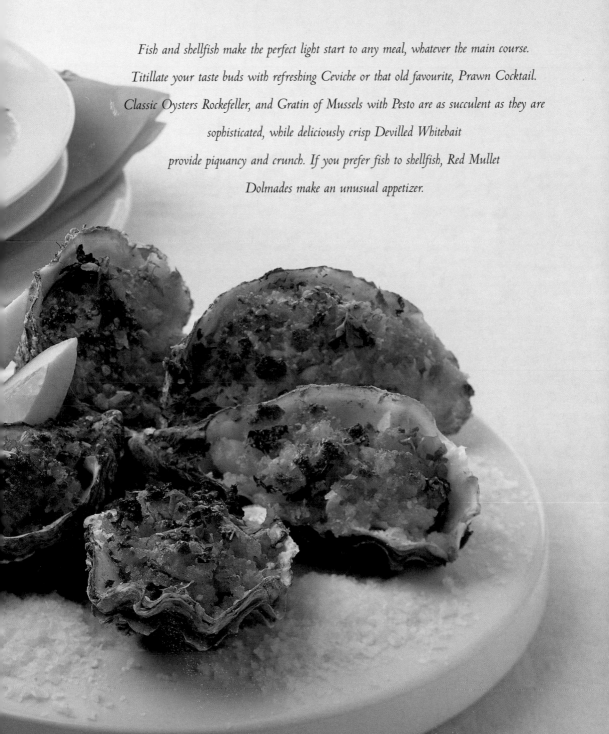

CEVICHE

You can use almost any firm-fleshed fish for this South American dish, provided that it is perfectly fresh. The fish is "cooked" by the action of the acidic lime juice. Adjust the amount of chilli according to your taste.

SERVES SIX

INGREDIENTS

675g/1½lb halibut, turbot,
  sea bass or salmon
  fillets, skinned
juice of 3 limes
1–2 fresh red chillies, seeded and
  very finely chopped
15ml/1 tbsp olive oil
salt
For the garnish
  4 large firm tomatoes, peeled, seeded
    and diced
  1 ripe avocado, peeled, stoned
    (pitted) and diced
  15ml/1 tbsp lemon juice
  30ml/2 tbsp olive oil
  30ml/2 tbsp fresh coriander
    (cilantro) leaves

1 Cut the fish into strips measuring about 5 × 1cm/2 × ½in. Lay these in a shallow dish and pour over the lime juice, turning the strips to coat them all over in the juice. Cover with clear film (plastic wrap) and leave for 1 hour.

2 Combine all the garnish ingredients, except the coriander. Set aside.

3 Season the fish with salt and sprinkle over the chillies. Drizzle with the olive oil. Toss the fish in the mixture, then re-cover. Leave to marinate in the refrigerator for 15–30 minutes more.

4 To serve, divide the garnish among six plates. Spoon on the ceviche, sprinkle with coriander and serve.

Energy 224kcal/939kJ; Protein 25.1g; Carbohydrate 2.5g, of which sugars 2.2g; Fat 12.7g, of which saturates 2.2g; Cholesterol 39mg; Calcium 40mg; Fibre 1.5g; Sodium 75mg.

MARINATED SMOKED HADDOCK FILLETS

THIS SIMPLE DISH COULD MAKE A LIGHT LUNCH, SERVED WITH A GREEN SALAD, AS WELL AS AN APPETIZER. EITHER WAY IT IS AN EXCELLENT SUMMER DISH AND CAN BE PREPARED IN ADVANCE.

SERVES SIX

INGREDIENTS

450g/1lb undyed smoked haddock
  fillet, skinned
1 onion, very thinly sliced
  into rings
5–10ml/1–2 tsp Dijon mustard
30ml/2 tbsp lemon juice
90ml/6 tbsp olive oil
45ml/3 tbsp dark rum
12 small new potatoes, scrubbed
30ml/2 tbsp chopped fresh dill, plus
  6 dill sprigs to garnish
ground black pepper

COOK'S TIP

Try to get a large, thick haddock fillet. If all you can find are small pieces, you can still make the dish, but serve the pieces whole instead of slicing them.

1 Cut the fish fillet in half lengthways. Arrange the pieces in a single layer in a shallow non-metallic dish. Sprinkle the onion rings evenly over the top.

2 Whisk together the mustard, lemon juice and some pepper. Gradually add the oil, whisking constantly. Pour two-thirds of the dressing over the fish. Cover the dish with clear film (plastic wrap) and leave the fish to marinate for 2 hours in a cool place. Sprinkle on the rum and leave for 1 hour more.

3 Cook the potatoes in salted, boiling water until tender. Drain, cut in half and tip into a bowl. Cool until warm, then toss in the remaining dressing. Stir in the dill, cover and set aside.

4 Slice the haddock thinly, as for smoked salmon, or leave whole. Arrange on small plates and spoon over some marinade and onion rings. Pile the potato halves on one side of each plate and garnish each portion with dill. Serve chilled or at room temperature.

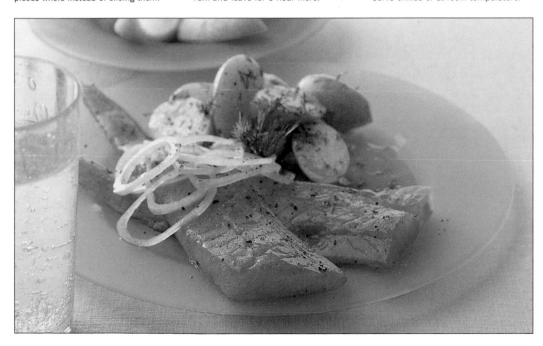

Energy 212kcal/884kJ; Protein 15.3g; Carbohydrate 7.7g, of which sugars 1.3g; Fat 11.7g, of which saturates 1.7g; Cholesterol 27mg; Calcium 37mg; Fibre 0.9g; Sodium 577mg.

MOULES PROVENÇALES

EATING THESE DELECTABLE MUSSELS IS A MESSY AFFAIR, WHICH IS PART OF THEIR CHARM. HAND ROUND PLENTY OF CRUSTY FRENCH BREAD FOR MOPPING UP THE JUICES AND DON'T FORGET FINGERBOWLS OF WARM WATER AND A PLATE FOR DISCARDED SHELLS.

SERVES FOUR

INGREDIENTS

30ml/2 tbsp olive oil
200g/7oz rindless unsmoked streaky (fatty) bacon, cubed
1 onion, finely chopped
3 garlic cloves, finely chopped
1 bay leaf
15ml/1 tbsp chopped fresh mixed Provençal herbs, thyme, marjoram, basil, oregano and savory
15–30ml/1–2 tbsp sun-dried tomatoes in oil, chopped
4 large, very ripe tomatoes, peeled, seeded and chopped
50g/2oz/½ cup pitted black olives, chopped
105ml/7 tbsp dry white wine
2.25kg/5–5¼lb fresh mussels, scrubbed and bearded
salt and ground black pepper
60ml/4 tbsp coarsely chopped fresh parsley, to garnish

1 Heat the oil in a large pan. Cook the bacon until golden and crisp. Remove with a slotted spoon and set aside. Add the onion and garlic to the pan and cook gently until softened. Add the herbs, with both types of tomatoes. Cook gently for 5 minutes, stirring frequently. Stir in the olives and season.

2 Put the wine and mussels in another pan. Cover and shake over a high heat for 5 minutes, until the mussels open. Discard any which remain closed.

3 Strain the cooking liquid into the pan containing the tomato sauce and boil until reduced by about one-third. Add the mussels and stir to coat them thoroughly with the sauce. Remove and discard the bay leaf.

4 Divide the mussels and sauce equally among four warm individual dishes. Sprinkle over the crispy bacon and chopped parsley and serve piping hot.

Energy 439kcal/1836kJ; Protein 34.9g; Carbohydrate 12.8g, of which sugars 6.9g; Fat 25.9g, of which saturates 6.2g; Cholesterol 123mg; Calcium 112mg; Fibre 2.4g; Sodium 1467mg.

OYSTERS ROCKEFELLER

THIS IS THE PERFECT DISH FOR THOSE WHO PREFER THEIR OYSTERS LIGHTLY COOKED. AS A CHEAPER ALTERNATIVE, FOR THOSE WHO ARE NOT "SO RICH AS ROCKEFELLER", GIVE MUSSELS OR CLAMS THE SAME TREATMENT; THEY WILL ALSO TASTE DELICIOUS.

SERVES SIX

INGREDIENTS

450g/1lb/3 cups coarse salt, plus
   extra to serve
24 oysters, opened
115g/4oz/½ cup butter
2 shallots, finely chopped
500g/1¼lb spinach leaves,
   finely chopped
60ml/4 tbsp chopped fresh parsley
60ml/4 tbsp chopped celery leaves
90ml/6 tbsp fresh white breadcrumbs
Tabasco sauce or cayenne pepper
10–20ml/2–4 tsp Pernod or Ricard
salt and ground black pepper
lemon wedges, to serve

COOK'S TIP
If you prefer a smoother stuffing, process to a paste in a food processor or blender.

1 Preheat the oven to 220°C/425°F/ Gas 7. Make a bed of coarse salt on two large baking sheets. Set the oysters in the half-shell in the bed of salt to keep them steady. Set aside.

2 Melt the butter in a frying pan. Add the finely chopped shallots and cook them over a low heat for 2–3 minutes, until they are softened. Stir in the spinach and let it wilt.

3 Add the parsley, celery leaves and breadcrumbs to the pan and cook gently for 5 minutes. Season with salt, pepper and Tabasco or cayenne.

4 Divide the stuffing among the oysters. Drizzle a few drops of Pernod or Ricard over each oyster, then bake for about 5 minutes, until bubbling and golden brown. Serve on a heated platter on a shallow salt bed with lemon wedges.

Energy 210kcal/867kJ; Protein 6.4g; Carbohydrate 3.4g, of which sugars 2.1g; Fat 17g, of which saturates 10.1g; Cholesterol 60mg; Calcium 211mg; Fibre 2.3g; Sodium 406mg.

AROMATIC TIGER PRAWNS

THERE IS NO ELEGANT WAY TO EAT THESE AROMATIC PRAWNS — JUST HOLD THEM BY THE TAILS, PULL THEM OFF THE STICKS WITH YOUR FINGERS AND POP THEM INTO YOUR MOUTH.

SERVES FOUR

INGREDIENTS
16 farmed raw tiger prawns (jumbo
   shrimp) or scampi (jumbo shrimp) tails
2.5ml/½ tsp chilli powder
5ml/1 tsp fennel seeds
5 Sichuan or black peppercorns
1 star anise, broken into segments
1 cinnamon stick, broken into pieces
30ml/2 tbsp groundnut (peanut) or
   sunflower oil
2 garlic cloves, chopped
2cm/¾in piece fresh root ginger,
   peeled and finely chopped
1 shallot, chopped
30ml/2 tbsp water
30ml/2 tbsp rice vinegar
30ml/2 tbsp soft brown or palm sugar
salt and ground black pepper
lime slices and chopped spring onion
   (scallion), to garnish

1 Thread the prawns or scampi tails in pairs on eight wooden cocktail sticks (toothpicks). Set aside. Heat a frying pan, put in all the chilli powder, fennel seeds, Sichuan or black peppercorns, star anise and cinnamon stick and dry-fry for 1–2 minutes to release the flavours. Leave to cool, then grind the spices coarsely in a grinder or tip into a mortar and crush with a pestle.

2 Heat the groundnut or sunflower oil in a shallow pan, add the garlic, ginger and chopped shallot and then cook gently until very lightly coloured. Add the crushed spices and seasoning and cook the mixture gently for 2 minutes. Pour in the water and simmer, stirring, for 5 minutes.

3 Add the rice vinegar and soft brown or palm sugar, stir until dissolved, then add the prawns or scampi tails. Cook for 3–5 minutes, until the shellfish has turned pink, but is still very juicy. Serve hot, garnished with lime slices and spring onion.

COOK'S TIP
If you buy whole prawns (shrimp), remove the heads before cooking them.

PRAWN AND VEGETABLE CROSTINI

USE BOTTLED CARCIOFINI (TINY ARTICHOKE HEARTS PRESERVED IN OLIVE OIL) FOR THIS SIMPLE APPETIZER, WHICH CAN BE PREPARED VERY QUICKLY.

SERVES FOUR

INGREDIENTS
450g/1lb whole cooked prawns
   (shrimp), in the shell
4 thick slices of ciabatta bread, cut
   diagonally across
3 garlic cloves, peeled and
   2 halved lengthways
60ml/4 tbsp olive oil
200g/7oz/2 cups small button (white)
   mushrooms, trimmed
12 drained bottled *carciofini*
60ml/4 tbsp chopped flat leaf parsley
salt and ground black pepper

COOK'S TIP
Don't be tempted to use thawed frozen prawns (shrimp), especially those that have been peeled; freshly cooked prawns in their shells are infinitely nicer.

1 Peel the prawns and remove the heads. Rub the ciabatta slices on both sides with the cut sides of the halved garlic cloves, drizzle with a little of the olive oil and toast in the oven or grill (broil) until lightly browned. Keep hot.

2 Finely chop the remaining garlic. Heat the remaining oil in a pan and gently cook the garlic until golden, but do not allow it to brown.

3 Add the mushrooms and stir to coat with oil. Season and sauté for about 2–3 minutes. Gently stir in the drained *carciofini*, then add the chopped flat leaf parsley.

4 Season again, then stir in the prawns and sauté briefly to warm through. Pile the prawn mixture on to the ciabatta, pour over any remaining cooking juices and serve immediately.

Top: Energy 142kcal/593kJ; Protein 13.4g; Carbohydrate 9g, of which sugars 8.7g; Fat 6g, of which saturates 0.7g; Cholesterol 146mg; Calcium 67mg; Fibre 0.2g; Sodium 144mg.
Bottom: Energy 264kcal/1104kJ; Protein 23.7g; Carbohydrate 13.6g, of which sugars 1.2g; Fat 13.1g, of which saturates 1.9g; Cholesterol 219mg; Calcium 152mg; Fibre 1.9g; Sodium 356mg.

SCALLOPS WITH SAMPHIRE AND LIME

SAMPHIRE HAS A WONDERFUL TASTE AND AROMA OF THE SEA. HIGH-QUALITY FISHMONGERS SOMETIMES STOCK IT. IT IS THE PERFECT COMPLEMENT TO SCALLOPS AND HELPS TO CREATE A VERY ATTRACTIVE APPETIZER.

SERVES FOUR

INGREDIENTS

225g/8oz fresh samphire
12 large or 24 queen scallops, out of the shell
300ml/½ pint/1¼ cups dry white wine
juice of 2 limes
15ml/1 tbsp groundnut (peanut) or vegetable oil
½ cucumber, peeled, seeded and diced
ground black pepper
chopped fresh parsley, to garnish

1 Wash the fresh samphire in several changes of cold water. Drain, then trim off any woody ends. Bring a pan of water to the boil, then drop in the samphire and cook for 3–5 minutes, until tender but still crisp. Drain, refresh under cold water and drain again.

2 If the scallops are large, cut them in half horizontally. Detach the corals. In a shallow pan, bring the wine to the boil and cook until it is reduced by about one-third. Lower the heat and add the lime juice to the pan.

3 Add the scallops and corals and poach them gently for 3–4 minutes, until the scallops are just cooked, but still opaque. Using a slotted spoon, lift out the scallops and corals and set them aside.

COOK'S TIP
Samphire grows wild in estuaries and salt marshes in Europe and North America.

4 Leave the cooking liquid to cool until tepid, then whisk in the groundnut or vegetable oil. Add the samphire, cucumber, scallops and corals and toss lightly to mix. Grind over some black pepper, cover and leave at room temperature for about 1 hour to allow the flavours to develop. Divide the mixture among four individual dishes and then garnish with chopped fresh parsley. Serve the dish at room temperature.

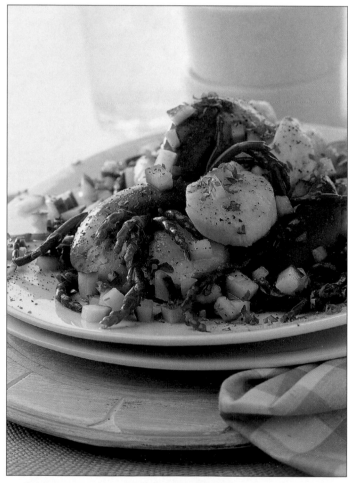

Energy 192kcal/801kJ; Protein 16.5g; Carbohydrate 4.2g, of which sugars 2g; Fat 6.9g, of which saturates 1g; Cholesterol 29mg; Calcium 130mg; Fibre 1.5g; Sodium 196mg.

GRATIN OF MUSSELS WITH PESTO

THIS IS THE PERFECT APPETIZER FOR SERVING WHEN YOUR TIME IS SHORT, SINCE BOTH THE PESTO AND THE MUSSELS CAN BE PREPARED IN ADVANCE, AND THE DISH ASSEMBLED AND COOKED AT THE LAST MINUTE.

SERVES FOUR

INGREDIENTS
    36 large fresh mussels, scrubbed
      and bearded
    105ml/7 tbsp dry white wine
    60ml/4 tbsp finely chopped fresh
      flat leaf parsley
    1 garlic clove, finely chopped
    30ml/2 tbsp fresh white breadcrumbs
    60ml/4 tbsp olive oil
    chopped fresh basil, to garnish
    crusty bread, to serve
For the pesto
    2 fat garlic cloves, chopped
    2.5ml/½ tsp coarse salt
    100g/3¾oz/3 cups basil leaves
    25g/1oz/¼ cup pine nuts, chopped
    50g/2oz/⅔ cup freshly grated
      Parmesan cheese
    120ml/4fl oz/½ cup extra virgin
      olive oil

1 Put the mussels in a pan with the wine, clamp on the lid and shake over high heat for 3–4 minutes until the mussels have opened. Discard any that remain closed.

2 As soon as the mussels are cool enough to handle, strain the cooking liquid and keep it for another recipe. Discard the empty half-shells. Arrange the mussels in their half-shells in a single layer in four individual gratin dishes. Cover and set aside.

COOK'S TIP
Home-made pesto is best, but when basil is out of season – or you are in a hurry – a jar may be used instead.

3 To make the pesto, put the chopped garlic and salt in a mortar and pound to a purée with a pestle. Then add the basil leaves and chopped pine nuts and crush to a thick paste. Work in the Parmesan cheese and, finally, gradually drip in enough olive oil to make a smooth and creamy paste. Alternatively, use a food processor.

4 Spoon pesto over the mussels placed in gratin dishes. Mix the parsley, garlic and breadcrumbs. Sprinkle over the mussels. Drizzle with the oil.

5 Preheat the grill (broiler) to high. Stand the dishes on a baking sheet and grill (broil) for 3 minutes. Garnish with basil and serve with crusty bread.

Energy 454kcal/1876kJ; Protein 11.7g; Carbohydrate 7.2g, of which sugars 1.4g; Fat 40.4g, of which saturates 7.4g; Cholesterol 22mg; Calcium 277mg; Fibre 2g; Sodium 253mg.

PRAWN COCKTAIL

THERE IS NO NICER APPETIZER THAN A GOOD, FRESH PRAWN COCKTAIL — AND NOTHING NASTIER THAN ONE IN WHICH SOGGY PRAWNS SWIM IN A THIN, VINEGARY SAUCE EMBEDDED IN LIMP LETTUCE. THIS RECIPE SHOWS JUST HOW GOOD A PRAWN COCKTAIL CAN BE.

SERVES SIX

INGREDIENTS
60ml/4 tbsp double (heavy) cream,
   lightly whipped
60ml/4 tbsp mayonnaise, preferably
   home-made
60ml/4 tbsp tomato ketchup
5–10ml/1–2 tsp Worcestershire sauce
juice of 1 lemon
½ cos or romaine lettuce or other
   very crisp lettuce
450g/1lb/4 cups cooked peeled
   prawns (shrimp)
salt, ground black pepper
   and paprika
6 large whole cooked prawns (shrimp)
   in the shell, to garnish (optional)
thinly sliced brown bread with butter
   and lemon wedges, to serve

1 Place the lightly whipped cream, mayonnaise and tomato ketchup in a small bowl and whisk lightly to combine. Add Worcestershire sauce to taste, then whisk in enough of the lemon juice to make a really tangy sauce.

COOK'S TIP
Partly peeled prawns (shrimp) make a pretty garnish. To prepare, carefully peel the body shell from the prawns and leave the tail "fan" for decoration.

2 Finely shred the lettuce and fill six individual glasses one-third full.

3 Stir the prawns into the sauce, then check the seasoning and spoon the prawn mixture generously over the lettuce. If you like, drape a whole cooked prawn over the edge of each glass and sprinkle each of the cocktails with ground black pepper and/or paprika. Serve immediately, with thinly sliced brown bread with butter and lemon wedges.

CRAB SALAD WITH ROCKET

IF THE DRESSED CRABS ARE REALLY SMALL, PILE THE SALAD BACK INTO THE SHELLS FOR AN ATTRACTIVE ALTERNATIVE PRESENTATION.

SERVES FOUR

INGREDIENTS
4 small fresh dressed crabs
1 small red (bell) pepper, seeded and
   finely chopped
1 small red onion, finely chopped
30ml/2 tbsp drained capers
30ml/2 tbsp chopped fresh
   coriander (cilantro)
grated rind and juice of 2 lemons
Tabasco sauce
salt and ground black pepper
lemon rind strips, to garnish
For the rocket (arugula) salad
40g/1½oz rocket (arugula) leaves
30ml/2 tbsp sunflower oil
15ml/1 tbsp fresh lime juice

1 Put the white and brown crab meat, red pepper, onion, capers and chopped coriander in a bowl. Add the lemon rind and juice and toss gently to mix together. Season with a few drops of Tabasco sauce, according to taste, and a little salt and pepper.

2 Wash the rocket leaves and pat dry on kitchen paper. Divide them among four plates. Mix together the oil and lime juice in a small bowl. Dress the rocket leaves, then pile the crab salad on top and serve garnished with lemon rind strips.

Top: Energy 193kcal/802kJ; Protein 13.9g; Carbohydrate 4g, of which sugars 3.9g; Fat 13.6g, of which saturates 4.6g; Cholesterol 167mg; Calcium 79mg; Fibre 0.4g; Sodium 374mg.
Bottom: Energy 106kcal/443kJ; Protein 14.2g; Carbohydrate 2.1g, of which sugars 2g; Fat 4.6g, of which saturates 0.6g; Cholesterol 54mg; Calcium 114mg; Fibre 0.7g; Sodium 431mg.

RED MULLET DOLMADES

*IF YOU CANNOT FIND PREPARED VINE LEAVES, USE BLANCHED CABBAGE OR LARGE SPINACH LEAVES
INSTEAD. PLAICE, FLOUNDER OR LEMON SOLE CAN BE SUBSTITUTED FOR THE RED MULLET.*

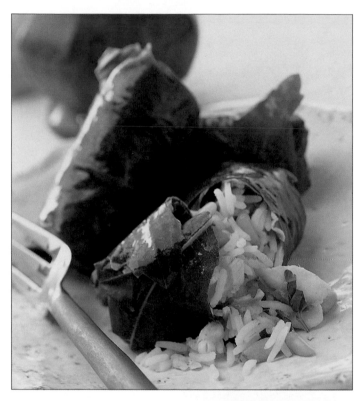

2 Remove the skin from the fish fillets and flake the flesh into a bowl. Gently stir in the cooked rice, pine nuts, the chopped parsley, and lemon rind and juice. Season the filling to taste with salt and ground black pepper.

3 Spoon 30–45ml/2–3 tbsp of the filling into the middle of each vine leaf. Roll up each filled leaf, tucking in the ends to make a secure package. Arrange the dolmades in an ovenproof dish, with the joins underneath. Then pour over the reserved cooking liquid and place the dolmades in the preheated oven for about 5 minutes, until they are thoroughly heated through.

4 Meanwhile, make the sauce. Mix the orange rind and juice and the shallots in a small pan and boil vigorously for a few minutes until the mixture is reduced and syrupy.

5 Strain the sauce into a clean pan, discarding the shallots. Beat in the butter, one piece at a time. Reheat gently, but do not let the sauce boil. Drizzle the sauce over the hot dolmades and serve immediately.

SERVES FOUR

INGREDIENTS
    225g/8oz red mullet or red snapper
        fillets, scaled
    45ml/3 tbsp dry white wine
    115g/4oz/1 cup cooked long
        grain rice
    25g/1oz/¼ cup pine nuts
    45ml/3 tbsp chopped fresh parsley
    grated rind and juice of ½ lemon
    8 vine (grape) leaves in brine, rinsed
        and dried
    salt and ground black pepper
For the orange butter sauce
    grated rind and juice of 2 oranges
    2 shallots, very finely chopped
    25g/1oz/2 tbsp chilled
        butter, diced

1 Preheat the oven to 200ºC/400ºF/Gas 6. Put the fish fillets in a shallow pan and season with salt and pepper. Pour over the wine, bring to the boil, then lower the heat and poach the fish gently for about 3 minutes, until it is just cooked. Strain, reserving the cooking liquid.

Energy 185kcal/772kJ; Protein 7.7g; Carbohydrate 12.4g, of which sugars 3.4g; Fat 11.2g, of which saturates 3.6g; Cholesterol 13mg; Calcium 59mg; Fibre 1g; Sodium 74mg.

SALMON AND SCALLOP BROCHETTES

WITH THEIR DELICATE COLOURS AND SUPERB FLAVOUR, THESE SKEWERS MAKE THE PERFECT OPENER FOR A SOPHISTICATED MEAL AND ARE ABSOLUTELY IRRESISTIBLE.

SERVES FOUR

INGREDIENTS

8 lemon grass stalks
225g/8oz salmon fillet, skinned
8 queen scallops, with their corals
  if possible
8 baby (pearl) onions, peeled
  and blanched
½ yellow (bell) pepper, cut into
  8 squares
25g/1oz/2 tbsp butter
juice of ½ lemon
salt, ground white pepper
  and paprika
For the sauce
30ml/2 tbsp dry vermouth
50g/2oz/¼ cup butter
5ml/1 tsp chopped fresh tarragon

1 Preheat the grill (broiler) to medium-high. Cut off the top 7.5–10cm/3–4in of each lemon grass stalk. Reserve the bulb ends for another dish. Cut the salmon fillet into twelve 2cm/¾in cubes. Thread the salmon, scallops, corals if available, onions and pepper squares on to the lemon grass and arrange the brochettes in a grill pan.

2 Melt the butter in a small pan, add the lemon juice and a pinch of paprika and then brush all over the brochettes. Grill (broil) the skewers for about 2–3 minutes on each side, turning and basting the brochettes every minute, until the fish and scallops are just cooked, but are still very juicy. Transfer to a platter and keep hot while you make the tarragon butter sauce.

3 Pour the dry vermouth and all the leftover cooking juices from the brochettes into a small pan and boil quite fiercely to reduce by half. Add the butter and melt, stirring constantly. Stir in the chopped fresh tarragon and add salt and ground white pepper to taste. Pour the tarragon butter sauce over the brochettes and serve.

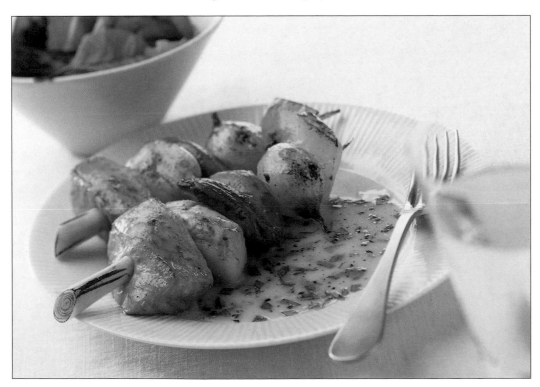

Energy 321kcal/1336kJ; Protein 23.5g; Carbohydrate 4.8g, of which sugars 2.7g; Fat 22.4g, of which saturates 11.1g; Cholesterol 92mg; Calcium 36mg; Fibre 0.6g; Sodium 231mg.

SOFT-SHELL CRABS WITH CHILLI AND SALT

*IF FRESH SOFT-SHELL CRABS ARE UNAVAILABLE, YOU CAN BUY FROZEN ONES IN ASIAN SUPERMARKETS.
ALLOW TWO SMALL CRABS PER SERVING, OR ONE IF THEY ARE QUITE LARGE. ADJUST THE QUANTITY OF
CHILLI ACCORDING TO HOW HOT YOU LIKE YOUR FOOD.*

SERVES FOUR

INGREDIENTS
8 small soft-shell crabs, thawed
    if frozen
50g/2oz/½ cup plain (all-purpose) flour
60ml/4 tbsp groundnut (peanut) or
    vegetable oil
2 large fresh red chillies, or 1 green
    and 1 red, seeded and thinly sliced
4 spring onions (scallions) or a small
    bunch of garlic chives, chopped
    sea salt and ground black pepper
To serve
    shredded lettuce, mooli (daikon)
    and carrot
    light soy sauce

COOK'S TIP
The vegetables make a colourful bed for
the crabs. If you can't locate any mooli
(daikon), use celeriac instead.

1 Pat the crabs dry with kitchen paper.
Season the flour with pepper and coat
the crabs lightly with the mixture.

2 Heat the oil in a shallow pan until
very hot, then put in the crabs (you may
need to do this in two batches). Cook
for 2–3 minutes on each side, until the
crabs are golden brown but still juicy in
the middle. Drain the cooked crabs on
kitchen paper and keep hot.

3 Add the sliced chillies and spring
onions or garlic chives to the oil
remaining in the pan and cook gently
for about 2 minutes. Sprinkle over a
generous pinch of salt, then spread the
mixture on to the crabs.

4 Mix the shredded lettuce, mooli and
carrot together. Arrange on plates, top
each portion with two crabs and serve,
with light soy sauce for dipping.

DEVILLED WHITEBAIT

*SERVE THESE DELICIOUSLY CRISP LITTLE FISH WITH LEMON WEDGES AND THINLY SLICED BROWN BREAD
AND BUTTER, AND EAT THEM WITH YOUR FINGERS.*

SERVES FOUR

INGREDIENTS
oil for deep-frying
150ml/¼ pint/⅔ cup milk
115g/4oz/1 cup plain (all-
    purpose) flour
450g/1lb whitebait
salt, ground black pepper and
    cayenne pepper

1 Heat the oil in a large pan or deep-
fryer. Put the milk in a shallow bowl and
the flour into a paper bag. Season it
with salt, pepper and a little cayenne.

COOK'S TIP
Most whitebait are sold frozen. Thaw
them before use and dry them thoroughly
on kitchen paper.

2 Dip a handful of the whitebait into the
bowl of milk, drain them well, then pop
them into the paper bag. Shake gently
to coat them evenly in the seasoned
flour. Repeat until all the fish have been
coated with flour. This is the easiest
method of flouring whitebait, but don't
add too many at once, or they will
stick together.

3 Heat the oil for deep-frying to 190°C/
375°F or until a small cube of stale
bread, dropped into the oil, browns in
20 seconds. Add a batch of whitebait,
preferably in a frying basket, and fry for
2–3 minutes, until crisp and golden
brown. Drain and keep hot while you fry
the rest. Sprinkle with more cayenne
and serve very hot.

MOUSSES, PÂTÉS AND TERRINES

Soft-textured fish and shellfish can be puréed to produce attractive light-textured mousses, such as Smoked Fish and Asparagus Mousse. Hot Crab Soufflés make a substantial appetizer or light lunch or supper dish for a chilly day, and chunky Haddock and Smoked Salmon Terrine is ideal when the weather warms up. Celebrate summer with cold creamy Sea Trout Mousse. For the simplest of dishes, Fiery Mackerel Pâté takes only moments to prepare and is perennially popular.

SEA TROUT MOUSSE

THIS DELICIOUSLY CREAMY MOUSSE MAKES A LITTLE SEA TROUT GO A LONG WAY. IT IS EQUALLY GOOD MADE WITH SALMON IF SEA TROUT IS UNAVAILABLE.

SERVES SIX

INGREDIENTS
    250g/9oz sea trout fillet
    120ml/4fl oz/½ cup fish stock
    2 gelatine leaves, or 15ml/1 tbsp
      powdered gelatine
    juice of ½ lemon
    30ml/2 tbsp dry sherry or
      dry vermouth
    30ml/2 tbsp freshly grated Parmesan
    300ml/½ pint/1¼ cups
      whipping cream
    2 egg whites
    15ml/1 tbsp sunflower oil
    salt and ground white pepper
For the garnish
    5cm/2in piece of cucumber, with
      peel, thinly sliced and halved
    fresh dill or chervil

1 Put the sea trout in a shallow pan. Pour in the fish stock and heat to simmering point. Poach the fish for about 3–4 minutes, until it is lightly cooked. Strain the stock into a jug (pitcher) and leave the trout to cool.

2 Add the gelatine to the hot stock and stir until it has dissolved completely. Set aside until required.

COOK'S TIP
Serve the mousse with Melba toast, if you like. Toast thin slices of bread on both sides under the grill (broiler), then cut off the crusts and slice each piece of toast in half horizontally. Return to the grill pan, untoasted sides up, and grill (broil) again. The thin slices will swiftly brown and curl, so watch them closely.

3 When the trout is cool enough to handle, remove the skin and flake the flesh. Pour the stock into a food processor or blender. Process briefly, then gradually add the flaked trout, lemon juice, sherry or vermouth and Parmesan through the feeder tube, continuing to process the mixture until it is smooth. Scrape into a large bowl and leave to cool completely.

4 Lightly whip the cream in a bowl; fold it into the cold trout mixture. Season to taste, then cover with clear film (plastic wrap) and chill until the mousse is just beginning to set. It should have the consistency of mayonnaise.

5 In a grease-free bowl, beat the egg whites with a pinch of salt until softly peaking. Using a large metal spoon, stir one-third into the trout mixture to slacken it, then fold in the rest.

6 Lightly grease six ramekins with the sunflower oil. Divide the mousse among the ramekins and level the surface. Place in the refrigerator for 2–3 hours, until set. Just before serving, arrange a few slices of cucumber and a small herb sprig on each mousse and add a little chopped dill or chervil.

Energy 241kcal/999kJ; Protein 12.3g; Carbohydrate 1.8g, of which sugars 1.8g; Fat 20g, of which saturates 14.5g; Cholesterol 9mg; Calcium 104mg; Fibre 0.1g; Sodium 127mg.

QUENELLES OF SOLE

TRADITIONALLY, THESE LIGHT FISH "DUMPLINGS" ARE MADE WITH PIKE, BUT THEY ARE EVEN BETTER MADE WITH SOLE OR OTHER WHITE FISH. IF YOU ARE FEELING EXTRAVAGANT, SERVE THEM WITH A CREAMY SHELLFISH SAUCE STUDDED WITH CRAYFISH TAILS OR PRAWNS.

SERVES SIX

INGREDIENTS
   450g/1lb sole fillets, skinned and cut
     into large pieces
   4 egg whites
   600ml/1 pint/2½ cups double
     (heavy) cream
   salt, ground white pepper and
     grated nutmeg
For the sauce
   1 small shallot, finely chopped
   60ml/4 tbsp dry vermouth
   120ml/4fl oz/½ cup fish stock
   150ml/¼ pint/⅔ cup double
     (heavy) cream
   50g/2oz/¼ cup cold butter, diced
   chopped fresh parsley, to garnish

1 Check the sole for stray bones, then put the pieces in a blender or food processor. Add a generous pinch of salt and a grinding of pepper. Switch on and, with the motor running, add the egg whites one at a time through the feeder tube to make a smooth purée. Press the purée through a metal sieve placed over a bowl. Stand the bowl of purée in a larger bowl and surround it with plenty of crushed ice or ice cubes.

2 Whip the cream until very thick and floppy, but not stiff. Gradually fold it into the fish mousse, making sure each spoonful has been absorbed completely before adding the next. Season with salt and pepper, then stir in nutmeg to taste. Cover the bowl of mousse and transfer it, still in its bowl of ice, to the refrigerator. Chill for several hours.

3 To make the sauce, combine the shallot, vermouth and fish stock in a small pan. Bring to the boil and cook until reduced by half. Add the cream and boil again until the sauce has the consistency of single (light) cream. Strain, return to the pan and whisk in the butter, one piece at a time, until the sauce is very creamy. Season and keep hot, but do not let it boil.

4 Bring a wide shallow pan of lightly salted water to the boil, then reduce the heat so that the water surface barely trembles. Using two tablespoons dipped in hot water, shape the fish mousse into ovals. As each quenelle is shaped, slip it into the simmering water.

5 Poach the quenelles, in batches, for 8–10 minutes, until they feel just firm to the touch, but are still slightly creamy inside. As each is cooked, lift it out on a slotted spoon, drain on kitchen paper and keep hot. When all the quenelles are cooked, arrange them on heated plates. Pour the sauce around. Serve garnished with parsley.

COOK'S TIP
Keep the heat low when poaching; quenelles disintegrate in boiling water.

Energy 767kcal/3165kJ; Protein 17.6g; Carbohydrate 2.5g, of which sugars 2.5g; Fat 75.3g, of which saturates 46.1g; Cholesterol 227mg; Calcium 86mg; Fibre 0g; Sodium 195mg.

FIERY MACKEREL PÂTÉ

SOME OF THE MOST DELICIOUS DISHES ARE ALSO THE SIMPLEST TO MAKE. SERVE THIS POPULAR PÂTÉ WITH WARMED MELBA TOAST AS AN APPETIZER, OR FOR A LIGHT LUNCH WITH WHOLEMEAL TOAST.

SERVES SIX

INGREDIENTS
   4 smoked mackerel fillets, skinned
   225g/8oz/1 cup cream cheese
   1–2 garlic cloves, finely chopped
   juice of 1 lemon
   30ml/2 tbsp chopped fresh chervil,
      parsley or chives
   15ml/1 tbsp Worcestershire sauce
   salt and cayenne pepper
   fresh chives, to garnish
   warmed Melba toast, to serve

VARIATION
Use peppered mackerel fillets for a more piquant flavour. This pâté can be made with smoked haddock or kipper (smoked herring) fillets.

1 Break up the mackerel and put it in a food processor. Add the cream cheese, garlic, lemon juice and herbs.

2 Process the mixture until it is fairly smooth but still has a slightly chunky texture, then add Worcestershire sauce, salt and cayenne pepper to taste. Process to mix, then spoon the pâté into a dish, cover with clear film (plastic wrap) and chill. Garnish with chives and serve with Melba toast.

BRANDADE OF SALT COD

THERE ARE ALMOST AS MANY VERSIONS OF THIS CREAMY SALT COD PURÉE AS THERE ARE REGIONS OF FRANCE. SOME CONTAIN MASHED POTATOES, OTHERS TRUFFLES. THIS COMPARATIVELY LIGHT RECIPE INCLUDES GARLIC, BUT YOU CAN OMIT IT AND SERVE THE BRANDADE ON TOASTED SLICES OF FRENCH BREAD RUBBED WITH GARLIC IF YOU LIKE.

SERVES SIX

INGREDIENTS
   200g/7oz salt cod
   250ml/8fl oz/1 cup extra virgin
      olive oil
   4 garlic cloves, crushed
   250ml/8fl oz/1 cup double (heavy) or
      whipping cream
   ground white pepper
   shredded spring onions (scallions),
      to garnish
   herbed crispbread, to serve

COOK'S TIP
You can purée the fish mixture in a mortar with a pestle. This gives a better texture, but is notoriously hard work.

1 Soak the fish in cold water for 24 hours, changing the water often. Drain. Cut into pieces, place in a shallow pan and pour in cold water to cover. Heat the water until simmering, then poach the fish for 8 minutes, until just cooked. Drain, then remove the skin and bones.

2 Combine the olive oil and garlic in a small pan and heat to just below boiling point. In another pan, heat the cream until it starts to simmer.

3 Put the cod into a food processor, process it briefly, then gradually add alternate amounts of the garlic-flavoured olive oil and cream, while continuing to process the mixture. The aim is to create a purée with the consistency of mashed potatoes.

4 Add pepper to taste, then scoop the brandade into a serving bowl. Garnish with shredded spring onions and serve warm with herbed crispbread.

Top: Energy 344kcal/1421kJ; Protein 10.7g; Carbohydrate 0.5g, of which sugars 0.4g; Fat 33.3g, of which saturates 14.3g; Cholesterol 88mg; Calcium 57mg; Fibre 0.1g; Sodium 518mg.
Bottom: Energy 467kcal/1927kJ; Protein 11.7g; Carbohydrate 1.1g, of which sugars 1.1g; Fat 46.2g, of which saturates 14.8g; Cholesterol 63mg; Calcium 32mg; Fibre 0g; Sodium 144mg.

HOT CRAB SOUFFLÉS

THESE DELICIOUS LITTLE SOUFFLÉS MUST BE SERVED AS SOON AS THEY ARE READY, SO SEAT YOUR GUESTS AT THE TABLE BEFORE TAKING THE SOUFFLÉS OUT OF THE OVEN.

SERVES SIX

INGREDIENTS

50g/2oz/¼ cup butter
45ml/3 tbsp fine wholemeal (whole-
    wheat) breadcrumbs
4 spring onions (scallions),
    finely chopped
15ml/1 tbsp Malaysian or mild
    Madras curry powder
25g/1oz/2 tbsp plain (all-
    purpose) flour
105ml/7 tbsp coconut milk or milk
150ml/¼ pint/⅔ cup
    whipping cream
4 egg yolks
225g/8oz white crab meat
mild green Tabasco sauce
6 egg whites
salt and ground black pepper

1 Use some of the butter to grease six ramekins or a 1.75 litre/3 pint/7 cup soufflé dish. Sprinkle in the fine wholemeal breadcrumbs, roll the dishes or dish around to coat the base and sides completely, then tip out the excess breadcrumbs. Preheat the oven to 200°C/400°F/Gas 6.

2 Melt the remaining butter in a pan, add the spring onions and Malaysian or mild Madras curry powder and cook over a low heat for about 1 minute, until softened. Stir in the flour and cook for 1 minute more.

3 Gradually add the coconut milk or milk and cream, stirring constantly. Cook until smooth and thick. Remove the pan from the heat, stir in the egg yolks, then the crab. Season with salt, black pepper and Tabasco sauce.

4 In a grease-free bowl, beat the egg whites stiffly with a pinch of salt. Using a metal spoon, stir one-third into the mixture to slacken it; fold in the rest. Spoon into the dishes or dish.

5 Bake until well-risen and golden brown, and just firm to the touch. Individual soufflés will be ready in about 8 minutes; a large soufflé will take 15–20 minutes. Serve immediately.

Energy 270kcal/1122kJ; Protein 14g; Carbohydrate 11.6g, of which sugars 2.2g; Fat 18.9g, of which saturates 12.1g; Cholesterol 181mg; Calcium 123mg; Fibre 1g; Sodium 426mg.

SMOKED FISH AND ASPARAGUS MOUSSE

THIS ELEGANT MOUSSE LOOKS VERY SPECIAL WITH ITS STUDDING OF ASPARAGUS AND SMOKED SALMON.
SERVE A MUSTARD AND DILL DRESSING SEPARATELY IF YOU LIKE.

SERVES EIGHT

INGREDIENTS
    15ml/1 tbsp powdered gelatine
    juice of 1 lemon
    105ml/7 tbsp fish stock
    50g/2oz/¼ cup butter, plus extra
        for greasing
    2 shallots, finely chopped
    225g/8oz smoked trout fillets
    105ml/7 tbsp sour cream
    225g/8oz/1 cup low-fat cream cheese
        or cottage cheese
    1 egg white
    12 spinach leaves, blanched
    12 fresh asparagus spears,
        lightly cooked
    115g/4oz smoked salmon, cut into
        long strips
    salt
    shredded beetroot (beet) and leaves,
        to garnish

4 Grease a 1 litre/1¾ pint/4 cup loaf tin (pan) or terrine with butter, then line it with the spinach leaves. Carefully spread half the trout mousse over the spinach-covered base, arrange the asparagus spears on top, then cover with the remaining trout mousse.

5 Arrange the smoked salmon strips lengthways on the mousse and fold over the overhanging spinach leaves. Cover with clear film (plastic wrap) and chill for 4 hours, until set. To serve, remove the clear film, turn out on to a serving dish and garnish.

1 Sprinkle the gelatine over the lemon juice and leave until spongy. In a small pan, heat the fish stock, then add the soaked gelatine and stir to dissolve completely. Set aside. Melt the butter in a small pan, add the shallots and cook gently until softened but not coloured.

2 Break up the smoked trout fillets and put them in a food processor with the shallots, sour cream, stock mixture and cream or cottage cheese. Process until smooth, then spoon into a bowl.

3 In a clean bowl, beat the egg white with a pinch of salt to soft peaks. Fold into the fish. Cover the bowl; chill for 30 minutes or until starting to set.

Energy 174kcal/723kJ; Protein 15.8g; Carbohydrate 2.8g, of which sugars 2.6g; Fat 11g, of which saturates 6g; Cholesterol 58mg; Calcium 75mg; Fibre 0.8g; Sodium 432mg.

STRIPED FISH TERRINE

*SERVE THIS ATTRACTIVE TERRINE COLD OR JUST WARM, WITH A HOLLANDAISE SAUCE IF YOU LIKE.
IT IS IDEAL AS AN APPETIZER OR LIGHT LUNCH DISH.*

SERVES EIGHT

INGREDIENTS

15ml/1 tbsp sunflower oil
450g/1lb salmon fillet, skinned
450g/1lb sole fillets, skinned
3 egg whites
105ml/7 tbsp double (heavy) cream
15ml/1 tbsp finely chopped
  fresh chives
juice of 1 lemon
115g/4oz/1 cup fresh or frozen
  peas, cooked
5ml/1 tsp chopped fresh mint leaves
salt, ground white pepper and
  grated nutmeg
thinly sliced cucumber, salad cress
  and chives, to garnish

3 In a grease-free bowl, beat the egg whites with a pinch of salt until they form soft peaks. Purée the remaining sole in a food processor. Spoon into a mixing bowl, season, then fold in two-thirds of the egg whites, followed by two-thirds of the cream. Put half the mixture into a second bowl; stir in the chives. Add nutmeg to the first bowl.

6 Add the salmon mixture, then finish with the plain sole mixture. Cover with the overhanging fish fillets and make a lid of oiled foil. Stand the terrine in a roasting pan and pour in enough boiling water to come halfway up the sides.

7 Bake for 15–20 minutes, until the top fillets are just cooked and the mousse feels springy. Remove the foil, lay a wire rack over the top of the terrine and invert both rack and terrine on to a lipped baking sheet to catch the cooking juices that drain out. Keep these to make fish stock or soup.

8 Leaving the tin in place, let the terrine stand for about 15 minutes, then turn the terrine over again. Invert it on to a serving dish and lift off the tin carefully. Serve warm, or chill in the refrigerator first and serve cold. Garnish with thinly sliced cucumber, salad cress and chives before serving.

1 Grease a 1 litre/1¾ pint/4 cup loaf tin (pan) or terrine with the oil. Slice the salmon thinly; cut it and the sole into long strips, 2.5cm/1in wide. Preheat the oven to 200°C/400°F/Gas 6.

4 Purée the remaining salmon, scrape it into a bowl; add the lemon juice. Fold in the remaining whites, then cream.

2 Line the terrine neatly with alternate slices of salmon and sole, leaving the ends overhanging the edge. You should be left with about a third of the salmon and half the sole.

5 Purée the peas with the mint. Season the mixture and spread it over the base of the terrine, smoothing the surface with a spatula. Spoon over the sole with chives mixture and spread evenly.

COOK'S TIPS
• Pop the salmon into the freezer about 1 hour before slicing it. If it is almost frozen, it will be much easier to slice.
• You can line the tin (pan) or terrine with oven-safe clear film (plastic wrap) after greasing and before adding the salmon and sole strips. This makes it easier to turn out the terrine.

Energy 248kcal/1030kJ; Protein 24g; Carbohydrate 2.2g, of which sugars 0.6g; Fat 15.9g, of which saturates 5.7g; Cholesterol 74mg; Calcium 51mg; Fibre 0.7g; Sodium 108mg.

HADDOCK AND SMOKED SALMON TERRINE

THIS SUBSTANTIAL TERRINE MAKES A SUPERB DISH FOR A SUMMER BUFFET, ACCOMPANIED BY DILL MAYONNAISE OR A FRESH MANGO SALSA.

SERVES TEN TO TWELVE AS AN APPETIZER,
SIX TO EIGHT AS A MAIN COURSE

INGREDIENTS
    15ml/1 tbsp sunflower oil,
        for greasing
    350g/12oz oak-smoked salmon
    900g/2lb haddock fillets, skinned
    2 eggs, lightly beaten
    105ml/7 tbsp crème fraîche
    30ml/2 tbsp drained capers
    30ml/2 tbsp drained soft green or
        pink peppercorns
    salt and ground white pepper
    crème fraîche, peppercorns and fresh
        dill and rocket (arugula), to garnish

3 Combine the eggs, crème fraîche, capers and green or pink peppercorns in a bowl. Season with salt and pepper; stir in the small pieces of haddock. Spoon the mixture into the mould until it is one-third full. Smooth the surface with a spatula.

6 Stand the terrine in a roasting pan and pour in boiling water to come halfway up the sides. Place in the oven and cook for 45 minutes–1 hour, until the filling is just set.

1 Preheat the oven to 200°C/400°F/ Gas 6. Grease a 1 litre/1¾ pint/4 cup loaf tin (pan) or terrine with the oil. Use some of the salmon to line the tin or terrine; let some of the ends overhang the mould. Reserve the remaining smoked salmon until needed.

2 Cut two long slices of haddock the length of the tin or terrine and set aside. Cut the rest of the haddock into small pieces. Season all the haddock with salt and pepper.

4 Wrap the long haddock fillets in the reserved smoked salmon. Lay them on top of the layer of the fish mixture in the tin or terrine.

5 Fill the tin or terrine with the rest of the fish mixture, smooth the surface and fold the overhanging pieces of smoked salmon over the top. Cover tightly with a double thickness of foil. Tap the terrine to settle the contents.

7 Take the terrine out of the roasting pan, but do not remove the foil cover. Place two or three large heavy cans on the foil to weight it and leave until cold. Chill in the refrigerator for 24 hours.

8 About an hour before serving, remove the terrine from the refrigerator, lift off the weights and remove the foil. Carefully invert the terrine on to a serving plate and lift off the loaf tin.

9 Cut the terrine into thick slices using a sharp knife and serve, garnished with crème fraîche, peppercorns and fronds of dill and rocket leaves.

VARIATION
Use any thick white fish fillets for this terrine: try halibut or Arctic bass.

Energy 154kcal/647kJ; Protein 22.4g; Carbohydrate 0.3g, of which sugars 0.3g; Fat 7.1g, of which saturates 3g; Cholesterol 78mg; Calcium 34mg; Fibre 0.2g; Sodium 571mg.

SMOKED HADDOCK AND AVOCADO MOUSSE

THE FRESH-TASTING SALSA COMPLEMENTS THE SMOOTH CREAMINESS OF THE MOUSSE.

SERVES SIX

INGREDIENTS

225g/8oz undyed smoked haddock
   fillets, skinned
½ onion, cut into thick rings
25g/1oz/2 tbsp butter
1 bay leaf
150ml/¼ pint/⅔ cup milk
1 ripe avocado
2 gelatine leaves, or 15ml/1 tbsp
   powdered gelatine
30ml/2 tbsp dry white wine
105ml/7 tbsp double (heavy) cream
1 egg white
salt, ground white pepper and
   grated nutmeg
For the salsa
3 tomatoes, peeled, seeded
   and diced
1 avocado
1 small red onion, finely chopped
1–2 garlic cloves, finely chopped
1 large fresh green chilli, seeded and
   finely chopped
45ml/3 tbsp extra virgin olive oil
juice of 1 lime
12 lime slices, to garnish

1 Arrange the fish in a single layer in a large shallow pan and lay the onion rings on top. Dot with butter, season with pepper, add the bay leaf and pour over the milk. Poach gently over a low heat for 5 minutes, or until the fish flakes easily when tested with the tip of a sharp knife. Remove the fish using a slotted spoon and leave to cool.

VARIATION
Undyed smoked cod can be used instead of the smoked haddock.

2 Using a slotted spoon, lift out and discard the bay leaf and onion. Set the pan over a high heat and boil the milk until it has reduced by about two-thirds. Flake the fish into a food processor and strain over the reduced milk. Process until smooth.

3 Spoon the fish mixture into a bowl. Peel the avocado and cut the flesh into 5mm/¼in dice. Fold into the fish purée.

4 In a small pan, soak the gelatine leaves in a little cold water until softened. If using powdered gelatine, sprinkle it over 30ml/2 tbsp cold water and leave until spongy. Add the wine to the softened gelatine and heat gently until completely dissolved, stirring constantly. Pour on to the fish mixture and mix well.

5 Lightly whip the cream in a bowl. In a second, grease-free bowl, beat the egg white with a pinch of salt until stiff. Fold the cream, then the egg white into the fish mixture. Season with salt and pepper and add a little nutmeg.

6 Pour the mixture into six ramekins or moulds, cover with clear film (plastic wrap) and chill for about 1 hour.

7 Meanwhile, make the salsa. Put the diced tomatoes in a bowl. Peel and dice the avocado and add it to the tomatoes with the onion, garlic and chilli. Add the olive oil and lime juice, with salt and pepper to taste. Chill until needed.

8 To release the mousse, dip the moulds into hot water for a couple of seconds, invert on to individual plates and give each mould a sharp tap. Put a spoonful of salsa on each plate and a little on the top of each mousse. Make a cut to the centre of each slice of lime and twist a couple of slices on to each plate. Serve with the remaining salsa.

Energy 248kcal/1029kJ; Protein 9.2g; Carbohydrate 4g, of which sugars 3g; Fat 21.4g, of which saturates 9.8g; Cholesterol 46mg; Calcium 31mg; Fibre 2.1g; Sodium 331mg.

SALADS

What could be nicer on a warm day than a refreshing fish or shellfish salad? Take a fresh look at fish as a salad ingredient. Meaty tuna, swordfish, skate and hake make ideal main-course medleys, while lighter offerings such as Insalata di Mare and Asparagus and Langoustine Salad are perfect for summertime al fresco lunches. If you're looking for something out of the ordinary, Warm Monkfish Salad with pine nuts makes an unusual and delicious dish, and Red Mullet with Raspberry Dressing is an unexpected delight.

FRESH TUNA SALADE NIÇOISE

FRESH TUNA TRANSFORMS THIS CLASSIC AND EVER-POPULAR COLOURFUL SALAD FROM THE SOUTH OF FRANCE INTO SOMETHING REALLY SPECIAL.

SERVES FOUR

INGREDIENTS

    4 tuna steaks, about 150g/5oz each
    30ml/2 tbsp olive oil
    225g/8oz fine green beans, trimmed
    1 small cos or romaine lettuce or
      2 Little Gem (Bibb) lettuces
    4 new potatoes, boiled
    4 ripe tomatoes, or
      12 cherry tomatoes
    2 red (bell) peppers, seeded and cut
      into thin strips
    4 hard-boiled eggs
    8 drained anchovy fillets in oil,
      halved lengthways
    16 large black olives
    salt and ground black pepper
    12 fresh basil leaves, to garnish
For the dressing
    15ml/1 tbsp red wine vinegar
    90ml/6 tbsp olive oil
    1 fat garlic clove, crushed

1 Brush the tuna on both sides with a little olive oil and season with salt and pepper. Heat a ridged griddle pan or the grill (broiler) until very hot, then cook the tuna steaks for 1–2 minutes on each side; the flesh should still be pink and juicy in the middle. Set aside.

2 Cook the beans in a pan of lightly salted boiling water for 4–5 minutes or until crisp-tender. Drain, refresh under cold water and drain again.

3 Separate the lettuce leaves and wash and dry them. Arrange them on four individual serving plates. Slice the potatoes and tomatoes, if large (leave cherry tomatoes whole) and divide them among the plates. Arrange the fine green beans and red pepper strips over them.

4 Shell the hard-boiled eggs, cut them into thick slices. Place two half eggs on each plate with an anchovy fillet draped over. Sprinkle four olives on to each plate.

5 To make the dressing, whisk together the vinegar, olive oil and garlic and seasoning to taste. Drizzle over the salads, arrange the tuna steaks on top, sprinkle over the basil and serve.

COOK'S TIP
To intensify the flavour of the (bell) peppers and improve their texture, grill (broil) them until the skins are charred, then put them in a bowl and cover with several layers of kitchen paper. Leave for 10–15 minutes, then rub off the skins.

Energy 578kcal/2408kJ; Protein 46.4g; Carbohydrate 15g, of which sugars 10.6g; Fat 37.5g, of which saturates 7.1g; Cholesterol 235mg; Calcium 127mg; Fibre 4.7g; Sodium 585mg.

INSALATA DI MARE

YOU CAN VARY THE FISH IN THIS ITALIAN SALAD ACCORDING TO WHAT IS AVAILABLE, BUT TRY TO INCLUDE AT LEAST TWO KINDS OF SHELLFISH AND SOME SQUID. THE SALAD IS GOOD WARM OR COLD.

SERVES SIX AS AN APPETIZER,
FOUR AS A MAIN COURSE

INGREDIENTS
   450g/1lb fresh mussels, scrubbed
      and bearded
   450g/1lb small clams, scrubbed
   105ml/7 tbsp dry white wine
   225g/8oz squid, cleaned
   4 large scallops, with their corals
   30ml/2 tbsp olive oil
   2 garlic cloves, finely chopped
   1 small dried red chilli, crumbled
   225g/8oz whole cooked prawns
      (shrimp), in the shell
   6–8 large chicory (Belgian
      endive) leaves
   6–8 radicchio leaves
   15ml/1 tbsp chopped flat leaf
      parsley, to garnish
For the dressing
   5ml/1 tsp Dijon mustard
   30ml/2 tbsp white wine vinegar
   5ml/1 tsp lemon juice
   120ml/4fl oz/½ cup extra virgin
      olive oil
   salt and ground black pepper

1 Put the mussels and clams in a large pan with the white wine. Cover and cook over a high heat, shaking the pan occasionally, for about 4 minutes, until they have opened. Discard any that remain closed. Use a slotted spoon to transfer the shellfish to a bowl, then strain and reserve the cooking liquid and set it aside.

2 Cut the squid into thin rings; chop the tentacles. Leave small squid whole. Halve the scallops horizontally.

3 Heat the oil in a frying pan, add the garlic, chilli, squid, scallops and corals, and sauté for about 2 minutes, until just cooked and tender. Lift the squid and scallops out of the pan; reserve the oil.

4 When the shellfish are cool enough to handle, shell them, keeping a dozen of each in the shell. Peel all but 6–8 of the prawns. Pour the shellfish cooking liquid into a small pan, set over a high heat and reduce by half. Mix all the shelled and unshelled mussels and clams with the squid and scallops, then add the prawns.

5 To make the dressing, whisk the mustard with the vinegar and lemon juice and season to taste. Add the olive oil, whisk vigorously, then whisk in the reserved cooking liquid and the oil from the frying pan. Pour the dressing over the shellfish mixture and toss lightly to coat well.

6 Arrange the chicory and radicchio leaves around the edge of a large serving dish and pile the mixed shellfish salad into the centre. Sprinkle with the chopped flat leaf parsley and serve immediately or chill first.

Energy 445kcal/1861kJ; Protein 41.1g; Carbohydrate 3.7g, of which sugars 1g; Fat 27.9g, of which saturates 4.3g; Cholesterol 241mg; Calcium 219mg; Fibre 0.5g; Sodium 585mg.

QUEEN SCALLOP AND GREEN BEAN SALAD

IF YOU LIKE, USE LIGHTLY COOKED MANGETOUTS INSTEAD OF THE FINE GREEN BEANS.

SERVES FOUR

INGREDIENTS
    115g/4oz fine green beans, trimmed
    2 good handfuls of frisée or Batavia
        lettuce leaves, finely shredded
    15g/½oz/1 tbsp butter
    15ml/1 tbsp hazelnut oil
    20 shelled queen scallops, with
        corals if possible
    2 spring onions (scallions), very
        thinly sliced
    salt and ground black pepper
    4 fresh chervil sprigs, to garnish
For the dressing
    10ml/2 tsp sherry vinegar
    30ml/2 tbsp hazelnut oil
    15ml/1 tbsp finely chopped fresh
        mint leaves

1 Cook the beans in a pan of lightly salted boiling water for about 5 minutes, until crisp-tender. Drain, refresh under cold water, drain again and set aside.

2 Wash and dry the salad leaves; put in a bowl. Mix the dressing, season, pour over the salad and toss. Divide the salad among four serving plates.

3 Heat the butter and hazelnut oil in a frying pan until sizzling, then add the scallops and their corals and sauté for about 1 minute, tossing the scallops in the fat until they have just turned opaque. Stir in the green beans and spring onions. Spoon the vegetables over the salad and pile the scallops and corals into a tower. Garnish and serve.

RED MULLET WITH RASPBERRY DRESSING

THE COMBINATION OF RED MULLET AND RASPBERRY VINEGAR IS DELICIOUS IN THIS FIRST-COURSE SALAD. KEEP TO THE "RED" THEME BY INCLUDING SALAD LEAVES SUCH AS RED OAKLEAF LETTUCE AND BABY RED-STEMMED CHARD. IF RED MULLET IS NOT AVAILABLE, USE SMALL RED SNAPPER FILLETS.

SERVES FOUR

INGREDIENTS
    8 red mullet or red snapper
        fillets, scaled
    15ml/1 tbsp olive oil
    15ml/1 tbsp raspberry vinegar
    175g/6oz mixed dark green and red
        salad leaves, such as lamb's lettuce
        (corn salad), radicchio, oakleaf
        lettuce and rocket (arugula)
    salt and ground black pepper
For the raspberry dressing
    115g/4oz/1 cup raspberries, puréed
        and sieved
    30ml/2 tbsp raspberry vinegar
    60ml/4 tbsp extra virgin olive oil
    2.5ml/½ tsp caster (superfine) sugar

COOK'S TIP
To make the raspberry purée, process the fruit in a blender or food processor, then press it through a strainer.

1 Lay the fish fillets in a shallow dish. Whisk together the olive oil and raspberry vinegar, add a pinch of salt and drizzle the mixture over the fish. Cover and leave to marinate for 1 hour.

2 Meanwhile, whisk together the dressing ingredients and season to taste.

3 Wash and dry the salad leaves, put them in a bowl, pour over most of the dressing and toss lightly.

4 Heat a ridged griddle pan or frying pan until very hot, put in the fish fillets and cook for 2–3 minutes on each side, until just tender. Cut the fillets diagonally in half to make rough diamond shapes.

5 Arrange a tall heap of salad in the middle of each serving plate. Prop up four fish fillet halves on the salad on each plate with the reserved dressing spooned around. Serve immediately.

Top: Energy 213kcal/887kJ; Protein 19g; Carbohydrate 5.4g, of which sugars 2.3g; Fat 12.9g, of which saturates 3.4g; Cholesterol 43mg; Calcium 59mg; Fibre 1.8g; Sodium 160mg.
Bottom: Energy 333kcal/1391kJ; Protein 38.2g; Carbohydrate 2.1g, of which sugars 2.1g; Fat 19.2g, of which saturates 1.7g; Cholesterol 0mg; Calcium 152mg; Fibre 1.1g; Sodium 184mg.

PIQUANT PRAWN SALAD

THE THAI-INSPIRED DRESSING ADDS A SUPERB FLAVOUR TO THE NOODLES AND PRAWNS. THIS DELICIOUS SALAD CAN BE SERVED WARM OR COLD, AND WILL SERVE SIX AS AN APPETIZER.

SERVES FOUR

INGREDIENTS
    200g/7oz rice vermicelli
    8 baby corn cobs, halved
    150g/5oz mangetouts (snow peas)
    15ml/1 tbsp stir-fry oil
    2 garlic cloves, finely chopped
    2.5cm/1in piece fresh root ginger,
        peeled and finely chopped
    1 fresh red or green chilli, seeded
        and finely chopped
    450g/1lb farmed raw peeled tiger
        prawns (jumbo shrimp)
    4 spring onions (scallions), thinly sliced
    15ml/1 tbsp sesame seeds, toasted
    1 lemon grass stalk, thinly shredded,
        to garnish
For the dressing
    15ml/1 tbsp chopped fresh chives
    15ml/1 tbsp Thai fish sauce
    5ml/1 tsp soy sauce
    45ml/3 tbsp groundnut (peanut) oil
    5ml/1 tsp sesame oil
    30ml/2 tbsp rice vinegar

1 Put the rice vermicelli in a wide heatproof bowl, pour over boiling water and leave for 5 minutes. Drain, refresh under cold water and drain well again. Tip back into the bowl and set aside until required.

2 Boil or steam the corn cobs and mangetouts for about 3 minutes; they should still be crunchy. Refresh under cold water and drain. Now make the dressing. Mix all the ingredients in a screw-top jar, close tightly and shake well to combine.

3 Heat the oil in a large frying pan or wok. Add the garlic, ginger and red or green chilli and cook for 1 minute. Add the tiger prawns and stir-fry for about 3 minutes, until they have just turned pink. Stir in the spring onions, corn cobs, mangetouts and sesame seeds, and toss lightly to mix.

4 Tip the contents of the pan or wok over the rice vermicelli or noodles. Pour the dressing on top and toss well. Serve, garnished with lemon grass, or chill for an hour before serving.

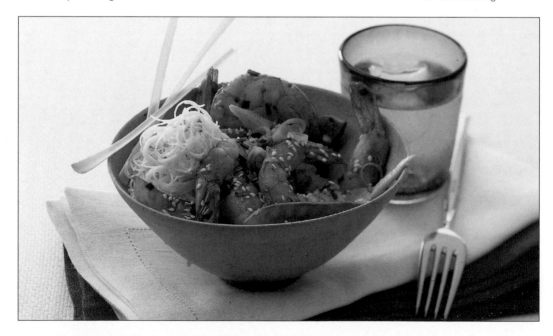

Energy 298kcal/1241kJ; Protein 18.8g; Carbohydrate 28.1g, of which sugars 1.6g; Fat 12.1g, of which saturates 2g; Cholesterol 146mg; Calcium 102mg; Fibre 1.4g; Sodium 587mg.

HAKE AND POTATO SALAD

*HAKE IS A "MEATY" FISH THAT IS EXCELLENT SERVED COLD IN A SALAD. HERE THE FLAVOUR IS
ENHANCED WITH A PIQUANT DRESSING.*

SERVES FOUR

INGREDIENTS
   450g/1lb hake fillets
   150ml/¼ pint/⅔ cup fish stock
   1 onion, thinly sliced
   1 bay leaf
   450g/1lb cooked baby new potatoes,
     halved unless tiny
   1 red (bell) pepper, seeded and diced
   115g/4oz/1 cup petits pois (baby
     peas), cooked
   2 spring onions (scallions), sliced
   ½ cucumber, unpeeled and diced
   4 large red lettuce leaves
   salt and ground black pepper
For the dressing
   150ml/¼ pint/⅔ cup Greek
     (US strained plain) yogurt
   30ml/2 tbsp olive oil
   juice of ½ lemon
   15–30ml/1–2 tbsp capers
To garnish
   2 hard-boiled eggs, finely chopped
   15ml/1 tbsp chopped fresh parsley
   15ml/1 tbsp finely chopped
     fresh chives

1 Put the hake fillets in a large, shallow
pan with the fish stock, onion slices
and bay leaf. Bring to the boil over
a medium heat, then lower the heat
and poach the fish gently for about
10 minutes until it flakes easily when
tested with the tip of a sharp knife.
Leave it to cool, then remove the skin
and any bones and separate the flesh
into large flakes.

2 Put the baby new potatoes in a bowl
with the red pepper, petits pois, spring
onions and cucumber. Gently stir in
the flaked hake and season with salt
and pepper.

3 Make the dressing by stirring all the
ingredients together in a bowl or jug
(pitcher). Season and spoon or pour
over the salad. Toss gently.

4 Place a lettuce leaf on each plate and
spoon the salad over it. Mix the finely
chopped hard-boiled eggs for the
garnish with the parsley and chives.
Sprinkle the mixture over each salad.

VARIATION
This is equally good made with halibut,
monkfish, pollack or Pacific cod. For a
change, try it with a dressing of home-
made mayonnaise mixed with capers.

Energy 318kcal/1335kJ; Protein 27.8g; Carbohydrate 32.3g, of which sugars 11.7g; Fat 9.6g, of which saturates 1.6g; Cholesterol 26mg; Calcium 134mg; Fibre 4.5g; Sodium 162mg.

WARM SWORDFISH <u>AND</u> ROCKET SALAD

SWORDFISH IS ROBUST ENOUGH TO TAKE THE SHARP FLAVOURS OF ROCKET AND PECORINO CHEESE. IF YOU CAN'T FIND PECORINO, USE A GOOD PARMESAN INSTEAD. YOU COULD SUBSTITUTE MARLIN OR SHARK FOR THE SWORDFISH, IF YOU LIKE.

SERVES FOUR

INGREDIENTS

4 swordfish steaks, about
    175g/6oz each
75ml/5 tbsp extra virgin olive oil,
    plus extra for serving
juice of 1 lemon
30ml/2 tbsp finely chopped
    fresh parsley
115g/4oz rocket (arugula) leaves,
    stalks snipped off
115g/4oz Pecorino cheese
salt and ground black pepper

1 Lay the swordfish steaks in a dish. Mix 60ml/4 tbsp of the olive oil with the lemon juice. Pour over the fish. Season, sprinkle on the parsley and turn the fish to coat, cover with clear film (plastic wrap) and marinate for 10 minutes.

2 Heat a ridged griddle pan or the grill (broiler) until very hot. Take the fish out of the marinade and pat it dry with kitchen paper. Grill (broil) for 2–3 minutes on each side until the swordfish is just cooked through, but still juicy.

3 Meanwhile, put the rocket leaves in a bowl and season with a little salt and plenty of pepper. Add the remaining 15ml/1 tbsp olive oil and toss well. Shave the Pecorino over the top.

4 Place the swordfish steaks on four individual plates and arrange a little pile of salad on each steak. Serve extra olive oil separately so it may be drizzled over the swordfish.

VARIATION
Tuna or marlin steaks would be equally good in this recipe.

Energy 452kcal/1880kJ; Protein 43.6g; Carbohydrate 0.5g, of which sugars 0.4g; Fat 30.6g, of which saturates 9.5g; Cholesterol 101mg; Calcium 401mg; Fibre 0.6g; Sodium 581mg.

PROVENÇAL AIOLI <u>WITH</u> SALT COD

THIS SUBSTANTIAL SALAD CONSTITUTES A MEAL ON ITS OWN AND IS ONE OF THE NICEST DISHES FOR SUMMER ENTERTAINING. VARY THE VEGETABLES ACCORDING TO WHAT IS IN SEASON; IF YOU LIKE RAW VEGETABLES, INCLUDE RADISHES, YELLOW PEPPER AND CELERY FOR COLOUR CONTRAST.

SERVES SIX

INGREDIENTS

1kg/2¼lb salt cod, soaked overnight in water to cover
1 fresh bouquet garni
18 small new potatoes, scrubbed
1 large fresh mint sprig, torn
225g/8oz green beans, trimmed
225g/8oz broccoli florets
6 hard-boiled eggs
12 baby carrots, with leaves if possible, scrubbed
1 large red (bell) pepper, seeded and cut into strips
2 fennel bulbs, cut into strips
18 red or yellow cherry tomatoes
6 large whole cooked prawns (shrimp) or langoustines, in the shell, to garnish (optional)
For the aioli
600ml/1 pint/2½ cups home-made mayonnaise
2 fat garlic cloves (or more if you are feeling brave), crushed
cayenne pepper

1 Drain the cod and put it into a shallow pan. Pour in barely enough water to cover the fish and add the bouquet garni. Bring to the boil, then cover and poach very gently for about 10 minutes, until the fish flakes easily when tested with the tip of a sharp knife. Drain and set aside until required.

2 Cook the potatoes with the mint in a pan of lightly salted, boiling water until just tender. Drain and set aside. Cook the beans and broccoli in separate pans of lightly salted, boiling water for about 3–5 minutes. They should still be very crisp. Refresh under cold water and drain again, then set aside.

3 Remove the skin from the cod and break the flesh into large flakes. Shell and halve the eggs lengthways.

4 Pile the cod in the middle of a large serving platter and arrange the eggs and all the vegetables around the edges or randomly. Garnish with the prawns or langoustines if you are using them.

5 To make the aioli, put the home-made mayonnaise in a bowl and stir in the crushed garlic and cayenne pepper to taste. Serve in individual bowls or one large bowl to hand around.

Energy 1099kcal/4567kJ; Protein 66.5g; Carbohydrate 21.4g, of which sugars 10.2g; Fat 83.9g, of which saturates 13.6g; Cholesterol 364mg; Calcium 140mg; Fibre 5.6g; Sodium 1217mg.

SMOKED EEL AND CHICORY SALAD

SMOKED EEL HAS BECOME INCREASINGLY POPULAR RECENTLY AND IS SEEN ON SOME OF THE MOST SOPHISTICATED TABLES. IT TASTES MARVELLOUS IN A SALAD WITH A REFRESHING CITRUS DRESSING.

SERVES FOUR

INGREDIENTS
    450g/1lb smoked eel fillets, skinned
    2 large heads of chicory (Belgian
      endive), separated
    4 radicchio leaves
    flat leaf parsley leaves, to garnish
For the citrus dressing
    1 lemon
    1 orange
    5ml/1 tsp sugar
    5ml/1 tsp Dijon mustard
    90ml/6 tbsp sunflower oil
    15ml/1 tbsp chopped fresh parsley
    salt and ground black pepper

VARIATION
This salad can also be made with other hot-smoked fish such as trout or mackerel.

1 Cut the eel fillets diagonally into eight pieces. Make the dressing. Using a zester, carefully remove the rind in strips from the lemon and the orange. Squeeze the juice of both fruit. Set the lemon juice aside and pour the orange juice into a small pan. Stir in the rinds and sugar. Bring to the boil and reduce by half. Leave to cool.

2 Whisk the Dijon mustard, reserved lemon juice and the sunflower oil together in a bowl. Add the orange juice mixture, then stir in the chopped fresh parsley. Season to taste with salt and ground black pepper and whisk again.

3 Arrange the chicory leaves in a circle on individual plates, with the pointed ends radiating outwards like the spokes of a wheel. Take the radicchio leaves and arrange them on the plates, between the chicory leaves.

4 Drizzle a little of the dressing over the leaves and place four pieces of eel in a star-shape in the middle. Garnish with the parsley leaves and serve. Offer the remaining dressing separately.

RAY WITH BITTER SALAD LEAVES

RAY HAS A DELICIOUSLY SWEET FLAVOUR WHICH CONTRASTS WELL WITH THE BITTERNESS OF SALAD LEAVES SUCH AS ESCAROLE, ROCKET, FRISÉE AND RADICCHIO. SERVE WITH TOASTED FRENCH BREAD.

SERVES FOUR

INGREDIENTS
    800g/1¾lb ray wings
    15ml/1 tbsp white wine vinegar
    4 black peppercorns
    1 fresh thyme sprig
    175g/6oz bag of ready-prepared
      bitter salad leaves, such as frisée,
      rocket (arugula), radicchio, escarole
      and lamb's lettuce (corn salad)
    1 orange
    2 tomatoes, peeled, seeded
      and diced
For the dressing
    15ml/1 tbsp white wine vinegar
    45ml/3 tbsp olive oil
    2 shallots, finely chopped
    salt and ground black pepper

1 Put the ray wings into a large shallow pan, cover with cold water and add the vinegar, peppercorns and thyme. Bring to the boil, then poach the fish gently for 8–10 minutes, until the flesh comes away easily from the bones.

2 Meanwhile, make the dressing. Whisk the vinegar, olive oil and shallots together in a bowl. Season to taste. Tip the salad leaves into a bowl, pour over the dressing and toss well.

3 Using a zester, remove the outer rind from the orange, then peel it, removing all the pith. Slice into thin rounds.

4 When the ray is cooked, flake the flesh and mix it into the salad. Add the orange rind shreds, the orange slices and tomatoes, toss gently and serve.

COOK'S TIP
When peeling the orange, take care not to include any of the bitter white pith.

Top: Energy 368kcal/1526kJ; Protein 19.9g; Carbohydrate 6.1g, of which sugars 5g; Fat 29.9g, of which saturates 5.4g; Cholesterol 169mg; Calcium 69mg; Fibre 1.6g; Sodium 142mg.
Bottom: Energy 230kcal/965kJ; Protein 31.6g; Carbohydrate 4.8g, of which sugars 4.8g; Fat 9.5g, of which saturates 1.3g; Cholesterol 0mg; Calcium 118mg; Fibre 1.5g; Sodium 247mg.

WARM MONKFISH SALAD

MONKFISH HAS A MATCHLESS FLAVOUR AND BENEFITS FROM BEING COOKED SIMPLY. TEAMING IT WITH WILTED BABY SPINACH AND TOASTED PINE NUTS IS INSPIRATIONAL.

3 Make the dressing by whisking all the ingredients together until smooth and creamy. Pour the dressing into a small pan, season to taste with salt and pepper and heat gently.

4 Heat the oil and butter in a ridged griddle pan or frying pan until sizzling. Add the fish; sauté for 20–30 seconds on each side.

SERVES FOUR

INGREDIENTS

    2 monkfish fillets, about
       350g/12oz each
    25g/1oz/¼ cup pine nuts
    15ml/1 tbsp olive oil
    15g/½oz/1 tbsp butter
    225g/8oz baby spinach leaves,
       washed and stalks removed
    salt and ground black pepper
For the dressing
    5ml/1 tsp Dijon mustard
    5ml/1 tsp sherry vinegar
    60ml/4 tbsp olive oil
    1 garlic clove, crushed

VARIATION
Substitute salad leaves for the spinach.

1 Holding the knife at a slight angle, cut each monkfish fillet into 12 diagonal slices. Season lightly and set aside.

2 Heat an empty frying pan, put in the pine nuts and shake them about for a while, until golden brown. Do not burn. Transfer to a plate; set aside.

5 Put the spinach leaves in a large bowl and pour over the warm dressing. Sprinkle on the toasted pine nuts, reserving a few, and toss together well. Divide the dressed spinach leaves among four serving plates and arrange the monkfish slices on top. Sprinkle the reserved pine nuts on top and serve.

Energy 331kcal/1379kJ; Protein 29.9g; Carbohydrate 1.2g, of which sugars 1.1g; Fat 23g, of which saturates 4.9g; Cholesterol 34mg; Calcium 110mg; Fibre 1.3g; Sodium 137mg.

ASPARAGUS AND LANGOUSTINE SALAD

FOR A REALLY EXTRAVAGANT TREAT, YOU COULD MAKE THIS ATTRACTIVE SALAD WITH MEDALLIONS OF LOBSTER. FOR A CHEAPER VERSION, USE LARGE PRAWNS, ALLOWING SIX PER SERVING.

SERVES FOUR

INGREDIENTS

16 langoustines
16 fresh asparagus spears, trimmed
2 carrots
30ml/2 tbsp olive oil
1 garlic clove, peeled
15ml/1 tbsp chopped fresh tarragon
4 fresh tarragon sprigs and some
    chopped, to garnish
For the dressing
30ml/2 tbsp tarragon vinegar
120ml/4fl oz/½ cup olive oil
salt and ground black pepper

1 Shell the langoustines and keep the discarded parts for stock. Set aside.

2 Steam the asparagus over salted, boiling water until just tender, but still a little crisp. Refresh under cold water, drain and place in a shallow dish.

3 Peel the carrots and cut into fine julienne shreds. Cook in a pan of salted, boiling water for about 3 minutes, until tender but still crunchy. Drain, refresh under cold water and drain again. Place in the dish with the asparagus.

4 Make the dressing. Whisk the vinegar with the oil in a jug (pitcher). Season to taste. Pour over the asparagus and carrots and leave to marinate.

5 Heat the oil with the garlic in a frying pan until very hot. Add the langoustines and sauté quickly until just heated through. Discard the garlic.

6 Cut the asparagus spears in half and arrange on four individual plates with the carrots. Drizzle over the dressing left in the dish and top each portion with four langoustine tails. Top with the tarragon sprigs and sprinkle the chopped tarragon on top. Serve.

COOK'S TIP
Most of the langoustines we buy have been cooked at sea; this is necessary because the flesh deteriorates rapidly after death. Bear this in mind when you cook the shellfish. Because they have already been cooked, they will need only to be lightly sautéed until heated through. If you are lucky enough to buy live langoustines, kill them quickly by immersing them in boiling water, then sauté until cooked through.

Energy 320kcal/1323kJ; Protein 16.3g; Carbohydrate 4g, of which sugars 3.8g; Fat 26.6g, of which saturates 3.9g; Cholesterol 146mg; Calcium 93mg; Fibre 2.3g; Sodium 150mg.

EVERYDAY
MAIN COURSES

Healthy everyday eating becomes a treat when you serve interesting, affordable fish dishes.

Quick to prepare, low in fat and packed with nutrients, fish makes the perfect

family meal. From simple-to-cook old favourites, such as Fish Pie and

Salmon Fish Cakes, to Trout with Tamarind and Chilli Sauce, and Green

Fish Curry, there's a dish to suit everyone, even those who profess not to like

fish. You will be surprised how little time it takes to

make these delicious everyday meals.

SALMON FISH CAKES

THE SECRET OF A GOOD FISH CAKE IS TO MAKE IT WITH FRESHLY PREPARED FISH AND POTATOES,
HOME-MADE BREADCRUMBS AND PLENTY OF INTERESTING SEASONING.

<u>SERVES FOUR</u>

INGREDIENTS

    450g/1lb cooked salmon fillet
    450g/1lb freshly cooked
      potatoes, mashed
    25g/1oz/2 tbsp butter, melted
    10ml/2 tsp wholegrain mustard
    15ml/1 tbsp each chopped fresh dill
      and chopped fresh parsley
    grated rind and juice of ½ lemon
    15ml/1 tbsp plain (all-purpose) flour
    1 egg, lightly beaten
    150g/5oz/1¼ cups dried breadcrumbs
    60ml/4 tbsp sunflower oil
    salt and ground black pepper
    rocket (arugula) and chives, to garnish
    lemon wedges, to serve

1 Flake the cooked salmon, discarding any skin and bones. Put it in a bowl with the mashed potato, melted butter and wholegrain mustard and mix well. Stir in the dill and parsley and lemon rind and juice. Season to taste with salt and pepper.

2 Divide the mixture into eight portions and shape each into a ball, then flatten into a round. Dip the fish cakes in flour, then in egg and finally in breadcrumbs, making sure that they are evenly coated.

3 Heat the oil in a frying pan until it is very hot. Fry the fish cakes, in batches, until golden brown and crisp all over. As each batch is ready, drain on kitchen paper and keep hot. Garnish with rocket leaves and chives and serve with lemon wedges.

COOK'S TIP
Almost any fresh white or hot-smoked fish is suitable; smoked cod and haddock are particularly good.

Energy 586kcal/2453kJ; Protein 29.8g; Carbohydrate 49.9g, of which sugars 3.2g; Fat 31g, of which saturates 7.2g; Cholesterol 117mg; Calcium 79mg; Fibre 1.3g; Sodium 266mg.

CRAB CAKES

UNLIKE FISH CAKES, CRAB CAKES ARE BOUND WITH EGG AND MAYONNAISE OR TARTARE SAUCE INSTEAD OF POTATOES, WHICH MAKES THEM LIGHT IN TEXTURE. IF YOU LIKE, THEY CAN BE GRILLED INSTEAD OF FRIED; BRUSH WITH A LITTLE OIL FIRST.

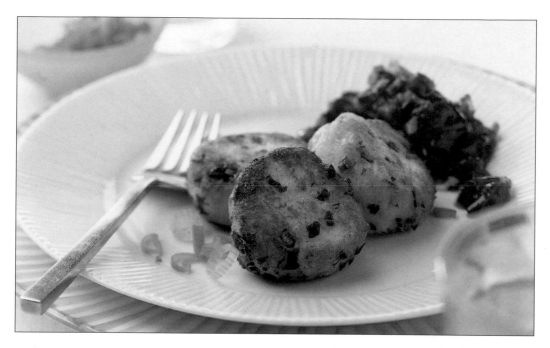

SERVES FOUR

INGREDIENTS
    450g/1lb mixed brown and white
        crab meat
    30ml/2 tbsp mayonnaise or
        tartare sauce
    2.5–5ml/½–1 tsp mustard powder
    1 egg, lightly beaten
    Tabasco sauce
    45ml/3 tbsp chopped fresh parsley
    4 spring onions (scallions), finely
        chopped (optional)
    50–75g/2–3oz/½–¾ cup dried
        breadcrumbs, preferably home-made
    sunflower oil, for frying
    salt, ground black pepper and
        cayenne pepper
    chopped spring onions (scallions),
        to garnish
    red onion marmalade, to serve

1 Put the crabmeat in a bowl and stir in the mayonnaise or tartar sauce, with the mustard and egg. Season with Tabasco, salt, pepper and cayenne.

2 Stir in the parsley, spring onions, if using, and 50g/2oz/½ cup of the breadcrumbs. The mixture should be just firm enough to hold together; depending on how much brown crab meat there is, you may need to add some more breadcrumbs.

3 Divide the mixture into eight portions, roll each into a ball and flatten slightly to make a thick flat disc. Spread out the crab cakes on a platter and put in the refrigerator for 30 minutes before frying.

4 Pour the oil into a shallow pan to a depth of about 5mm/¼in. Fry the crab cakes in two batches until golden brown all over. Drain on kitchen paper and keep hot. Serve with a spring onion garnish and red onion marmalade.

Energy 285kcal/1187kJ; Protein 23.9g; Carbohydrate 10.3g, of which sugars 0.9g; Fat 16.7g, of which saturates 2.4g; Cholesterol 134mg; Calcium 178mg; Fibre 0.8g; Sodium 768mg.

SARDINE FRITTATA

IT MAY SEEM ODD TO COOK SARDINES IN AN OMELETTE, BUT THEY ARE SURPRISINGLY DELICIOUS THIS WAY. FROZEN SARDINES ARE FINE FOR THIS DISH. SERVE THE FRITTATA WITH CRISP SAUTÉED POTATOES AND THINLY SLICED CUCUMBER CRESCENTS.

SERVES FOUR

INGREDIENTS

    4 fat sardines, cleaned, filleted and
      with heads removed, thawed
      if frozen
    juice of 1 lemon
    45ml/3 tbsp olive oil
    6 large (US extra large) eggs
    30ml/2 tbsp chopped fresh parsley
    30ml/2 tbsp chopped fresh chives
    1 garlic clove, chopped
    salt, ground black pepper
      and paprika

1 Open out the sardines and sprinkle the fish with lemon juice, a little salt and paprika. Heat 15ml/1 tbsp olive oil in a frying pan and fry the sardines for about 1–2 minutes on each side to seal them. Drain on kitchen paper, trim off the tails and set aside until required.

2 Separate the eggs. In a bowl, whisk the yolks lightly with the parsley, chives and a little salt and pepper. Beat the whites in a separate bowl with a pinch of salt until fairly stiff. Preheat the grill (broiler) to medium-high.

3 Heat the remaining olive oil in a large frying pan, add the garlic and cook over a low heat until just golden. Gently mix together the egg yolks and whites and ladle half the mixture into the pan. Cook gently until just beginning to set on the base, then lay the sardines on the frittata and sprinkle lightly with paprika. Pour over the remaining egg mixture and cook gently until the frittata has browned underneath and is beginning to set on the top.

4 Put the pan under the grill and cook until the top of the frittata is golden. Cut into wedges and serve immediately.

COOK'S TIP

It is important to use a frying pan with a handle that can safely be used under the grill (broiler). If your frying pan has a wooden handle, protect it with foil.

FISH PIE

FISH PIE CAN BE VARIED TO SUIT YOUR TASTE AND POCKET. THIS IS A SIMPLE VERSION, BUT YOU COULD ADD PRAWNS OR HARD-BOILED EGGS, OR MIX THE POTATO TOPPING WITH SPRING ONIONS.

SERVES FOUR

INGREDIENTS
450g/1lb cod or haddock fillets
225g/8oz smoked cod fillets
300ml/½ pint/1¼ cups milk
½ lemon, sliced
1 bay leaf
1 fresh thyme sprig
4–5 black peppercorns
50g/2oz/¼ cup butter
25g/1oz/¼ cup plain (all-purpose) flour
30ml/2 tbsp chopped fresh parsley
5ml/1 tsp anchovy essence (extract)
150g/5oz/2 cups shiitake or chestnut
   mushrooms, sliced
salt, ground black pepper and
   cayenne pepper
For the topping
450g/1lb potatoes, cooked and
   mashed with milk
50g/2oz/¼ cup butter
2 tomatoes, sliced
25g/1oz/¼ cup grated Cheddar
   cheese (optional)

3 Heat the remaining butter in a frying pan, add the sliced mushrooms and sauté until tender. Season and add to the flaked fish. Mix the sauce into the fish and stir gently to combine. Transfer the mixture to an ovenproof casserole.

4 Preheat the oven to 200°C/400°F/ Gas 6. Beat the mashed potato with the butter until very creamy. Season, then spread the topping evenly over the fish. Fork up the surface and arrange the sliced tomatoes around the edge. Sprinkle the exposed topping with the grated cheese, if using.

5 Bake for 20–25 minutes, until the topping is lightly browned.

VARIATION
Instead of using plain mashed potatoes for the topping, try a mixture of mashed potato and mashed swede (rutabaga) or sweet potato.

1 Put the fish, skin-side down, in a shallow pan. Add the milk, lemon slices, bay leaf, thyme and peppercorns. Bring to the boil, then lower the heat and poach gently for about 5 minutes, until just cooked. Strain off and reserve the milk. Remove the fish skin and flake the flesh, discarding any bones.

2 Melt half the butter in a small pan, stir in the flour and cook gently for 1 minute. Add the milk and boil, whisking, until smooth and creamy. Stir in the parsley and anchovy essence and season to taste.

Energy 458kcal/1921kJ; Protein 29.5g; Carbohydrate 32.8g, of which sugars 5.8g; Fat 25g, of which saturates 3.7g; Cholesterol 74mg; Calcium 216mg; Fibre 1g; Sodium 867mg.

SALMON AND PRAWN TART

THIS TART IS UNUSUAL BECAUSE IT IS MADE WITH RAW SALMON, WHICH MEANS THAT THE FISH STAYS MOIST. COOKING IT THIS WAY GIVES A LOVELY SUCCULENT RESULT. THIS VERSATILE DISH MAY BE SERVED HOT WITH VEGETABLES OR COOL WITH MIXED SALAD LEAVES AND TOMATO WEDGES.

SERVES SIX

INGREDIENTS
  350g/12oz shortcrust pastry, thawed
    if frozen
  225g/8oz salmon fillet, skinned
  225g/8oz/2 cups cooked peeled
    prawns (shrimp)
  2 eggs, plus 2 egg yolks
  150ml/¼ pint/⅔ cup
    whipping cream
  200ml/7fl oz/scant 1 cup milk
  15ml/1 tbsp chopped fresh dill
  salt, ground black pepper and paprika
  lime slices, tomato wedges and fresh
    dill sprigs, to garnish

VARIATION
For a more economical version of this
flan, omit the prawns (shrimp) and use
some extra salmon instead, or use a
mixture of salmon and white fish.

1 Roll out the pastry on a floured work
surface and use it to line a 20cm/8in
quiche dish or tin (pan). Prick the base
all over and mark the edges with the
tines of the fork. It need not be too
neat. Chill for about 30 minutes.
Meanwhile, preheat the oven to 180°C/
350°F/Gas 4. Bake the pastry case (pie
shell) for about 30 minutes, until golden
brown. Reduce the oven temperature to
160°C/325°F/Gas 3.

2 Cut the salmon into 2cm/¾in cubes.
Arrange the salmon and prawns evenly
in the pastry case. Dust with paprika.

3 In a bowl, beat together the eggs and
yolks, cream, milk and dill and season
to taste. Pour over the salmon and
prawns. Bake for about 30 minutes,
until the filling is just set. Serve hot or
at room temperature, garnished with
lime slices, tomato wedges and dill.

COCONUT BAKED SNAPPER

ADDING A COUPLE OF FRESH RED CHILLIES TO THE MARINADE GIVES THIS DISH A REALLY SPICY FLAVOUR. SERVE THE BAKED SNAPPER WITH PLAIN BOILED RICE.

SERVES FOUR

INGREDIENTS
  1 snapper, about 1kg/2¼lb, scaled
    and cleaned
  400ml/14fl oz/1⅔ cups coconut milk
  105ml/7 tbsp dry white wine
  juice of 1 lime
  45ml/3 tbsp light soy sauce
  1–2 fresh red chillies, seeded and
    thinly sliced (optional)
  60ml/4 tbsp chopped fresh parsley
  45ml/3 tbsp chopped fresh
    coriander (cilantro)
  salt and ground black pepper

COOK'S TIP
Any type of snapper or trout can be used
for this recipe. If you like, use one small
fish per person.

1 Lay the snapper in an ovenproof
shallow dish and season with a little salt
and plenty of pepper. Mix together the
coconut milk, wine, lime juice, soy
sauce and chillies, if using. Stir in the
herbs and pour over the fish. Cover with
clear film (plastic wrap) and marinate in
the refrigerator for about 4 hours,
turning the fish over halfway through.

2 Preheat the oven to 190°C/375°F/
Gas 5. Take the fish out of the marinade
and wrap loosely in foil, spooning over
the marinade before sealing the parcel.
Support the fish on a clean dish and
bake for 30–40 minutes, until the flesh
comes away easily from the bone.

FRIED PLAICE WITH TOMATO SAUCE

THIS SIMPLE DISH IS PERENNIALLY POPULAR WITH CHILDREN. IT WORKS EQUALLY WELL WITH LEMON SOLE OR DABS (THESE DO NOT NEED SKINNING), OR FILLETS OF HADDOCK AND WHITING.

SERVES FOUR

INGREDIENTS

25g/1oz/¼ cup plain (all-purpose) flour
2 eggs, beaten
75g/3oz/¾ cup dried breadcrumbs, preferably home-made
4 small plaice or flounder, skinned
15g/½oz/1 tbsp butter
15ml/1 tbsp sunflower oil
salt and ground black pepper
1 lemon, quartered, to serve
fresh basil leaves, to garnish
For the tomato sauce
30ml/2 tbsp olive oil
1 red onion, finely chopped
1 garlic clove, finely chopped
400g/14oz can chopped tomatoes
15ml/1 tbsp tomato purée (paste)
15ml/1 tbsp torn fresh basil leaves

1 First make the tomato sauce. Heat the olive oil in a large pan, add the finely chopped onion and garlic and cook gently for about 5 minutes, until softened and pale golden. Stir in the chopped tomatoes and tomato purée and simmer for 20–30 minutes, stirring occasionally. Season with salt and pepper and stir in the basil.

2 Spread out the flour in a shallow dish, pour the beaten eggs into another and spread out the breadcrumbs in a third. Season the fish with salt and pepper.

3 Hold a fish in your left hand and dip it first in flour, then in egg and finally, in the breadcrumbs, patting the crumbs on with your dry right hand.

4 Heat the butter and oil in a frying pan until foaming. Fry the fish one at a time in the hot fat for about 5 minutes on each side, until golden brown and cooked through, but still juicy in the middle. Drain on kitchen paper and keep hot while you fry the rest. Serve with lemon wedges and the tomato sauce, garnished with basil leaves.

Energy 333kcal/1390kJ; Protein 22.5g; Carbohydrate 14.2g, of which sugars 3.9g; Fat 21.1g, of which saturates 2.5g; Cholesterol 0mg; Calcium 90mg; Fibre 1.3g; Sodium 279mg.

COD CARAMBA

THIS COLOURFUL MEXICAN DISH, WITH ITS CONTRASTING CRUNCHY TOPPING AND TENDER FISH FILLING, CAN BE MADE WITH ANY ECONOMICAL WHITE FISH SUCH AS COLEY OR HADDOCK.

SERVES FOUR TO SIX

INGREDIENTS

450g/1lb Pacific cod fillets
225g/8oz smoked Pacific cod fillets
300ml/½ pint/1¼ cups fish stock
50g/2oz/¼ cup butter
1 onion, sliced
2 garlic cloves, crushed
1 green and 1 red (bell) pepper,
   seeded and diced
2 courgettes (zucchini), diced
115g/4oz/⅔ cup drained canned or
   thawed frozen corn kernels
2 tomatoes, peeled and chopped
juice of 1 lime
Tabasco sauce
salt, ground black pepper and
   cayenne pepper
For the topping
75g/3oz tortilla chips
50g/2oz/½ cup grated
   Cheddar cheese
coriander (cilantro) sprigs, to garnish
lime wedges, to serve

1 Lay the fish in a shallow pan and pour over the fish stock. Bring to the boil, lower the heat, cover and poach for about 8 minutes, until the flesh flakes easily when tested with the tip of a sharp knife. Leave to cool slightly, then remove the skin and separate the flesh into large flakes. Keep hot.

2 Melt the butter in a pan, add the onion and garlic and cook over a low heat until soft. Add the peppers, stir and cook for 2 minutes. Stir in the courgettes and cook for 3 minutes more, until all the vegetables are tender.

3 Stir in the corn and tomatoes, then add lime juice and Tabasco to taste. Season with salt, black pepper and cayenne. Cook for a few minutes to heat the corn and tomatoes, then stir in the fish and transfer to a dish that can safely be used under the grill (broiler).

4 Preheat the grill. Make the topping by crushing the tortilla chips, then mixing in the grated cheese. Add cayenne pepper to taste and sprinkle over the fish. Place the dish under the grill until the topping is crisp and brown. Garnish with coriander sprigs and lime wedges.

Energy 293kcal/1223kJ; Protein 26.6g; Carbohydrate 15.8g, of which sugars 7.5g; Fat 13.9g, of which saturates 6.9g; Cholesterol 78mg; Calcium 123mg; Fibre 3.2g; Sodium 927mg.

HERRINGS <u>IN</u> OATMEAL <u>WITH</u> BACON

THIS TRADITIONAL SCOTTISH DISH IS CHEAP AND NUTRITIOUS. FOR EASE OF EATING, BONE THE HERRINGS BEFORE COATING THEM IN THE OATMEAL. IF YOU DON'T LIKE HERRINGS, USE TROUT OR MACKEREL INSTEAD. FOR EXTRA COLOUR AND FLAVOUR, SERVE WITH GRILLED TOMATOES.

SERVES FOUR

INGREDIENTS
115–150g/4–5oz/1–1¼ cups
    medium oatmeal
10ml/2 tsp mustard powder
4 herrings, about 225g/8oz each,
    cleaned, boned, heads and
    tails removed
30ml/2 tbsp sunflower oil
8 rindless streaky (fatty) bacon
    rashers (strips)
salt and ground black pepper
lemon wedges, to serve

COOK'S TIPS
• Use tongs to turn the herrings so as
not to dislodge the oatmeal.
• Cook the herrings two at a time.
• Don't overcrowd the frying pan.

1 In a shallow dish, mix together the oatmeal and mustard powder with salt and pepper. Press the herrings into the mixture, one at a time, to coat them thickly on both sides. Shake off the excess oatmeal mixture and set the herrings aside.

2 Heat the oil in a large frying pan and fry the bacon until crisp. Drain on kitchen paper and keep hot.

3 Put the herrings into the pan and fry them for 3–4 minutes on each side, until crisp and golden brown. Serve the herrings with the streaky bacon rashers and lemon wedges.

RAY <u>WITH</u> BLACK BUTTER

RAY CAN BE QUITE INEXPENSIVE, AND THIS CLASSIC DISH IS PERFECT FOR A FAMILY SUPPER. SERVE IT WITH STEAMED LEEKS AND PLAIN BOILED POTATOES.

SERVES FOUR

INGREDIENTS
4 ray wings, about
    225g/8oz each
60ml/4 tbsp red wine vinegar
    or malt vinegar
30ml/2 tbsp drained capers in
    vinegar, chopped if large
30ml/2 tbsp chopped fresh parsley
150g/5oz/⅔ cup butter
salt and ground black pepper

COOK'S TIP
Despite the title of the recipe, the butter should be a rich golden brown. It should never be allowed to blacken, or it will taste unpleasantly bitter.

1 Put the ray wings in a large, shallow pan, cover with cold water and add a pinch of salt and 15ml/1 tbsp of the red wine or malt vinegar.

2 Bring to the boil, skim the surface, then lower the heat and simmer gently for about 10–12 minutes, until the ray flesh comes away from the bone easily. Carefully drain the ray and peel off the skin.

3 Transfer the ray to a warmed serving dish, season with salt and pepper and sprinkle over the capers and parsley. Keep hot.

4 In a small pan, heat the butter until it foams and turns a rich nutty brown. Pour it over the ray. Pour the remaining vinegar into the pan and boil until reduced by about two-thirds. Drizzle over the ray and serve.

Top: *Energy 700kcal/2917kJ; Protein 51.9g; Carbohydrate 20.9g, of which sugars 0g; Fat 46g, of which saturates 11.2g; Cholesterol 139mg; Calcium 153mg; Fibre 2g; Sodium 1050mg.*
Bottom: *Energy 246kcal/1029kJ; Protein 35.5g; Carbohydrate 0.5g, of which sugars 0.4g; Fat 11.2g, of which saturates 6.5g; Cholesterol 27mg; Calcium 125mg; Fibre 0.8g; Sodium 356mg.*

TROUT WITH TAMARIND AND CHILLI SAUCE

TROUT IS A VERY ECONOMICAL FISH, BUT CAN TASTE RATHER BLAND. THIS SPICY, THAI-INSPIRED SAUCE REALLY GIVES IT A ZING. IF YOU LIKE YOUR FOOD VERY SPICY, ADD AN EXTRA CHILLI.

SERVES FOUR

INGREDIENTS

    4 trout, about 350g/12oz
      each, cleaned
    6 spring onions (scallions), sliced
    60ml/4 tbsp soy sauce
    15ml/1 tbsp stir-fry oil
    30ml/2 tbsp chopped fresh
      coriander (cilantro)
For the sauce
    50g/2oz tamarind pulp
    105ml/7 tbsp boiling water
    2 shallots, coarsely chopped
    1 fresh red chilli, seeded and chopped
    1cm/½in piece fresh root ginger,
      peeled and chopped
    5ml/1 tsp soft brown sugar
    45ml/3 tbsp Thai fish sauce

1 Slash the trout diagonally four or five times on each side with a sharp knife and place in a shallow dish.

2 Fill the cavities with spring onions and douse each fish with soy sauce. Carefully turn the fish over to coat both sides with the sauce. Sprinkle on any remaining spring onions and set aside until required.

3 Make the sauce. Put the tamarind pulp in a small bowl and pour on the boiling water. Mash well with a fork until soft. Tip the mixture into a food processor or blender, then add the shallots, fresh chilli, ginger, sugar and fish sauce and process to a fairly coarse pulp.

4 Heat the stir-fry oil in a large frying pan or wok and fry the trout, one at a time if necessary, for about 5 minutes on each side, until the skin is crisp and browned and the flesh cooked. Put on warmed plates and spoon over some sauce. Sprinkle with the coriander and serve with the remaining sauce.

Energy 352kcal/1481kJ; Protein 55g; Carbohydrate 3.3g, of which sugars 2.8g; Fat 13.4g, of which saturates 2.8g; Cholesterol 224mg; Calcium 95mg; Fibre 0.4g; Sodium 721mg.

HOKI CURRY WITH HERBS

HOKI IS AN IDEAL FIRM-FLESHED FISH TO USE FOR THIS DELICIOUS CURRY, WHICH GAINS ITS RICH COLOUR FROM A MIXTURE OF FRESH HERBS; TRY OTHER EXOTICS, SUCH AS MAHI MAHI OR SWORDFISH, OR HUMBLER FISH, SUCH AS COLEY. SERVE IT WITH BASMATI OR THAI FRAGRANT RICE AND LIME WEDGES.

SERVES FOUR

INGREDIENTS

4 garlic cloves, coarsely chopped
5cm/2in piece fresh root ginger,
  peeled and coarsely chopped
2 fresh green chillies, seeded and
  coarsely chopped
grated rind and juice of 1 lime
5–10ml/1–2 tsp shrimp paste (optional)
5ml/1 tsp coriander seeds
5ml/1 tsp Chinese five-spice powder
75ml/5 tbsp sesame oil
2 red onions, finely chopped
900g/2lb hoki fillets, skinned
400ml/14fl oz/1⅔ cups coconut milk
45ml/3 tbsp Thai fish sauce
50g/2oz/1 cup fresh coriander
  (cilantro) leaves
50g/2oz/1 cup fresh mint leaves
50g/2oz/1 cup fresh basil leaves
6 spring onions (scallions), chopped
150ml/¼ pint/⅔ cup sunflower or
  groundnut (peanut) oil
sliced fresh green chilli and chopped
  fresh coriander (cilantro), to garnish
cooked basmati or Thai fragrant rice
  and lime wedges, to serve

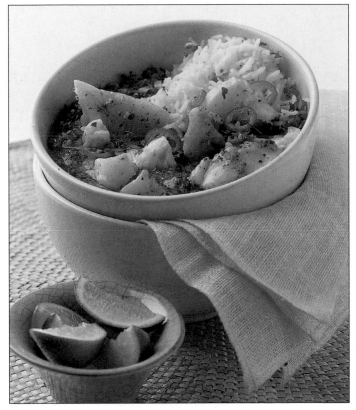

1 First make the curry paste. Combine the garlic, fresh root ginger, green chillies, the lime juice and shrimp paste, if using, in a food processor. Add the coriander seeds and five-spice powder, with half the sesame oil. Process to a fine paste, then set aside until required.

2 Heat a wok or large shallow pan and pour in the remaining sesame oil. When it is hot, stir-fry the red onions over a high heat for 2 minutes. Add the fish and stir-fry for 1–2 minutes to seal the fillets on all sides.

3 Lift out the red onions and fish and put them on a plate. Add the curry paste to the wok or pan and fry for 1 minute, stirring. Return the hoki fillets and red onions to the wok or pan, pour in the coconut milk and bring to the boil. Lower the heat, add the fish sauce and simmer for 5–7 minutes, until the fish is cooked through.

4 Meanwhile, process the herbs, spring onions, lime rind and oil in a food processor to a coarse paste. Stir into the fish curry. Garnish with chilli and coriander and serve with rice and lime wedges.

Energy 608kcal/2527kJ; Protein 41g; Carbohydrate 13.3g, of which sugars 9.5g; Fat 43.8g, of which saturates 5.9g; Cholesterol 0mg; Calcium 168mg; Fibre 1.3g; Sodium 313mg.

KEDGEREE

THIS CLASSIC DISH ORIGINATED IN INDIA. IT IS BEST MADE WITH BASMATI RICE, WHICH GOES WELL WITH THE MILD CURRY FLAVOUR, BUT OTHER LONG GRAIN RICE WILL DO. FOR A COLOURFUL GARNISH, ADD SOME FINELY SLICED RED ONION AND A LITTLE RED ONION MARMALADE.

SERVES FOUR

INGREDIENTS

450g/1lb undyed smoked
  haddock fillet
750ml/1¼ pints/3 cups milk
2 bay leaves
½ lemon, sliced
50g/2oz/¼ cup butter
1 onion, chopped
2.5ml/½ tsp ground turmeric
5ml/1 tsp mild Madras curry powder
2 green cardamom pods
350g/12oz/1¾ cups basmati or long
  grain rice, washed and drained
4 hard-boiled eggs,
  coarsely chopped
150ml/¼ pint/⅔ cup single (light)
  cream (optional)
30ml/2 tbsp chopped fresh parsley
salt and ground black pepper

1 Put the haddock in a shallow pan and add the milk, bay leaves and lemon slices. Poach gently for 8–10 minutes, until the haddock flakes easily when tested with the tip of a sharp knife. Strain the milk into a jug (pitcher), discarding the bay leaves and lemon slices. Remove the skin from the haddock and flake the flesh into large pieces. Keep hot until required.

2 Melt the butter in the pan, add the onion and cook over a low heat for about 3 minutes, until softened. Stir in the turmeric, the curry powder and cardamom pods and cook for 1 minute.

3 Add the rice, stirring to coat it well with the butter. Pour in the reserved milk, stir and bring to the boil. Lower the heat and simmer the rice for 10–12 minutes, until all the milk has been absorbed and the rice is tender. Season to taste, going easy on the salt.

4 Gently stir in the fish and hard-boiled eggs, with the cream, if using. Sprinkle with the parsley and serve.

VARIATION
Use smoked and poached fresh salmon for a delicious change from haddock.

Energy 320kcal/1336kJ; Protein 15.6g; Carbohydrate 46.6g, of which sugars 0g; Fat 7.6g, of which saturates 3.3g; Cholesterol 149mg; Calcium 39mg; Fibre 0g; Sodium 357mg.

GRILLED MACKEREL WITH SPICY DHAL

OILY FISH LIKE MACKEREL ARE CHEAP AND NUTRITIOUS. THEY ARE COMPLEMENTED BY A TART OR SOUR ACCOMPANIMENT, LIKE THESE TAMARIND-FLAVOURED LENTILS. SERVE WITH CHOPPED FRESH TOMATOES, ONION SALAD AND FLAT BREAD.

SERVES FOUR

INGREDIENTS
    250g/9oz/1 cup red lentils, or yellow
        split peas (soaked overnight)
    1 litre/1¾ pints/4 cups water
    30ml/2 tbsp sunflower oil
    2.5ml/½ tsp each mustard seeds,
        cumin seeds, fennel seeds, and
        fenugreek or cardamom seeds
    5ml/1 tsp ground turmeric
    3–4 dried red chillies, crumbled
    30ml/2 tbsp tamarind paste
    5ml/1 tsp soft brown sugar
    30ml/2 tbsp chopped fresh
        coriander (cilantro)
    4 mackerel or 8 large sardines
    salt and ground black pepper
    fresh red chilli slices and chopped
        coriander (cilantro), to garnish

1 Rinse the lentils or split peas, drain them thoroughly and put them in a pan. Pour in the water and bring to the boil. Lower the heat, partially cover the pan and simmer for 30–40 minutes, stirring occasionally, until the pulses are tender and soft.

2 Heat the oil in a wok or shallow pan. Add the mustard seeds, then cover and cook for a few seconds, until they pop. Remove the lid, add the rest of the seeds, with the turmeric and chillies and cook for a few more seconds.

3 Stir in the pulses, with salt to taste. Mix well; stir in the tamarind paste and sugar. Bring to the boil, then simmer for 10 minutes, until thick. Stir in the chopped fresh coriander.

4 Meanwhile, clean the fish, then heat a ridged griddle pan or the grill (broiler) until very hot. Make six diagonal slashes on either side of each fish and remove the heads if you like. Season inside and out, then grill (broil) for 5–7 minutes on each side, until the skin is crisp. Serve with the dhal, garnished with red chilli and chopped coriander.

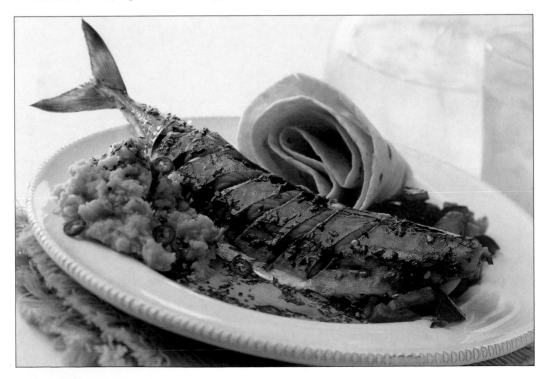

Energy 468kcal/1963kJ; Protein 33.6g; Carbohydrate 35.2g, of which sugars 1.5g; Fat 22.4g, of which saturates 4.1g; Cholesterol 54mg; Calcium 43mg; Fibre 3.1g; Sodium 86mg.

PASTA AND RICE DISHES

Fish and shellfish make perfect partners for pasta and rice, their lightness and freshness balancing the heaviness of the starch. From simple Pappardelle, Sardine and Fennel Bake to the ultra-luxurious Lobster Ravioli, there are pasta dishes to suit every occasion and palate. Risotto appears in two guises — dramatically coloured and flavoured with squid ink, and as a simple version that uses the ready-prepared shellfish that most supermarkets now stock.

SEAFOOD LASAGNE

THIS DISH CAN BE AS SIMPLE OR AS ELEGANT AS YOU LIKE. FOR A DINNER PARTY, DRESS IT UP WITH SCALLOPS, MUSSELS OR PRAWNS AND A REALLY GENEROUS PINCH OF SAFFRON IN THE SAUCE; FOR A FAMILY SUPPER, USE SIMPLE FISH, SUCH AS COD AND SMOKED HADDOCK. THE LASAGNE CAN BE PREPARED IN ADVANCE AND BAKED AT THE LAST MOMENT.

SERVES EIGHT

INGREDIENTS
    350g/12oz monkfish
    350g/12oz salmon fillet
    350g/12oz undyed smoked haddock
    1 litre/1¾ pints/4 cups milk
    500ml/17fl oz/generous 2 cups
      fish stock
    2 bay leaves or a good pinch of
      saffron threads
    1 small onion, peeled and halved
    75g/3oz/6 tbsp butter, plus extra
      for greasing
    45ml/3 tbsp plain (all-purpose) flour
    150g/5oz/2 cups mushrooms, sliced
    225–300g/8–11oz no-precook or
      fresh lasagne
    60ml/4 tbsp freshly grated
      Parmesan cheese
    salt, ground black pepper, grated
      nutmeg and paprika
    rocket (arugula) leaves, to garnish
For the tomato sauce
    30ml/2 tbsp olive oil
    1 red onion, finely chopped
    1 garlic clove, finely chopped
    400g/14oz can chopped tomatoes
    15ml/1 tbsp tomato purée (paste)
    15ml/1 tbsp torn fresh basil leaves

1 Make the tomato sauce. Heat the oil in a pan and cook the onion and garlic over a low heat for 5 minutes, until softened and golden. Stir in the tomatoes and tomato purée and simmer for 20–30 minutes, stirring occasionally. Season and stir in the basil.

2 Put all the fish in a shallow flameproof dish or pan with the milk, stock, bay leaves or saffron and onion. Bring to the boil over a medium heat; poach for 5 minutes, until almost cooked. Leave to cool.

3 When the fish is almost cold, strain it, reserving the liquid. Remove the skin and any bones and flake the flesh.

4 Preheat the oven to 180°C/350°F/ Gas 4. Melt the butter in a pan, stir in the flour; cook for 2 minutes, stirring. Gradually add the poaching liquid and bring to the boil, stirring. Add the mushrooms, cook for 2–3 minutes; season with salt, pepper and nutmeg.

5 Lightly grease a shallow ovenproof dish. Spoon a thin layer of the mushroom sauce over the base of the dish and spread it with a spatula. Stir the fish into the remaining mushroom sauce in the pan.

6 Make a layer of lasagne, then a layer of fish and sauce. Add another layer of lasagne, then spread over all the tomato sauce. Continue to layer the lasagne and fish, finishing with a layer of fish.

7 Sprinkle over the grated Parmesan cheese. Bake for 30–45 minutes, until bubbling and golden. Before serving, sprinkle with paprika and garnish with rocket leaves.

COOK'S TIP
It is preferable to use fresh lasagne, if available. Cook the sheets in a large pan of lightly salted boiling water for 3 minutes. Do not overcrowd the pan, or the sheets will stick together.

Energy 411kcal/1724kJ; Protein 32.2g; Carbohydrate 29.8g, of which sugars 3.6g; Fat 18.9g, of which saturates 7.8g; Cholesterol 71mg; Calcium 143mg; Fibre 1.9g; Sodium 525mg.

SEAFOOD SPAGHETTI PARCELS

IN THIS RECIPE, THE COOKING IS FINISHED IN A PAPER PARCEL. WHEN THE PARCEL IS OPENED, THE MOST WONDERFUL AROMA WAFTS OUT. TO SERVE AS AN APPETIZER, BAKE IN TWO LARGER PARCELS.

SERVES FOUR AS A MAIN COURSE,
SIX AS AN APPETIZER

INGREDIENTS
   500g/1¼lb fresh mussels, scrubbed
    and bearded
   500g/1¼lb small clams, scrubbed
   105ml/7 tbsp dry white wine
   60ml/4 tbsp olive oil
   2 fat garlic cloves, chopped
   2 dried red chillies, crumbled
   200g/7oz squid, cut into rings
   200g/7oz raw peeled prawns (shrimp)
   400g/14oz dried spaghetti
   30ml/2 tbsp chopped fresh parsley
   5ml/1 tsp chopped fresh oregano or
    2.5ml/½ tsp dried
   salt and ground black pepper
For the tomato sauce
   30ml/2 tbsp olive oil
   1 red onion, finely chopped
   1 garlic clove, finely chopped
   400g/14oz can chopped tomatoes
   15ml/1 tbsp tomato purée (paste)
   15ml/1 tbsp torn fresh basil leaves

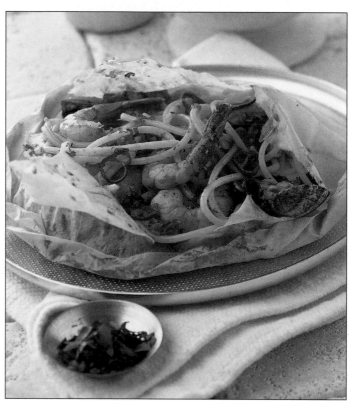

1 Make the tomato sauce. Heat the oil in a pan and cook the onion and garlic over a low heat for 5 minutes. Stir in the tomatoes and tomato purée and simmer for 20–30 minutes, stirring occasionally. Season and add the basil.

2 Put the mussels, clams and wine in a large pan and bring to the boil. Put on the lid and shake the pan until all the shells have opened. Discard any that remain closed. Remove most of the mussels and clams from the shells, leaving about a dozen of each in the shell. Strain the juices and set aside.

3 Heat the olive oil in a frying pan, add the garlic and cook until lightly coloured. Add the chillies, then add the squid and prawns and sauté for 2–3 minutes, until the squid is opaque and the prawns have turned pink. Add the shellfish and their reserved juices, then stir in the tomato sauce. Set aside.

4 Preheat the oven to 240°C/475°F/ Gas 9 or the grill (broiler) to hot. Cook the spaghetti in a pan of lightly salted, boiling water for about 12 minutes, or until it is just tender. Drain very thoroughly, then return to the clean pan and stir in the shellfish sauce, tossing to coat all the strands of spaghetti. Stir in the parsley and oregano, with some seasoning.

5 Cut out four 25cm/10in square pieces of greaseproof (waxed) paper. Put a quarter of the spaghetti mixture into the middle of one piece and fold up the edges, pleating them to make a secure bag. Seal the sides first, then blow gently into the top to fill the bag with air. Fold over the top to seal. Make another three parcels with the rest of the spaghetti mixture.

6 Place the parcels on a baking sheet and cook in the hot oven or under the grill until the paper is browned and slightly charred at the edges. Transfer the parcels to serving plates and open them at the table so that you can enjoy the wonderful aromas.

Energy 681kcal/2875kJ; Protein 44.4g; Carbohydrate 80.5g, of which sugars 7.6g; Fat 20.6g, of which saturates 3g; Cholesterol 259mg; Calcium 201mg; Fibre 3.9g; Sodium 881mg.

PAPPARDELLE, SARDINE AND FENNEL BAKE

PAPPARDELLE ARE WIDE, FLAT NOODLES. THEY ARE PERFECT FOR THIS SICILIAN RECIPE. IF YOU CAN'T FIND THEM, ANY WIDE PASTA, SUCH AS MACCHERONCINI OR BUCATINI, WILL DO INSTEAD. THE DISH IS ALSO DELICIOUS MADE WITH FRESH ANCHOVIES.

SERVES SIX

INGREDIENTS

2 fennel bulbs, trimmed
large pinch of saffron threads
12 sardines, backbones and
   heads removed
60ml/4 tbsp olive oil
2 shallots, finely chopped
2 garlic cloves, finely chopped
2 fresh red chillies, seeded and
   finely chopped
4 drained canned anchovy fillets, or
   8–12 pitted black olives, chopped
30ml/2 tbsp capers
75g/3oz/¾ cup pine nuts
450g/1lb pappardelle
butter, for greasing
30ml/2 tbsp grated Pecorino cheese
salt and ground black pepper

1 Preheat the oven to 200°C/400°F/ Gas 6. Cut the fennel bulbs in half and cook them in a pan of lightly salted boiling water with the saffron threads for about 10 minutes, until tender. Drain, reserving the cooking liquid, and cut into small dice. Then finely chop the sardines, season with salt and ground black pepper and set aside until required.

2 Heat the olive oil in a pan, add the shallots and garlic and cook until lightly coloured. Add the chillies and sardines and cook for 3 minutes. Stir in the fennel and cook gently for 3 minutes. If the mixture seems dry, add a little of the reserved fennel water.

3 Add the anchovies or olives and cook for 1 minute; stir in the capers and pine nuts, and season. Simmer for 3 minutes more, then turn off the heat.

4 Meanwhile, pour the reserved fennel liquid into a pan and top it up with enough water to cook the pasta. Stir in a little salt, bring to the boil and add the pappardelle. Cook dried pasta for about 12 minutes; fresh pasta until it rises to the surface of the water. When the pasta is just tender, drain it.

5 Grease a shallow ovenproof dish and put in a layer of pasta, then make a layer of the sardine mixture. Continue until all the pasta and sardine mixture have been used, finishing with the fish. Sprinkle over the Pecorino; bake for 15 minutes, until bubbling and golden.

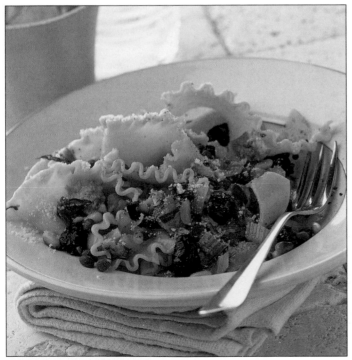

Energy 597kcal/2512kJ; Protein 41.3g; Carbohydrate 57.3g, of which sugars 4.1g; Fat 24.2g, of which saturates 5.4g; Cholesterol 6mg; Calcium 214mg; Fibre 4g; Sodium 303mg.

LOBSTER RAVIOLI

IT IS ESSENTIAL TO USE HOME-MADE PASTA TO OBTAIN THE DELICACY AND THINNESS THAT THIS SUPERB FILLING DESERVES. BEFORE YOU START THE RECIPE, MAKE A WELL-FLAVOURED FISH STOCK, INCLUDING THE LOBSTER SHELL AND HEAD.

SERVES SIX AS AN APPETIZER,
FOUR AS A MAIN COURSE

INGREDIENTS
    1 lobster, about 450g/1lb, cooked
    and taken out of the shell
    2 soft white bread slices, about
    50g/2oz, crusts removed
    200ml/7fl oz/scant 1 cup fish stock,
    made with the lobster shell
    1 egg
    250ml/8fl oz/1 cup double
    (heavy) cream
    15ml/1 tbsp chopped fresh chives,
    plus extra to garnish
    15ml/1 tbsp finely chopped fresh chervil
    salt and ground white pepper
    fresh chives, to garnish
For the pasta dough
    225g/8oz/2 cups strong plain (all-
    purpose) flour
    2 eggs, plus 2 egg yolks
For the mushroom sauce
    a large pinch of saffron threads
    25g/1oz/2 tbsp butter
    2 shallots, finely chopped
    200g/7oz/3 cups button (white)
    mushrooms, finely chopped
    juice of ½ lemon
    200ml/7fl oz/scant 1 cup double
    (heavy) cream

1 Make the pasta dough. Sift the flour with a pinch of salt. Put into a food processor with the eggs and extra yolks; process until the mixture resembles coarse breadcrumbs. Turn out on to a floured surface; knead to a smooth dough. Wrap in clear film (plastic wrap) and rest in the refrigerator for 1 hour.

2 Meanwhile, make the lobster filling. Cut the lobster meat into large chunks and place in a bowl. Tear the white bread into small pieces and soak them in 45ml/3 tbsp of the fish stock. Place in a food processor with half the egg and 30–45ml/2–3 tbsp of the double cream and process until smooth. Stir the mixture into the lobster meat, then add the chives and chervil and season to taste with salt and white pepper.

3 Roll the ravioli dough to a thickness of 3mm/⅛in, preferably using a pasta machine. The process can be done by hand with a rolling pin but is quite hard work. Divide the dough into four rectangles and dust each rectangle lightly with flour.

4 Spoon six equal heaps of filling on to one sheet of pasta, leaving about 3cm/1¼in between each pile of filling. Lightly beat the remaining egg with a tablespoon of water and brush it over the pasta between the piles of filling. Cover with a second sheet of pasta. Repeat with the other two sheets of pasta and remaining filling.

5 Using your fingertips, press the top layer of dough down well between the piles of filling, making sure each is well sealed. Cut between the heaps with a 7.5cm/3in fluted pastry cutter or a pasta wheel to make twelve ravioli.

6 Place the ravioli in a single layer on a baking sheet, cover with clear film or a damp cloth, and put in the refrigerator while you make the sauces.

7 Make the mushroom sauce. Soak the saffron in 15ml/1 tbsp warm water. Melt the butter in a pan and cook the shallots over a low heat until they are soft but not coloured.

8 Add the chopped mushrooms and lemon juice and continue to cook over a low heat until almost all the liquid has evaporated. Stir in the saffron, with its soaking water, and the cream, then cook gently, stirring occasionally, until the sauce has thickened. Keep warm while you cook the ravioli.

Energy 652kcal/2722kJ; Protein 23g; Carbohydrate 52.2g, of which sugars 3.1g; Fat 40.5g, of which saturates 22.2g; Cholesterol 361mg; Calcium 186mg; Fibre 2.9g; Sodium 298mg.

9 In another pan, bring the remaining fish stock to the boil, stir in the rest of the cream and bubble to make a slightly thickened sauce. Season to taste and keep warm. Bring a large pan of lightly salted water to a rolling boil. Gently drop in the ravioli (left) and cook for 3–4 minutes, until the pasta is just tender.

10 Place two ravioli (three for a main course) on to the centre of individual warmed plates, spoon over a little of the mushroom sauce and pour a ribbon of fish sauce around the edge. Serve immediately, garnished with chopped and whole fresh chives.

LINGUINE ALLE VONGOLE

USE THE SMALLEST CLAMS YOU CAN FIND FOR THIS RECIPE. YOU WILL HAVE GREAT FUN SUCKING
THEM OUT OF THEIR SHELLS. IF YOU CAN'T FIND LINGUINE, USE THIN SPAGHETTI.

SERVES FOUR AS A MAIN COURSE,
SIX AS AN APPETIZER

INGREDIENTS
  675g/1½lb small clams
  45ml/3 tbsp olive oil
  2 fat garlic cloves, finely chopped
  15ml/1 tbsp anchovy paste, or
    4 drained canned anchovy fillets,
    finely chopped
  400g/14oz can chopped tomatoes
  30ml/2 tbsp finely chopped fresh
    flat leaf parsley
  450g/1lb linguine
  salt and ground black pepper

1 Wash and scrub the clams, then put them in a large pan. Cover the pan and place it over a high heat for 3–4 minutes, shaking the pan occasionally, until all the clams have opened. Discard any that remain closed. Strain the clams, reserving the juices. Shell the clams, if you like.

2 Heat the oil in a pan, add the garlic and cook gently for 2 minutes, until lightly coloured. Stir in the anchovy paste or chopped fillets, then the tomatoes and the reserved clam juices. Add the parsley, bring to the boil, then lower the heat and simmer, uncovered, for 20 minutes, until the sauce is well reduced and full of flavour. Season to taste.

3 Cook the linguine in plenty of lightly salted, boiling water until just tender. Drain the pasta, then tip it back into the pan. Add the clams to the tomato and anchovy sauce, mix together well, then pour the sauce over the linguine and toss until the pasta is well coated. Serve immediately.

BLACK FETTUCINE WITH SEAFOOD

THE DRAMATIC BLACK PASTA MAKES A WONDERFUL CONTRASTING BACKGROUND FOR THE PINK, WHITE
AND GOLDEN SHELLFISH. USE WHATEVER SHELLFISH ARE AVAILABLE; TINY CUTTLEFISH, SMALL SQUID,
CLAMS OR RAZORSHELL CLAMS ARE DELICIOUS IN THIS DISH.

SERVES FOUR AS A MAIN COURSE,
SIX AS AN APPETIZER

INGREDIENTS
  800g/1¾lb fresh mussels, scrubbed
    and bearded
  45ml/3 tbsp olive oil
  105ml/7 tbsp dry white wine
  2 fat garlic cloves, chopped
  150g/5oz queen scallops
  200g/7oz raw prawns (shrimp),
    partially shelled
  400g/14oz black fettucine,
    preferably fresh
  salt and ground black pepper
  30ml/2 tbsp chopped fresh
    flat leaf parsley, to garnish

COOK'S TIP
If you can't find black pasta, use green spinach tagliatelle or fettucine instead.

1 Put the mussels in a pan with 15ml/ 1 tbsp of the oil. Add the wine, set over a high heat, cover and steam for about 3 minutes, shaking the pan occasionally, until all the mussels have opened. Discard any shellfish that remain closed. Leave to cool in the pan, then lift out and shell some of the mussels. Strain the cooking liquid and set it aside until required.

2 Heat the remaining oil in a large, deep frying pan. Add the chopped garlic and cook for 1 minute, without letting it brown. Add the queen scallops and cook for about 1–2 minutes, tossing them about until they turn opaque. Add the prawns and cook for 1 minute more, then remove the shellfish with a slotted spoon to a bowl and set it aside. Keep the frying pan handy; it will be needed for the sauce.

3 Meanwhile, cook the pasta in a large pan of lightly salted, boiling water according to the packet instructions until just tender; fresh pasta will take only about 2 minutes. Drain.

4 Pour the reserved mussel liquid into the frying pan and bring it to the boil. Lower the heat and season. Return the shellfish to the pan, heat for a few seconds, then stir in the pasta. Toss well, sprinkle the parsley on top and serve.

Top: Energy 579kcal/2441kJ; Protein 27.1g; Carbohydrate 79.2g, of which sugars 6.7g; Fat 19.3g, of which saturates 2.8g; Cholesterol 59mg; Calcium 122mg; Fibre 4.5g; Sodium 1066mg.
Bottom: Energy 552kcal/2337kJ; Protein 40g; Carbohydrate 75.5g, of which sugars 3.4g; Fat 12.1g, of which saturates 1.8g; Cholesterol 139mg; Calcium 201mg; Fibre 3.1g; Sodium 293mg.

STIR-FRIED NOODLES IN SHELLFISH SAUCE

THE CHINESE WOULD HAVE US BELIEVE THAT IT WAS THEY WHO INVENTED PASTA, SO IT SEEMS APPROPRIATE TO INCLUDE A CHINESE-STYLE PASTA DISH.

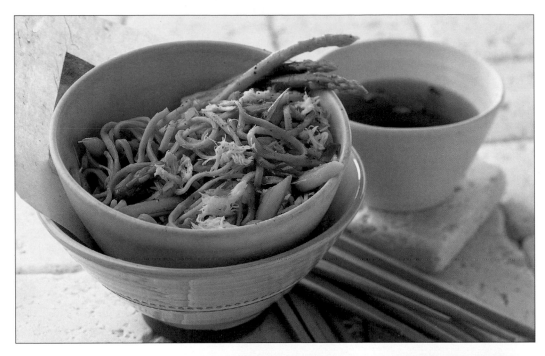

SERVES SIX TO EIGHT AS AN APPETIZER
FOUR AS A MAIN COURSE

INGREDIENTS
225g/8oz Chinese egg noodles
8 spring onions (scallions), trimmed
8 asparagus spears, plus extra
    steamed asparagus spears, to
    serve (optional)
30ml/2 tbsp stir-fry oil
5cm/2in piece fresh root ginger,
    peeled and cut into very fine batons
3 garlic cloves, chopped
60ml/4 tbsp oyster sauce
450g/1lb cooked crab meat (all
    white, or two-thirds white and
    one-third brown)
30ml/2 tbsp rice wine vinegar
15–30ml/1–2 tbsp light
    soy sauce

1 Put the noodles in a large pan or wok, cover with lightly salted, boiling water, place a lid on top and leave for 3–4 minutes, or for the time suggested on the packet. Drain and set aside.

2 Cut off the green spring onion tops and slice them thinly. Set aside. Cut the white parts into 2cm/¾in lengths and quarter them lengthways. Cut the asparagus spears on the diagonal into 2cm/¾in pieces.

3 Heat the stir-fry oil in a pan or wok until very hot, then add the ginger, garlic and white spring onion batons. Stir-fry over a high heat for 1 minute. Add the oyster sauce, crab meat, rice wine vinegar and soy sauce to taste. Stir-fry for about 2 minutes, until the crab and sauce are hot. Add the noodles and toss until heated through. At the last moment, toss in the spring onion tops and serve with a few extra asparagus spears, if you like.

Energy 385kcal/1622kJ; Protein 28.5g; Carbohydrate 45.9g, of which sugars 6.4g; Fat 10.9g, of which saturates 2.2g; Cholesterol 98mg; Calcium 167mg; Fibre 2.4g; Sodium 1233mg.

SHELLFISH PAELLA

THERE ARE AS MANY VERSIONS OF PAELLA AS THERE ARE REGIONS OF SPAIN. THOSE FROM NEAR THE COAST CONTAIN A LOT OF SHELLFISH, WHILE INLAND VERSIONS ADD CHICKEN OR PORK. HERE THE ONLY MEAT IS THE CHORIZO, ESSENTIAL FOR AN AUTHENTIC FLAVOUR.

SERVES FOUR

INGREDIENTS
- 45ml/3 tbsp olive oil
- 1 Spanish onion, chopped
- 2 fat garlic cloves, chopped
- 150g/5oz chorizo sausage, sliced
- 300g/11oz small squid, cleaned
- 1 red (bell) pepper, cut into strips
- 4 tomatoes, peeled, seeded and diced, or 200g/7oz can tomatoes
- 500ml/17fl oz/generous 2 cups chicken stock
- 105ml/7 tbsp dry white wine
- 200g/7oz/1 cup short grain Spanish rice or risotto rice
- a large pinch of saffron threads
- 150g/5oz/1 cup fresh or frozen peas
- 12 large cooked prawns (shrimp), in the shell, or 8 langoustines
- 450g/1lb fresh mussels, scrubbed
- 450g/1lb medium clams, scrubbed
- salt and ground black pepper

1 Heat the olive oil in a paella pan or wok, add the onion and garlic and cook until translucent. Add the chorizo and cook until lightly golden.

2 If the squid are very small, leave them whole, otherwise cut the bodies into rings and the tentacles into pieces. Add the squid to the pan and sauté over a high heat for 2 minutes.

3 Stir in the pepper strips and tomatoes and simmer gently for 5 minutes, until the pepper strips are tender. Pour in the stock and wine, stir well and bring to the boil.

4 Stir in the rice and saffron threads and season well with salt and pepper. Spread the contents of the pan evenly. Bring the liquid back to the boil, then lower the heat and simmer gently for about 10 minutes.

5 Add the peas, prawns or langoustines, mussels and clams, stirring them gently into the rice.

6 Cook the paella gently for a further 15–20 minutes, until the rice is tender and all the mussels and clams have opened. If any remain closed, discard them. If the paella seems dry, add a little more hot chicken stock. Gently stir everything together and serve piping hot.

Energy 585kcal/2445kJ; Protein 36.1g; Carbohydrate 60.9g, of which sugars 10.1g; Fat 20.4g, of which saturates 5.6g; Cholesterol 268mg; Calcium 132mg; Fibre 4.2g; Sodium 1055mg.

RISOTTO NERO

IF YOU HAPPEN TO HAVE SOME SQUID OR CUTTLEFISH COMPLETE WITH INK SACS, RETRIEVE THE INK YOURSELF TO MAKE THIS BLACK RISOTTO. OTHERWISE, YOU CAN BUY SACHETS OF SQUID OR CUTTLEFISH INK AT FISHMONGERS AND SOME DELICATESSENS.

SERVES FOUR

INGREDIENTS

450g/1lb small cuttlefish or squid,
   with their ink, or 350g/12oz
   cuttlefish and 4 sachets cuttlefish
   or squid ink
1.2 litres/2 pints/5 cups light
   fish stock
50g/2oz/¼ cup butter
30ml/2 tbsp olive oil
3 shallots, finely chopped
350g/12oz/1¾ cups risotto rice
105ml/7 tbsp dry white wine
30ml/2 tbsp chopped fresh
   flat leaf parsley
salt and ground black pepper

1 If the cuttlefish or squid contain ink, squeeze it out into a small bowl and set it aside. Cut the bodies into thin rings and chop the tentacles. Set aside.

2 Add the ink to the fish stock. Bring to the boil and lower the heat so that the liquid is at a gentle simmer. Heat half the butter and all the olive oil in a large pan. Add the chopped shallots and cook for about 3 minutes, until they are soft and translucent.

COOK'S TIP
If you prefer, make the risotto without the cuttlefish or squid and serve it with other fish or shellfish.

3 Add the cuttlefish or squid and cook very gently for 5–7 minutes, until tender. Add the rice and stir well to coat all the grains with fat. Pour in the wine and simmer until most of it has been absorbed by the rice. Add a ladleful of the hot stock and cook, stirring constantly, until it has been absorbed.

4 Continue cooking and stirring for 20–25 minutes, adding the remaining stock a ladleful at a time after the previous quantity has been absorbed.

5 Season to taste, then stir in the parsley. Beat in the remaining butter to make the risotto shiny. Spoon the risotto into four warmed dishes and serve.

Energy 571kcal/2382kJ; Protein 24.1g; Carbohydrate 72.6g, of which sugars 1.1g; Fat 18.2g, of which saturates 7.8g; Cholesterol 280mg; Calcium 40mg; Fibre 0.2g; Sodium 201mg.

SHELLFISH RISOTTO

MOST SUPERMARKETS NOW STOCK PACKS OF READY-PREPARED MIXED SHELLFISH, SUCH AS PRAWNS, SQUID AND MUSSELS, WHICH ARE IDEAL FOR MAKING THIS QUICK AND EASY RISOTTO.

SERVES FOUR

INGREDIENTS

1 litre/1¾ pints/4 cups fish or
  shellfish stock
50g/2oz/¼ cup butter
2 shallots, chopped
2 garlic cloves, chopped
350g/12oz/1¾ cups risotto rice
150ml/¼ pint/⅔ cup dry white wine
2.5ml/½ tsp powdered saffron, or a
  pinch of saffron threads
400g/14oz mixed prepared shellfish
30ml/2 tbsp freshly grated
  Parmesan cheese
30ml/2 tbsp chopped fresh
  flat leaf parsley, to garnish
salt and ground black pepper

1 Pour the fish or shellfish stock into a large pan. Bring it to the boil, then reduce the heat and keep it at a gentle simmer. The water needs to be hot when it is added to the rice.

2 Melt the butter in a heavy pan, add the shallots and garlic and cook over a low heat until soft but not coloured. Add the rice, stir well to coat the grains with butter, then pour in the wine. Cook over a medium heat, stirring occasionally, until all the wine has been absorbed by the rice.

COOK'S TIP
It is essential to use risotto rice for this dish. You can buy arborio or carnaroli risotto rice in an Italian delicatessen or a large supermarket.

3 Add a ladleful of hot stock and the saffron and cook, stirring constantly, until the liquid has been absorbed. Add the shellfish and stir well. Continue to add stock a ladleful at a time, waiting until each quantity has been absorbed before adding more. Stir the mixture for about 20 minutes, until the rice is swollen and creamy, but still with a little bite in the middle.

VARIATION
Use peeled prawns (shrimp), or cubes of fish, such as cod or salmon, in place of the mixed prepared shellfish.

4 Vigorously mix in the freshly grated Parmesan cheese and season to taste, then sprinkle over the chopped parsley and serve immediately.

Energy 404kcal/1693kJ; Protein 28.1g; Carbohydrate 56.3g, of which sugars 1.1g; Fat 3.9g, of which saturates 1.9g; Cholesterol 228mg; Calcium 200mg; Fibre 0.2g; Sodium 301mg.

LIGHT AND HEALTHY DISHES

What could be healthier than a meal based on simply cooked fish and shellfish?

We should all include fish in our diet at least twice a week, particularly the oily

fish that are so beneficial to health. Here are vibrant, attractive dishes certain to

inspire, such as Roast Cod with Pancetta and Beans, Moroccan Spiced Mackerel,

and Hoki Stir-Fry. All are quick to prepare and so full of fresh, natural

flavours that healthy eating becomes pure pleasure.

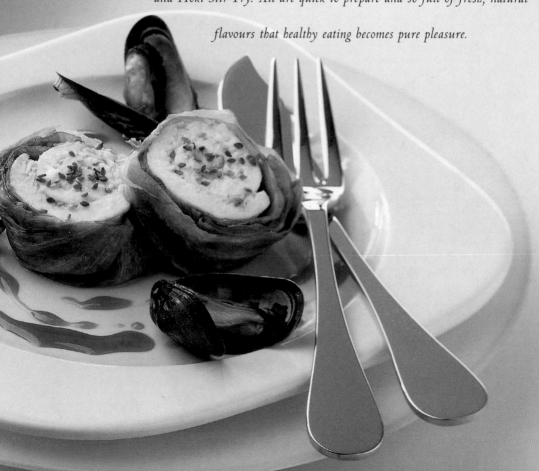

STEAMED LETTUCE-WRAPPED SOLE

IF YOU CAN AFFORD IT, USE DOVER SOLE FILLETS FOR THIS RECIPE; IF NOT, LEMON SOLE, TROUT, PLAICE, FLOUNDER AND BRILL ARE ALL EXCELLENT COOKED THIS WAY.

SERVES FOUR

INGREDIENTS

2 large sole fillets, skinned
15ml/1 tbsp sesame seeds
15ml/1 tbsp sunflower or
    groundnut (peanut) oil
10ml/2 tsp sesame oil
2.5cm/1in piece fresh root ginger,
    peeled and grated
3 garlic cloves, finely chopped
15ml/1 tbsp soy sauce or Thai
    fish sauce
juice of 1 lemon
2 spring onions (scallions), thinly sliced
8 large soft lettuce leaves
12 large fresh mussels, scrubbed
    and bearded

1 Cut the sole fillets in half lengthways. Season; set aside. Prepare a steamer.

2 Heat a heavy frying pan until hot. Toast the sesame seeds lightly but do not allow them to burn. Set aside in a bowl until required.

3 Heat the oils in the frying pan over a medium heat. Add the ginger and garlic and cook until lightly coloured; stir in the soy sauce or fish sauce, lemon juice and spring onions. Remove from the heat; stir in the toasted sesame seeds.

4 Lay the pieces of fish on baking parchment, skinned-side up; spread each evenly with the ginger mixture. Roll up each piece, starting at the tail end. Place on a baking sheet.

5 Plunge the lettuce leaves into the boiling water you have prepared for the steamer and immediately lift them out with tongs or a slotted spoon. Lay them out flat on kitchen paper and gently pat them dry. Wrap each sole parcel in two lettuce leaves, making sure that the filling is well covered to keep it in place.

6 Arrange the fish parcels in a steamer basket, cover and steam over simmering water for 8 minutes. Add the mussels and steam for 2–4 minutes, until opened. Discard any that remain closed. Put the parcels on individual warmed plates, halve and garnish with mussels. Serve immediately.

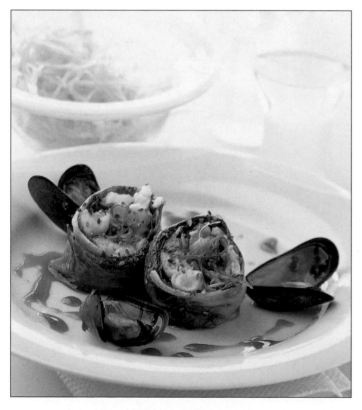

Energy 118kcal/492kJ; Protein 15.3g; Carbohydrate 0.9g, of which sugars 0.9g; Fat 5.9g, of which saturates 0.7g; Cholesterol 41mg; Calcium 46mg; Fibre 0.3g; Sodium 359mg.

SMOKED HADDOCK <u>WITH</u> MUSTARD CABBAGE

*THIS SIMPLE DISH TAKES LESS THAN TWENTY MINUTES TO MAKE AND IS QUITE DELICIOUS. SERVE IT
WITH NEW POTATOES.*

2 Meanwhile put the haddock in a large
shallow pan with the milk, onion and
bay leaves. Add the lemon slices
and peppercorns. Bring to simmering
point, cover and poach until the fish
flakes easily when tested with the tip
of a sharp knife. Depending on the
thickness of the fish, this takes
8–10 minutes. Remove the pan from
the heat. Preheat the grill (broiler).

3 Cut the tomatoes in half horizontally,
season them with salt and pepper and
grill (broil) until lightly browned. Drain
the cabbage, refresh under cold water
and drain again.

4 Melt the butter in a shallow pan or
wok, add the cabbage and toss over the
heat for 2 minutes. Mix in the mustard
and season to taste, then tip the
cabbage into a warmed serving dish.

5 Drain the haddock. Skin and cut the
fish into four pieces. Place on top of
the cabbage with some onion rings
and grilled tomato halves. Pour on the
lemon juice, then sprinkle with chopped
parsley and serve.

SERVES FOUR

INGREDIENTS

  1 Savoy or pointu cabbage
  675g/1½lb undyed smoked
    haddock fillet
  300ml/½ pint/1¼ cups milk
  ½ onion, sliced into rings
  2 bay leaves
  ½ lemon, sliced
  4 white peppercorns
  4 ripe tomatoes
  50g/2oz/¼ cup butter
  30ml/2 tbsp wholegrain mustard
  juice of 1 lemon
  salt and ground black pepper
  30ml/2 tbsp chopped fresh parsley,
    to garnish

1 Cut the cabbage in half, remove the
central core and thick ribs, then shred
the cabbage. Cook in a pan of lightly
salted, boiling water, or steam over
boiling water for about 10 minutes, until
just tender. Leave in the pan or steamer
until required.

Energy 319kcal/1340kJ; Protein 36.1g; Carbohydrate 14.2g, of which sugars 13.7g; Fat 13.1g, of which saturates 7.3g; Cholesterol 90mg; Calcium 146mg; Fibre 4.2g; Sodium 1512mg.

BAKED SEA BASS WITH FENNEL

SEA BASS HAS A WONDERFUL FLAVOUR, BUT CHEAPER ALTERNATIVES, SUCH AS SNAPPER, BREAM OR PORGY, CAN BE USED. SERVE WITH CRISPLY COOKED GREEN BEANS TOSSED IN OLIVE OIL AND GARLIC.

SERVES FOUR

INGREDIENTS
4 fennel bulbs, trimmed
4 tomatoes, peeled and diced
8 drained canned anchovy fillets,
  halved lengthways
a large pinch of saffron threads,
  soaked in 30ml/2 tbsp hot water
150ml/¼ pint/⅔ cup chicken or
  fish stock
2 red or yellow (bell) peppers, seeded
  and each cut into 12 strips
4 garlic cloves, chopped
15ml/1 tbsp chopped fresh marjoram
45ml/3 tbsp olive oil
1 sea bass, about 1.75kg/4–4½lb,
  scaled and cleaned
salt and ground black pepper
chopped parsley, to garnish

1 Preheat the oven to 200°C/400°F/ Gas 6. Quarter the fennel bulbs lengthways. Cook in lightly salted boiling water for 5 minutes, until barely tender. Drain and arrange in a shallow ovenproof dish. Season with pepper; set aside.

2 Spoon the diced tomatoes and anchovy strips on top of the fennel. Stir the saffron and its soaking water into the stock and pour the mixture over the tomatoes. Lay the strips of pepper alongside the fennel and sprinkle with the garlic and marjoram. Drizzle 30ml/ 2 tbsp of the olive oil over the peppers and season with salt and pepper.

VARIATION
If you like, use large pieces of thick-cut halibut or turbot for this dish.

3 Bake the vegetables for 15 minutes. Season the prepared sea bass inside and out and lay it on top of the fennel and pepper mixture. Drizzle the remaining olive oil over the fish and bake for 30–40 minutes more, until the sea bass flesh comes away easily from the bone when tested with the point of a sharp knife. Serve, garnished with parsley.

MOROCCAN SPICED MACKEREL

MACKEREL IS EXTREMELY GOOD FOR YOU, BUT SOME PEOPLE FIND ITS HEALTHY OILINESS TOO MUCH TO TAKE. THE MOROCCAN SPICES IN THIS RECIPE COUNTERACT THE RICHNESS OF THE FISH.

SERVES FOUR

INGREDIENTS
150ml/¼ pint/⅔ cup sunflower oil
15ml/1 tbsp paprika
5–10ml/1–2 tsp harissa (chilli sauce)
  or chilli powder
10ml/2 tsp ground cumin
10ml/2 tsp ground coriander
2 garlic cloves, crushed
juice of 2 lemons
30ml/2 tbsp chopped fresh
  mint leaves
30ml/2 tbsp chopped fresh
  coriander (cilantro)
4 mackerel, cleaned
salt and ground black pepper
mint sprigs, to garnish
lemon wedges, to serve

1 In a bowl, whisk together the oil, spices, garlic and lemon juice. Season, then stir in the mint and coriander.

2 Make two or three diagonal slashes on either side of each mackerel so that they will absorb the marinade. Pour the marinade into a shallow non-metallic dish that is large enough to hold the fish in a single layer.

3 Put in the mackerel and turn them over in the marinade, spooning it into the slashes. Cover the dish with clear film (plastic wrap) and place in the refrigerator for at least 3 hours.

4 When you are ready to cook the mackerel, preheat the grill (broiler) to medium-high. Transfer the fish to the grill rack and grill (broil) for 5–7 minutes on each side, until just cooked, turning the fish once and basting them several times with the marinade. Serve hot or cold with lemon wedges, garnished with mint. Herb-flavoured couscous or rice make good accompaniments.

COOK'S TIP
These spicy mackerel can be cooked on a barbecue. Make sure the coals are very hot before you begin cooking. Arrange the fish on a large hinged rack to make turning easier and barbecue (grill) for 5–7 minutes, turning once.

VARIATION
Trout, bonito, trevally or bluefish are also good cooked this way.

Top: Energy 296kcal/1241kJ; Protein 38.7g; Carbohydrate 12.3g, of which sugars 11.9g; Fat 10.5g, of which saturates 1.6g; Cholesterol 144mg; Calcium 308mg; Fibre 7.2g; Sodium 391mg.
Bottom: Energy 422kcal/1753kJ; Protein 31.8g; Carbohydrate 1.9g, of which sugars 0.1g; Fat 31.9g, of which saturates 6g; Cholesterol 86mg; Calcium 51mg; Fibre 1.3g; Sodium 117mg.

ASIAN FISH EN PAPILLOTE

THE AROMATIC SMELL THAT WAFTS OUT OF THESE FISH PARCELS AS YOU OPEN THEM IS DELICIOUSLY TEMPTING. IF YOU DON'T LIKE ASIAN FLAVOURS, USE WHITE WINE, HERBS AND THINLY SLICED VEGETABLES, OR MEDITERRANEAN INGREDIENTS, SUCH AS TOMATOES, BASIL AND OLIVES.

SERVES FOUR

INGREDIENTS
2 carrots
2 courgettes (zucchini)
6 spring onions (scallions)
2.5cm/1in piece fresh root
  ginger, peeled
1 lime
2 garlic cloves, thinly sliced
30ml/2 tbsp teriyaki marinade or
  Thai fish sauce
5–10ml/1–2 tsp clear sesame oil
4 salmon fillets, about
  200g/7oz each
ground black pepper
rice, to serve

VARIATION
Thick fillets of hake, halibut, hoki and fresh or undyed smoked haddock and cod can all be used for this dish.

1 Cut the carrots, courgettes and spring onions into thin sticks and set them aside. Cut the ginger into thin sticks and put these in a small bowl. Using a zester, pare the lime thinly. Add the pared rind to the ginger, with the garlic. Squeeze the lime juice.

2 Place the teriyaki marinade or fish sauce in a bowl and stir in the lime juice and sesame oil.

3 Preheat the oven to 220°C/425°F/Gas 7. Cut out four rounds of baking parchment, each with a diameter of 40cm/16in. Season the salmon with pepper. Lay a fillet on one side of each paper round, about 3cm/1¼in off centre. Sprinkle a quarter of the ginger mixture over each and pile a quarter of the vegetable sticks on top. Spoon a quarter of the teriyaki or fish sauce mixture over the top.

4 Fold the bare side of the baking parchment over the salmon and roll the edges of the parchment over to seal each parcel very tightly.

5 Place the salmon parcels on a baking sheet and cook in the oven for about 10–12 minutes, depending on the thickness of the fillets. Put the parcels on plates and serve with rice.

Energy 321kcal/1337kJ; Protein 31.6g; Carbohydrate 5.3g, of which sugars 4.8g; Fat 16.6g, of which saturates 2.9g; Cholesterol 75mg; Calcium 46mg; Fibre 0.6g; Sodium 873mg.

ROAST COD <u>WITH</u> PANCETTA <u>AND</u> BEANS

THICK COD STEAKS WRAPPED IN PANCETTA AND ROASTED MAKE A SUPERB SUPPER DISH WHEN SERVED ON A BED OF BUTTER BEANS, WITH SWEET AND JUICY CHERRY TOMATOES ON THE SIDE.

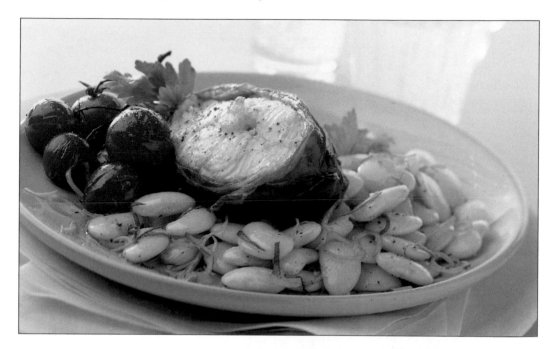

SERVES FOUR

INGREDIENTS
    200g/7oz/1 cup butter (lima) beans,
        soaked overnight in cold water
    2 leeks, thinly sliced
    2 garlic cloves, chopped
    8 fresh sage leaves
    90ml/6 tbsp fruity olive oil
    8 thin slices of pancetta
    4 thick Pacific cod steaks, skinned
    12 cherry tomatoes
    salt and ground black pepper

1 Drain the beans, tip into a pan and cover with cold water. Bring to the boil and skim off the foam on the surface. Lower the heat, then stir in the leeks, garlic, four sage leaves and 30ml/2 tbsp of the olive oil. Simmer for 1–1½ hours until the beans are tender, adding more water if necessary. Drain, return to the pan, season, stir in 30ml/2 tbsp olive oil and keep warm.

2 Preheat the oven to 200°C/400°F/ Gas 6. Wrap two slices of pancetta around the edge of each cod steak, tying it on with kitchen string or securing it with a wooden cocktail stick or toothpick. Insert a sage leaf between the pancetta and the cod. Season the fish.

VARIATION
You can use cannellini beans for this recipe, and streaky (fatty) bacon instead of pancetta. It is also good made with halibut, hake, haddock or salmon.

3 Heat a heavy frying pan, add 15ml/ 1 tbsp of the remaining oil and seal the cod steaks, two at a time, for 1 minute on each side. Transfer them to an ovenproof dish and roast in the oven for 5 minutes.

4 Add the tomatoes to the dish and drizzle over the remaining olive oil. Roast for 5 minutes more, until the cod steaks are cooked but still juicy. Serve them on a bed of butter beans with the roasted tomatoes. Garnish with parsley.

Energy 449kcal/1883kJ; Protein 44.5g; Carbohydrate 25.3g, of which sugars 3.9g; Fat 19.5g, of which saturates 3g; Cholesterol 84mg; Calcium 85mg; Fibre 9.8g; Sodium 403mg.

HERBED CHARGRILLED TUNA STEAKS

TUNA IS VERY LOW IN FAT, WITH DENSE, WELL-FLAVOURED FLESH. OTHER CLOSE-TEXTURED FISH LIKE BONITO AND MARLIN WORK EQUALLY WELL IN THIS RECIPE, WHICH IS IDEAL FOR A BARBECUE. SERVE THE FISH WITH A TANGY TOMATO SALAD.

SERVES FOUR

INGREDIENTS
  45ml/3 tbsp olive oil
  2 fresh bay leaves, chopped
  15ml/1 tbsp chopped fresh basil
  15ml/1 tbsp chopped fresh oregano
  30ml/2 tbsp chopped fresh parsley
  5ml/1 tsp finely chopped
    fresh rosemary
  5ml/1 tsp fresh thyme leaves
  2 garlic cloves, crushed
  4 pieces drained sun-dried tomatoes
    in oil, chopped
  4 tuna steaks, about 200g/7oz each
  juice of 1 lemon
  15ml/1 tbsp drained small
    capers in vinegar (optional)
  salt and ground black pepper

1 Whisk the oil, herbs, garlic and sun-dried tomatoes in a bowl, then pour the mixture into a shallow dish that is large enough to hold the tuna steaks in a single layer. Season the tuna steaks with salt and pepper and brush the lemon juice over both sides. Lay the fish in the dish, turning the steaks to coat them all over. Cover and marinate in the refrigerator for 1–2 hours.

2 Heat a ridged griddle pan or barbecue until it is very hot. Lift the tuna steaks out of the marinade, pat dry with kitchen paper and grill (broil) or cook on the barbecue for about 5 minutes on each side, until they are cooked through. Pour the marinade into a small pan and bring to the boil. Stir in the capers, if using. Spoon over the tuna steaks and serve immediately.

CHINESE-STYLE SCALLOPS AND PRAWNS

SERVE THIS LIGHT, DELICATE DISH FOR LUNCH OR SUPPER ACCOMPANIED BY AROMATIC STEAMED RICE OR FINE RICE NOODLES AND STIR-FRIED PAK CHOI.

SERVES FOUR

INGREDIENTS
  15ml/1 tbsp stir-fry or sunflower oil
  500g/1¼lb raw tiger prawns (jumbo
    shrimp), peeled
  1 star anise
  225g/8oz scallops, halved if large
  2.5cm/1in piece fresh root ginger,
    peeled and grated
  2 garlic cloves, thinly sliced
  1 red (bell) pepper, seeded and cut
    into thin strips
  115g/4oz/1¾ cups shiitake or button
    (white) mushrooms, thinly sliced
  juice of 1 lemon
  5ml/1 tsp cornflour (cornstarch),
    mixed with 30ml/2 tbsp cold water
  30ml/2 tbsp light soy sauce
  chopped fresh chives, to garnish
  salt and ground black pepper

1 Heat the oil in a wok until very hot. Put in the prawns and star anise and stir-fry over a high heat for 2 minutes. Add the scallops, ginger and garlic and stir-fry for 1 minute more, by which time the prawns should have turned pink and the scallops opaque. Season with a little salt and plenty of pepper and then remove from the wok using a slotted spoon. Discard the star anise.

2 Add the red pepper and mushrooms to the wok and stir-fry for 1–2 minutes. Pour in the lemon juice, cornflour paste and soy sauce, bring to the boil and bubble for 1–2 minutes, stirring constantly, until the sauce is smooth and slightly thickened.

3 Stir the prawns and scallops into the sauce, cook for a few seconds until heated through, then season with salt and ground black pepper and serve garnished with chopped chives.

VARIATIONS
Use other prepared shellfish in this dish; try thinly sliced rings of squid, or mussels or clams, or substitute chunks of firm white fish, such as monkfish fillet, for the scallops.

Top: Energy 239kcal/1006kJ; Protein 40.6g; Carbohydrate 0.7g, of which sugars 0.1g; Fat 7.5g, of which saturates 1.2g; Cholesterol 77mg; Calcium 33mg; Fibre 0.2g; Sodium 246mg.
Bottom: Energy 212kcal/892kJ; Protein 36.3g; Carbohydrate 6.6g, of which sugars 3.3g; Fat 4.6g, of which saturates 0.8g; Cholesterol 270mg; Calcium 122mg; Fibre 1g; Sodium 877mg.

FILO FISH PIES

THESE LIGHT FILO-WRAPPED FISH PIES CAN BE MADE WITH ANY FIRM WHITE FISH FILLETS, SUCH AS ORANGE ROUGHY, COD, HALIBUT OR HOKI. SERVE WITH SALAD LEAVES AND MAYONNAISE ON THE SIDE.

2 Brush the inside of six 13cm/5in tartlet tins (muffin pans) with a little of the melted butter. Fit a piece of filo pastry into the tins, draping it so that it hangs over the sides. Brush with butter, then add another sheet at right-angles to the first. Brush with butter. Continue to line the tins in this way.

3 Spread the spinach evenly over the pastry. Add the diced fish and season well. Stir the chives into the crème fraîche and spread the mixture over the top of the fish. Sprinkle the dill over.

SERVES SIX

INGREDIENTS
400g/14oz spinach, trimmed
1 egg, lightly beaten
2 garlic cloves, crushed
450g/1lb orange roughy or other
   white fish fillet
juice of 1 lemon
50g/2oz/¼ cup butter, melted
8–12 filo pastry sheets, thawed
   if frozen, quartered
15ml/1 tbsp finely chopped
   fresh chives
200ml/7fl oz/scant 1 cup half-fat
   crème fraîche
15ml/1 tbsp chopped fresh dill
salt and ground black pepper

VARIATION
To make one large pie, use a 20cm/8in tin (pan) and cook for 45 minutes.

1 Preheat the oven to 190°C/375°F/ Gas 5. Wash the spinach, then cook it in a lidded heavy pan with just the water that clings to the leaves. As soon as the leaves are tender, drain, squeeze as dry as possible and chop. Put the spinach in a bowl, add the egg and garlic, season with salt and pepper and set aside. Dice the fish and place it in a bowl. Stir in the lemon juice. Season with salt and pepper and toss lightly.

4 Draw the overhanging pieces of pastry together and scrunch lightly to make a lid. Brush with butter. Bake for about 15–20 minutes, until golden brown.

Energy 233kcal/972kJ; Protein 18.4g; Carbohydrate 9.1g, of which sugars 2.2g; Fat 14g, of which saturates 8.2g; Cholesterol 84mg; Calcium 170mg; Fibre 1.7g; Sodium 213mg.

HOKI STIR-FRY

ANY FIRM WHITE FISH, SUCH AS MONKFISH, HAKE OR COD, CAN BE USED FOR THIS ATTRACTIVE STIR-FRY. VARY THE VEGETABLES ACCORDING TO WHAT IS AVAILABLE, BUT TRY TO INCLUDE AT LEAST THREE DIFFERENT COLOURS. SHRIMP-FRIED RICE WOULD BE THE PERFECT ACCOMPANIMENT.

SERVES FOUR TO SIX

INGREDIENTS
    675g/1½lb hoki fillet, skinned
    pinch of five-spice powder
    2 carrots
    115g/4oz/1 cup mangetouts (snow peas)
    115g/4oz asparagus spears
    4 spring onions (scallions)
    45ml/3 tbsp groundnut (peanut) oil
    2.5cm/1in piece fresh root ginger,
       peeled and cut into thin slivers
    2 garlic cloves, finely chopped
    300g/11oz beansprouts
    8–12 small baby corn cobs
    15–30ml/1–2 tbsp light soy sauce
    salt and ground black pepper

1 Cut the hoki into finger-size strips and season with salt, pepper and five spice powder. Cut the carrots diagonally into slices as thin as the mangetouts.

2 Trim the mangetouts. Trim the asparagus spears and cut in half crossways. Trim the spring onions and cut them diagonally into 2cm/¾in pieces, keeping the white and green parts separate. Set aside.

3 Heat a wok, then pour in the oil. As soon as it is hot, add the ginger and garlic. Stir-fry for 1 minute, then add the white parts of the spring onions and cook for 1 minute more.

COOK'S TIP
When adding the oil to the hot wok, drizzle it around the inner rim like a necklace. The oil will run down to coat the entire surface of the wok. Swirl the wok to make sure the coating is even.

4 Add the hoki strips and stir-fry for 2–3 minutes, until all the pieces of fish are opaque. Add the beansprouts. Toss them around to coat them in the oil, then put in the carrots, mangetouts, asparagus and corn. Continue to stir-fry for 3–4 minutes, by which time the fish should be cooked, but all the vegetables will still be crunchy. Add soy sauce to taste, toss everything quickly together, then stir in the green parts of the spring onions. Serve immediately.

Energy 183kcal/764kJ; Protein 22.4g; Carbohydrate 5g, of which sugars 3.8g; Fat 8.2g, of which saturates 1.1g; Cholesterol 0mg; Calcium 49mg; Fibre 2.3g; Sodium 295mg.

BRAISED BREAM WITH SHELLFISH

THIS VERSATILE DISH IS EXTREMELY LOW IN CALORIES, BUT FULL OF FLAVOUR. USE ANY MIXTURE OF FRESH OR FROZEN SHELLFISH YOU LIKE (A FEW MUSSELS OR CLAMS IN THE SHELL ARE PARTICULARLY ATTRACTIVE). SERVE WITH NOODLES OR PASTA SHELLS.

SERVES FOUR

INGREDIENTS
30ml/2 tbsp olive oil
1 onion, thinly sliced
1 yellow or orange (bell) pepper, seeded and cut into strips
400ml/14fl oz/1⅔ cups well-reduced tomato sauce
45ml/3 tbsp dry white wine or fish stock
2 courgettes (zucchini), sliced
350g/12oz bream or porgy fillets, skinned and cut into 5cm/2in chunks
450g/1lb ready-prepared mixed shellfish, thawed if frozen
juice of ½ lemon
15ml/1 tbsp shredded fresh marjoram or basil leaves
salt and ground black pepper
basil leaves, to garnish
cooked pasta or noodles, to serve

1 Heat the olive oil in a large frying pan. Add the onion slices and yellow or orange pepper strips and stir-fry the vegetables for about 2 minutes, until the onion is translucent.

COOK'S TIP
If you are short of time, use a 400ml/14fl oz jar of good quality ready-prepared tomato sauce.

2 Stir in the tomato sauce, with the white wine or fish stock and bring to the boil. Lower the heat, then simmer for about 2 minutes.

3 Add the courgettes and the chunks of fish; cover and cook gently for about 5 minutes, stirring once or twice during this time. Add the shellfish and stir well to coat it with the sauce.

4 Season to taste with salt, pepper and lemon juice, cover the pan and simmer for 2–3 minutes, until heated through. Stir in the shredded marjoram or basil, and garnish with basil leaves. Serve with noodles or pasta.

VARIATIONS
Fillets of snapper, bass or red mullet could be used in place of the bream in this recipe.

MALAYSIAN STEAMED TROUT FILLETS

THIS SIMPLE DISH CAN BE PREPARED EXTREMELY QUICKLY, AND IS SUITABLE FOR ANY FISH FILLETS. SERVE IT ON A BED OF NOODLES ACCOMPANIED BY RIBBONS OF COLOURFUL VEGETABLES.

SERVES FOUR

INGREDIENTS
8 pink trout fillets of even thickness, about 115g/4oz each, skinned
45ml/3 tbsp grated creamed coconut (coconut cream)
grated rind and juice of 2 limes
45ml/3 tbsp chopped fresh coriander (cilantro)
15ml/1 tbsp sunflower oil
2.5–5ml/½–1 tsp chilli oil
salt and ground black pepper
lime slices and coriander (cilantro) sprigs, to garnish

1 Cut four rectangles of baking parchment, twice the size of the trout. Place a fillet on each piece and season.

2 Mix together the coconut, lime rind and chopped coriander and spread a quarter of the mixture over each trout fillet. Sandwich another trout fillet on top. Mix the lime juice with the oils, adjusting the quantity of chilli oil to your own taste, and drizzle the mixture over the trout "sandwiches".

3 Prepare a steamer. Fold up the edges of the parchment and pleat them over the trout to make parcels, making sure they are well sealed. Place in the steamer insert and steam over the simmering water for about 10–15 minutes, depending on the thickness of the fish. Serve immediately.

Top: Energy 342kcal/1437kJ; Protein 36.4g; Carbohydrate 14.8g, of which sugars 8.4g; Fat 15.9g, of which saturates 3.1g; Cholesterol 296mg; Calcium 89mg; Fibre 2.8g; Sodium 563mg.
Bottom: Energy 241kcal/1005kJ; Protein 25g; Carbohydrate 0.9g, of which sugars 0.9g; Fat 15.3g, of which saturates 7g; Cholesterol 0mg; Calcium 21mg; Fibre 0.2g; Sodium 75mg.

ELEGANT DISHES FOR ENTERTAINING

For sheer elegance, fish and shellfish are hard to beat and so quick to prepare that they make light work of entertaining. A whole fish baked in a salt crust looks intriguing and tastes superb. For breathtaking elegance and taste, treat your guests to Lobster Thermidor, Vegetable-stuffed Squid or Fillets of Turbot with Oysters. Whatever the occasion, delight your guests with these superb party dishes.

HAKE <u>AU</u> POIVRE <u>WITH</u> RED PEPPER RELISH

THIS PISCINE VERSION OF THE CLASSIC STEAK AU POIVRE CAN BE MADE WITH MONKFISH OR COD INSTEAD OF HAKE. VARY THE QUANTITY OF PEPPERCORNS ACCORDING TO YOUR PERSONAL TASTE.

SERVES FOUR

INGREDIENTS

    30–45ml/2–3 tbsp mixed peppercorns
      (black, white, pink and green)
    4 hake steaks, about 175g/6oz each
    30ml/2 tbsp olive oil
For the red (bell) pepper relish
    2 red (bell) peppers
    15ml/1 tbsp olive oil
    2 garlic cloves, chopped
    4 ripe tomatoes, peeled, seeded
      and quartered
    4 drained canned anchovy
      fillets, chopped
    5ml/1 tsp capers
    15ml/1 tbsp balsamic vinegar
    12 fresh basil leaves, shredded, plus
      a few extra to garnish
    salt and ground black pepper

1 Put the peppercorns in a mortar and crush them coarsely with a pestle. Alternatively, put them in a plastic bag and crush them with a rolling pin. Season the hake fillets lightly with salt, then coat them evenly on both sides with the crushed peppercorns. Set the coated fish steaks aside while you make the red pepper relish.

2 Make the relish. Cut the red peppers in half lengthways, remove the core and seeds from each and cut the flesh into 1cm/½in wide strips. Heat the olive oil in a wok or a shallow pan that has a lid. Add the peppers and stir them for about 5 minutes, until they are slightly softened. Stir in the chopped garlic, tomatoes and the anchovies, then cover the pan and simmer the mixture very gently for about 20 minutes, until the peppers are very soft.

3 Tip the contents of the pan into a food processor and process to a coarse purée. Transfer to a bowl and season to taste. Stir in the capers, balsamic vinegar and basil. Keep the relish hot.

4 Heat the olive oil in a shallow pan, add the hake steaks and cook them, in batches if necessary, for 5 minutes on each side, turning them once or twice, until they are just cooked through.

5 Place the fish on individual plates and spoon a little red pepper relish on to each plate. Garnish with basil leaves and a little extra balsamic vinegar. Serve the rest of the relish separately.

Energy 283kcal/1186kJ; Protein 33.7g; Carbohydrate 8.2g, of which sugars 8g; Fat 13g, of which saturates 1.9g; Cholesterol 42mg; Calcium 47mg; Fibre 2.3g; Sodium 304mg.

MOROCCAN FISH TAGINE

THIS SPICY, AROMATIC DISH PROVES JUST HOW EXCITING AN INGREDIENT FISH CAN BE. SERVE IT WITH COUSCOUS FLAVOURED WITH CHOPPED MINT, AND GARNISH WITH EXTRA CORIANDER SPRIGS.

SERVES EIGHT

INGREDIENTS

1.4kg/3lb firm fish fillets, skinned
3 large fresh red chillies, seeded
  and chopped
3 garlic cloves, peeled
15ml/1 tbsp ground coriander
30ml/2 tbsp ground cumin
5ml/1 tsp ground cinnamon
grated rind of 1 lemon
30ml/2 tbsp sunflower oil
60ml/4 tbsp olive oil
4 onions, chopped
1 large aubergine (eggplant), cut into
  1cm/½in cubes
2 courgettes (zucchini), cut into
  1cm/½in cubes
400g/14oz can chopped tomatoes
400ml/14fl oz/1⅔ cups passata
  (bottled strained tomatoes)
200ml/7fl oz/scant 1 cup fish stock
1 preserved lemon, chopped
90g/3½oz/scant 1 cup olives
60ml/4 tbsp chopped fresh
  coriander (cilantro)
salt and ground black pepper

1 Cut the fish into 5cm/2in chunks. Make a chilli sauce by processing the next seven ingredients in a blender to a smooth paste. Place the fish chunks in a wide bowl and add 30ml/2 tbsp of the sauce. Toss to coat, cover and chill for at least 1 hour, or overnight.

2 Heat half the olive oil in a shallow, heavy pan. Cook the onions over a low heat for 10 minutes, until golden brown. Stir in the remaining chilli sauce and cook for 5 minutes, stirring occasionally.

3 Heat the remaining olive oil in a separate shallow pan. Add the aubergine cubes and cook for about 10 minutes, until they are golden brown. Add the cubed courgettes and cook for a further 2 minutes.

4 Tip the mixture into the shallow pan and combine with the onions, then stir in the chopped tomatoes, the passata and fish stock. Bring to the boil, then lower the heat and simmer the mixture for about 20 minutes.

5 Stir the fish chunks and preserved lemon into the pan. Add the olives and stir gently. Cover and simmer over a low heat for about 15–20 minutes, until the fish is just cooked through. Season to taste. Stir in the chopped coriander. Serve with couscous and garnish with coriander sprigs, if you like.

COOK'S TIP
If you want to make the fish go further, you could add 225g/8oz/1¼ cups cooked chickpeas to the tagine.

Energy 174kcal/735kJ; Protein 33.7g; Carbohydrate 6.1g, of which sugars 5.9g; Fat 1.8g, of which saturates 0.4g; Cholesterol 81mg; Calcium 32mg; Fibre 2.5g; Sodium 134mg.

GRILLED SQUID WITH CHORIZO

THE BEST WAY TO COOK THIS DISH IS ON A GRIDDLE OR IN A RIDGED GRIDDLE PAN. IF YOU HAVE NEITHER, USE AN OVERHEAD GRILL, MAKING SURE IT IS VERY HOT. IF YOU CAN ONLY FIND MEDIUM-SIZE SQUID, ALLOW TWO PER SERVING AND HALVE THEM LENGTHWAYS FROM THE TAIL END TO THE CAVITY.

SERVES SIX

INGREDIENTS
24 small squid, cleaned
150ml/¼ pint/⅔ cup extra
   virgin olive oil
300g/11oz cooking chorizo, cut into
   12 slices
3 tomatoes, halved and seasoned
   with salt and pepper
juice of 1 lemon
24 cooked new potatoes, halved
fresh rocket (arugula) leaves
salt and ground black pepper
lemon slices, to garnish

1 Separate the body and tentacles of the squid and cut the bodies in half lengthways if they are large.

2 Pour half the oil into a bowl, season with salt and pepper, then toss all the squid in the oil. Heat a ridged griddle pan or grill (broiler) to very hot.

3 Grill (broil) the prepared squid bodies for about 45 seconds on each side until the flesh is opaque and tender. Then transfer to a plate and keep hot. Grill the tentacles for about 1 minute on each side, then place them on the plate. Grill the chorizo slices for about 30 seconds on each side, until golden brown, then set them aside with the squid. Grill the tomato halves for 1–2 minutes on each side, until they are softened and browned.

4 Place the potatoes and a handful of rocket in a large bowl.

5 Pour the lemon juice into a bowl and whisk in the remaining oil. Season. Reserve 30ml/2 tbsp of this dressing. Pour the dressing over the potatoes and rocket, toss lightly and divide among six plates. Pile a portion of the squid, tomatoes and chorizo on each salad, and drizzle over the reserved dressing. Garnish with lemon slices and serve immediately.

SOLE WITH WILD MUSHROOMS

IF POSSIBLE, USE CHANTERELLES FOR THIS DISH; THEIR GLOWING ORANGE COLOUR COMBINES REALLY WONDERFULLY WITH THE INTENSELY GOLDEN SAUCE. OTHERWISE, USE ANY PALE-COLOURED OR OYSTER MUSHROOMS THAT YOU CAN FIND INSTEAD.

SERVES FOUR

INGREDIENTS
4 Dover sole fillets, about 115g/4oz
   each, skinned
50g/2oz/4 tbsp butter
500ml/17fl oz/generous 2 cups
   fish stock
150g/5oz/2 cups chanterelles
a large pinch of saffron threads
150ml/¼ pint/⅔ cup double
   (heavy) cream
1 egg yolk
salt and ground white pepper
finely chopped fresh parsley, and
   parsley sprigs to garnish
boiled new potatoes, to serve

1 Preheat the oven to 200°C/400°F/ Gas 6. Cut the sole fillets in half lengthways and place them on a board with the skinned side uppermost. Season them with salt and white pepper, then roll them up. Use a little of the butter to grease an ovenproof dish just large enough to hold all the sole fillets in a single layer. Arrange the sole rolls in the dish, then pour over the fish stock. Cover tightly with foil and bake for 12–15 minutes, until cooked through.

2 Meanwhile, pick off any bits of fern or twig from the chanterelles and wipe the mushrooms with a damp cloth. Halve or quarter any large ones. Heat the remaining butter in a frying pan until foaming and sauté the mushrooms for 3–4 minutes, until just tender. Season with salt and pepper and keep hot.

3 Lift the cooked sole fillets out of the cooking liquid and place them on a heated serving dish. Keep hot. Strain the liquid into a small pan, add the saffron threads, set over a very high heat and boil until reduced to about 250ml/8fl oz/1 cup. Stir in the cream and then let the sauce bubble gently once or twice.

4 Lightly beat the egg yolk in a small bowl, pour on a little of the hot sauce and stir well. Stir the mixture into the remaining sauce in the pan and cook over a very low heat for 1–2 minutes, until slightly thickened. Season to taste. Stir the chanterelles into the sauce and pour it over the sole fillets. Garnish with fresh parsley sprigs and serve immediately. Boiled new potatoes make the perfect accompaniment.

Top: Energy 629kcal/2630kJ; Protein 39.3g; Carbohydrate 30.6g, of which sugars 4g; Fat 39.7g, of which saturates 10.6g; Cholesterol 417mg; Calcium 41mg; Fibre 2.2g; Sodium 1106mg.
Bottom: Energy 411kcal/1699kJ; Protein 24.7g; Carbohydrate 0.9g, of which sugars 0.8g; Fat 34.2g, of which saturates 19.5g; Cholesterol 191mg; Calcium 65mg; Fibre 0.4g; Sodium 213mg.

LOBSTER THERMIDOR

ONE OF THE CLASSIC FRENCH DISHES, LOBSTER THERMIDOR MAKES A LITTLE LOBSTER GO A LONG WAY.
IT IS BEST TO USE ONE BIG RATHER THAN TWO SMALL LOBSTERS, AS A LARGER LOBSTER WILL CONTAIN
A HIGHER PROPORTION OF FLESH AND THE MEAT WILL BE SWEETER. IDEALLY, USE A LIVE CRUSTACEAN
AND COOK IT YOURSELF, BUT A BOILED LOBSTER FROM THE FISHMONGER WILL DO.

SERVES TWO

INGREDIENTS

1 large lobster, about
   800g–1kg/1¾–2¼lb, boiled
45ml/3 tbsp brandy
25g/1oz/2 tbsp butter
2 shallots, finely chopped
115g/4oz/1½ cups button (white)
   mushrooms, thinly sliced
15ml/1 tbsp plain (all-purpose) flour
105ml/7 tbsp fish or shellfish stock
120ml/4fl oz/½ cup double
   (heavy) cream
5ml/1 tsp Dijon mustard
2 egg yolks, beaten
45ml/3 tbsp dry white wine
45ml/3 tbsp freshly grated Parmesan
salt, ground black pepper and
   cayenne pepper

1 Split the lobster in half lengthways; crack the claws. Discard the stomach sac; keep the coral for another dish. Keeping each half-shell intact, extract the meat from the tail and claws, then cut into large dice. Place in a shallow dish; sprinkle over the brandy. Cover and set aside. Wipe and dry the half-shells and set them aside.

2 Melt the butter in a pan and cook the shallots over a low heat until soft. Add the mushrooms and cook until just tender, stirring constantly. Stir in the flour and a pinch of cayenne; cook, stirring, for 2 minutes. Gradually add the stock, stirring until the sauce boils and thickens.

3 Stir in the cream and mustard and continue to cook until the sauce is smooth and thick. Season to taste with salt, black pepper and cayenne. Pour half the sauce on to the egg yolks, stir well and return the mixture to the pan. Stir in the wine; adjust the seasoning, being generous with the cayenne.

4 Preheat the grill (broiler) to medium-high. Stir the diced lobster and the brandy into the sauce. Arrange the lobster half-shells in a grill pan and divide the mixture among them. Sprinkle with Parmesan and place under the grill until browned. Serve with steamed rice and mixed salad leaves.

Energy 859kcal/3573kJ; Protein 56g; Carbohydrate 9.8g, of which sugars 2g; Fat 59.6g, of which saturates 33.8g; Cholesterol 536mg; Calcium 488mg; Fibre 1.2g; Sodium 976mg.

RED MULLET SALTIMBOCCA

THE RICH RED COLOUR OF THE MULLET IS INTENSIFIED BY RUBBING SAFFRON INTO THE SKIN, COMPLEMENTING THE PROSCIUTTO BEAUTIFULLY. SERVE WITH BRIGHTLY COLOURED ROASTED MEDITERRANEAN VEGETABLES AND CRISPLY COOKED GREEN BEANS, IF YOU LIKE.

SERVES FOUR

INGREDIENTS

    8 red mullet or red snapper fillets,
      scaled but not skinned
    a pinch of saffron threads or
      powdered saffron
    15ml/1 tbsp olive oil
    8 fresh sage leaves
    8 thin slices of prosciutto
    25g/1oz/2 tbsp butter
    115g/4oz/1 cup mixed olives
    salt and ground black pepper
For the dressing
    15ml/1 tbsp caster (superfine) sugar
    105ml/7 tbsp balsamic vinegar
    300ml/½ pint/1¼ cups extra virgin
      olive oil
    5cm/2in slice red (bell) pepper, diced
    1 small courgette (zucchini), diced
    1 ripe tomato, peeled, seeded and
      very finely diced

1 Score the fish skin lightly in three or four places. Season both sides of each fillet with salt and ground black pepper. If you are using saffron threads, crumble them over the skin side of each fish fillet, or sprinkle the powdered saffron over the skin. Drizzle on a little olive oil and then rub the saffron in well with your fingertips. This will dramatically enhance the colour of the fish skin.

2 Heat a non-stick frying pan until very hot, then put in the fillets, skin side down, and cook over a high heat for 2 minutes. Turn the fillets over and cook them for 2 minutes more. Drain on kitchen paper and leave until cool enough to handle.

3 Place a sage leaf on each cooked fillet, then wrap the fillets in a slice of prosciutto to cover them completely. Melt the butter in the frying pan and continue to heat until it foams. Fry the ham and red mullet parcels over a high heat for 1–2 minutes on each side, until the ham is pale golden. Transfer to warmed serving plates and keep hot while you make the dressing.

4 Mix the sugar and balsamic vinegar in a small pan, set over a high heat and boil until syrupy.

5 Meanwhile, pour the olive oil into a bowl, stir in the diced vegetables and season. Stir the vinegar syrup into the dressing. Drizzle it over and around the ham-wrapped fish. Place the olives on the plates and serve immediately.

Energy 773kcal/3203kJ; Protein 46.6g; Carbohydrate 1.8g, of which sugars 1.7g; Fat 64.4g, of which saturates 12.1g; Cholesterol 100mg; Calcium 123mg; Fibre 1.5g; Sodium 936mg.

ROAST MONKFISH WITH GARLIC

MONKFISH TIED UP AND COOKED IN THIS WAY IS KNOWN IN FRENCH AS A "GIGOT", BECAUSE IT RESEMBLES A LEG OF LAMB. THE COMBINATION OF MONKFISH AND GARLIC IS SUPERB. FOR A CONTRAST IN COLOUR, SERVE IT WITH VIBRANT GREEN BEANS.

SERVES FOUR TO SIX

INGREDIENTS
1kg/2¼lb monkfish tail, skinned
14 fat garlic cloves
5ml/1 tsp fresh thyme leaves
30ml/2 tbsp olive oil
juice of 1 lemon
2 bay leaves
salt and ground black pepper

1 Preheat the oven to 220°C/425°F/ Gas 7. Remove any membrane from the monkfish tail and cut out the central bone. Peel two garlic cloves and cut them into thin slivers. Sprinkle a quarter of these and half the thyme leaves over the cut side of the fish, then close it up and use fine kitchen string to tie it into a neat shape, like a boned piece of meat. Pat dry with kitchen paper.

2 Make incisions on either side of the fish and push in the remaining garlic slivers. Heat half the olive oil in a frying pan which can safely be used in the oven. When the oil is hot, put in the monkfish and brown it all over for about 5 minutes, until evenly coloured. Season with salt and pepper, sprinkle with lemon juice and sprinkle over the remaining thyme.

3 Tuck the bay leaves under the monkfish, arrange the remaining (unpeeled) garlic cloves around it and drizzle the remaining olive oil over the fish and the garlic. Transfer the frying pan to the oven and roast the monkfish for 20–25 minutes, until the flesh is cooked through.

4 Place on a warmed serving dish with the garlic and some green beans. To serve, remove the string and cut the monkfish into 2cm/¾in thick slices.

COOK'S TIPS
• The garlic heads can be used whole.
• When serving the monkfish, invite each guest to pop out the soft garlic pulp with a fork and spread it over the monkfish.
• Use two smaller monkfish tails.

Energy 259kcal/1091kJ; Protein 45.7g; Carbohydrate 4.1g, of which sugars 0.4g; Fat 6.7g, of which saturates 1.1g; Cholesterol 40mg; Calcium 27mg; Fibre 1g; Sodium 51mg.

SEA BASS WITH GINGER AND LEEKS

YOU CAN USE WHOLE FISH OR THICK FILLETS FOR THIS RECIPE, WHICH IS ALSO EXCELLENT MADE WITH BREAM, PORGY, SNAPPER, POMFRET AND TREVALLY. SERVE THE FISH WITH FRIED RICE AND STIR-FRIED CHINESE GREEN VEGETABLES, SUCH AS PAK CHOI, IF YOU LIKE.

SERVES FOUR

INGREDIENTS

    1 sea bass, about 1.4–1.5kg/
        3–3½lb, scaled and cleaned
    8 spring onions (scallions)
    60ml/4 tbsp teriyaki marinade or
        dark soy sauce
    30ml/2 tbsp cornflour (cornstarch)
    juice of 1 lemon
    30ml/2 tbsp rice wine vinegar
    5ml/1 tsp ground ginger
    60ml/4 tbsp groundnut (peanut) oil
    2 leeks, shredded
    2.5cm/1in piece fresh root ginger,
        peeled and grated
    105ml/7 tbsp chicken or fish stock
    30ml/2 tbsp rice wine or dry sherry
    5ml/1 tsp caster (superfine) sugar
    salt and ground black pepper

1 Make several diagonal slashes on either side of the sea bass so it can absorb the flavours, then season the fish inside and out with salt and ground black pepper. Trim the spring onions, cut them in half lengthways, then slice them diagonally into 2cm/¾in lengths. Put half of the spring onions in the cavity of the fish and reserve the rest for later use.

2 In a shallow dish, mix together the teriyaki marinade or dark soy sauce, the cornflour, lemon juice, rice wine vinegar and ground ginger to make a smooth, runny paste. Turn the fish in the marinade to coat it thoroughly, working it into the slashes, then leave it to marinate for 20–30 minutes, turning it several times.

3 Heat a wok or frying pan that is large enough to hold the sea bass comfortably. Add the oil, then the leeks and grated ginger. Cook gently for about 5 minutes, until the leeks are tender. Remove the leeks and ginger with a slotted spoon and drain on kitchen paper. leaving the oil in the wok or pan.

4 Lift the sea bass out of the marinade and lower it carefully into the hot oil. Cook over a medium heat for 2–3 minutes on each side. Stir the stock, rice wine or sherry and sugar into the marinade, with salt and pepper to taste. Pour the mixture over the fish. Return the leeks and ginger to the wok, together with the reserved spring onions. Cover and simmer for about 15 minutes, until the fish is cooked through. Serve.

Energy 300kcal/1253kJ; Protein 31.1g; Carbohydrate 7.5g, of which sugars 6.7g; Fat 15.4g, of which saturates 2g; Cholesterol 120mg; Calcium 229mg; Fibre 2.6g; Sodium 271mg.

GRILLED LANGOUSTINES WITH HERBS

THIS SIMPLE COOKING METHOD ENHANCES BOTH THE DELICATE COLOUR AND FLAVOUR OF THE LANGOUSTINES. TRY TO FIND LIVE LANGOUSTINES FOR THIS RECIPE. CHOOSE THE LARGEST YOU CAN FIND (OR AFFORD) FOR THIS DISH, AND ALLOW FIVE OR SIX PER SERVING. LOBSTER AND CRAYFISH ARE ALSO DELICIOUS COOKED THIS WAY.

SERVES FOUR AS A MAIN COURSE,
SIX AS AN APPETIZER

INGREDIENTS
  60ml/4 tbsp extra virgin olive oil
  60ml/4 tbsp hazelnut oil
  15ml/1 tbsp each finely chopped
    fresh basil, chives, chervil, parsley
    and tarragon
  pinch of ground ginger
  20–24 large langoustines,
    preferably live
  lemon wedges and rocket (arugula)
    leaves, to garnish
  salt and ground black pepper

COOK'S TIPS
• Don't forget to provide your guests with fingerbowls of warm water and plenty of paper napkins.
• If you use cooked langoustines, then grill (broil) them for just 2–3 minutes to warm them through.

1 Preheat the grill (broiler) to very hot. Mix together the olive and hazelnut oils in a small bowl. Add the herbs, a pinch of ground ginger and salt and pepper to taste. Whisk thoroughly until slightly thickened and emulsified.

2 If you are using live langoustines, immerse them in a pan of boiling water for 1–2 minutes, then drain and leave them to cool.

3 Split the langoustines lengthways using a large sharp knife and arrange them on a foil-lined grill pan. Spoon over the herb-flavoured oil.

4 Grill (broil) for 8–10 minutes, basting the langoustines two or three times until they are cooked and lightly browned.

5 Arrange the langoustines on a warmed serving dish, pour the juices from the grill pan over and serve immediately garnished with lemon wedges and rocket leaves.

SEA BASS IN A SALT CRUST

BAKING FISH IN A CRUST OF SEA SALT ENHANCES THE FLAVOUR AND BRINGS OUT THE TASTE OF THE SEA. ANY FIRM FISH CAN BE COOKED IN THIS WAY. BREAK OPEN THE CRUST AT THE TABLE TO RELEASE THE GLORIOUS AROMA.

SERVES FOUR

INGREDIENTS
  1 sea bass, about 1kg/2¼lb, cleaned
    and scaled
  1 sprig each of fresh fennel,
    rosemary and thyme
  2kg/4½lb/13½ cups coarse sea salt
  mixed peppercorns
  seaweed or samphire, blanched, and
    lemon slices, to garnish

1 Preheat the oven to 240°C/475°F/ Gas 9. Fill the cavity of the sea bass with all the herbs and grind over some of the mixed peppercorns.

2 Spread half the salt on a shallow baking tray (ideally oval) and lay the sea bass on it. Cover the fish all over with a 1cm/½in layer of salt, pressing it down firmly. Moisten the salt lightly by spraying with water from an atomizer. Bake the fish in the hot oven for 30–40 minutes, until the salt crust is just beginning to colour.

3 Garnish the baking tray with seaweed or samphire and bring the fish to the table in its salt crust. Use a sharp knife to break open the crust. Serve the fish, adding lemon slices to each plate.

Top: Energy 128kcal/536kJ; Protein 14.3g; Carbohydrate 0g, of which sugars 0g; Fat 7.8g, of which saturates 1.2g; Cholesterol 175mg; Calcium 72mg; Fibre 0g; Sodium 1000mg.
Bottom: Energy 150kcal/632kJ; Protein 29g; Carbohydrate 0g, of which sugars 0g; Fat 3.8g, of which saturates 0.6g; Cholesterol 120mg; Calcium 195mg; Fibre 0g; Sodium 595mg.

FILLETS OF BRILL IN RED WINE SAUCE

FORGET THE OLD MAXIM THAT RED WINE AND FISH DO NOT GO WELL TOGETHER. THE ROBUST SAUCE ADDS COLOUR AND RICHNESS TO THIS EXCELLENT DISH. TURBOT, HALIBUT AND JOHN DORY ARE ALSO GOOD COOKED THIS WAY.

SERVES FOUR

INGREDIENTS

    4 brill fillets, about 175–200g/6–7oz
      each, skinned
    150g/5oz/⅔ cup chilled butter,
      diced, plus extra for greasing
    115g/4oz shallots, thinly sliced
    200ml/7fl oz/scant 1 cup robust
      red wine
    200ml/7fl oz/scant 1 cup fish stock
    salt and ground white pepper
    fresh chervil or flat leaf parsley
      leaves, to garnish

3 Using a fish slice (spatula), carefully lift the fish and shallots on to a serving dish, cover with foil and keep hot.

4 Transfer the casserole to the hob (stovetop) and bring the cooking liquid to the boil over a high heat. Cook it until it has reduced by half. Lower the heat and whisk in the chilled butter, one piece at a time, to make a smooth, shiny sauce. Season with salt and white pepper, set aside and keep hot.

5 Divide the shallots among four warmed plates and lay the brill fillets on top. Pour the sauce over and around the fish and garnish with the chervil or flat leaf parsley.

1 Preheat the oven to 180°C/350°F/ Gas 4. Season the fish on both sides with salt and pepper. Generously butter a flameproof dish, which is large enough to take all the brill fillets in a single layer without overlapping. Spread the shallots over the base and lay the fish fillets on top. Season.

2 Pour in the red wine and fish stock, cover the dish and bring the liquid to just below boiling point. Transfer to the oven and bake for 6–8 minutes, until the brill is just cooked.

Energy 511kcal/2123kJ; Protein 35.7g; Carbohydrate 1.3g, of which sugars 1.3g; Fat 36.7g, of which saturates 19.5g; Cholesterol 156mg; Calcium 97mg; Fibre 0.4g; Sodium 454mg.

BAKED SEA BREAM <u>WITH</u> TOMATOES

JOHN DORY, TURBOT OR SEA BASS CAN ALL BE COOKED THIS WAY. IF YOU PREFER TO USE FILLETED FISH, CHOOSE A CHUNKY FILLET, LIKE COD, AND ROAST IT SKIN-SIDE UP. ROASTING THE TOMATOES BRINGS OUT THEIR SWEETNESS, WHICH CONTRASTS BEAUTIFULLY WITH THE FLAVOUR OF THE FISH.

2 Meanwhile, cut the potatoes into 1cm/½in slices. Par-boil for 5 minutes. Drain and set aside.

3 Grease an ovenproof dish with oil. Arrange the potatoes in a single layer with the lemon slices over them; sprinkle on the bay leaf, thyme and basil. Season and drizzle with half the remaining olive oil. Lay the fish on top, season; pour over the wine and the rest of the oil. Arrange the tomatoes around the fish.

SERVES FOUR TO SIX

INGREDIENTS
- 8 ripe tomatoes
- 10ml/2 tsp caster (superfine) sugar
- 200ml/7fl oz/scant 1 cup olive oil
- 450g/1lb new potatoes
- 1 lemon, sliced
- 1 bay leaf
- 1 fresh thyme sprig
- 8 fresh basil leaves
- 1 sea bream or porgy, about 900g–1kg/ 2–2¼lb, cleaned and scaled
- 150ml/¼ pint/⅔ cup dry white wine
- 30ml/2 tbsp fresh white breadcrumbs
- 2 garlic cloves, crushed
- 15ml/1 tbsp finely chopped fresh parsley
- salt and ground black pepper
- fresh flat parsley or basil leaves, chopped, to garnish

1 Preheat the oven to 240°C/475°F/ Gas 9. Cut the tomatoes in half lengthways and arrange them in a single layer in an ovenproof dish, cut side up. Sprinkle with sugar, salt and pepper and drizzle over a little of the olive oil. Roast for 30–40 minutes, until soft and lightly browned.

4 Mix together the breadcrumbs, garlic and parsley; sprinkle over the fish. Bake for 30 minutes, until the flesh comes away easily from the bone. Garnish with chopped parsley or basil.

Energy 571kcal/2383kJ; Protein 25.9g; Carbohydrate 29.4g, of which sugars 7.2g; Fat 37.1g, of which saturates 4.9g; Cholesterol 48mg; Calcium 82mg; Fibre 3g; Sodium 224mg.

FILLETS OF SEA BREAM IN FILO PASTRY

ANY FIRM FISH FILLETS CAN BE USED FOR THIS DISH — BASS, GROUPER, RED MULLET AND SNAPPER ARE PARTICULARLY GOOD. EACH LITTLE PARCEL IS A MEAL IN ITSELF AND CAN BE PREPARED SEVERAL HOURS IN ADVANCE, WHICH MAKES THIS AN IDEAL RECIPE FOR ENTERTAINING. IF YOU LIKE, SERVE THE PASTRIES WITH FENNEL BRAISED WITH ORANGE JUICE OR A MIXED LEAF SALAD.

2 Thinly slice the potatoes lengthways. Brush a baking sheet with a little of the oil. Lay a sheet of filo pastry on the sheet, brush it with oil, then lay a second sheet crossways over the first. Repeat with two more sheets. Arrange a quarter of the sliced potatoes in the centre, season and add a quarter of the shredded sorrel or spinach. Lay a fish fillet on top, skin-side up. Season.

3 Loosely fold the filo pastry up and over to make a neat parcel. Make three more parcels; place on the baking sheet. Brush with half the butter. Bake for about 20 minutes, until the filo is puffed up and golden brown.

SERVES FOUR

INGREDIENTS

8 small waxy salad potatoes,
   preferably red-skinned
200g/7oz sorrel or spinach,
   stalks removed
30ml/2 tbsp olive oil
16 filo pastry sheets, thawed
   if frozen
4 sea bream or porgy fillets, about
   175g/6oz each, scaled but
   not skinned
50g/2oz/¼ cup butter, melted
120ml/4fl oz/½ cup fish stock
250ml/8fl oz/1 cup whipping cream
salt and ground black pepper
finely diced red (bell) pepper,
   to garnish

1 Preheat the oven to 200°C/400°F/ Gas 6. Cook the potatoes in a pan of lightly salted boiling water for about 15–20 minutes, until just tender. Drain and leave to cool. Set about half the sorrel or spinach leaves aside. Shred the remaining leaves by piling up six at a time, rolling them up like a fat cigar and slicing them with a sharp knife.

4 Meanwhile, make the sorrel sauce. Heat the remaining butter in a pan, add the reserved sorrel and cook gently for 3 minutes, stirring, until it wilts. Stir in the stock and cream. Heat almost to boiling point, stirring so that the sorrel breaks down. Season to taste and keep hot until the fish parcels are ready. Serve garnished with red pepper. Hand around the sauce separately.

Energy 651kcal/2710kJ; Protein 35.8g; Carbohydrate 23.2g, of which sugars 3.3g; Fat 46.8g, of which saturates 23.2g; Cholesterol 159mg; Calcium 222mg; Fibre 2g; Sodium 359mg.

OCTOPUS STEW

THIS RUSTIC STEW IS A PERFECT DISH FOR ENTERTAINING, AS IT TASTES EVEN BETTER IF MADE A DAY IN ADVANCE. SERVE WITH A COLOURFUL SALAD OF BABY CHARD, ROCKET AND RADICCHIO.

SERVES FOUR TO SIX

INGREDIENTS
   1kg/2¼lb octopus, cleaned
   45ml/3 tbsp olive oil
   1 large red onion, chopped
   3 garlic cloves, finely chopped
   30ml/2 tbsp brandy
   300ml/½ pint/1¼ cups dry
      white wine
   800g/1¾lb ripe plum tomatoes,
      peeled and chopped, or two
      400g/14oz cans chopped tomatoes
   1 fresh red chilli, seeded and
      chopped (optional)
   450g/1lb small new potatoes
   15ml/1 tbsp chopped fresh rosemary
   15ml/1 tbsp fresh thyme leaves
   1.2 litres/2 pints/5 cups fish stock
   30ml/2 tbsp fresh flat leaf
      parsley leaves
   salt and ground black pepper
   rosemary sprigs, to garnish
For the garlic croûtes
   1 fat garlic clove, peeled
   8 thick slices of baguette or ciabatta
   30ml/2 tbsp olive oil

3 Pour the brandy over the octopus and ignite it. When the flames have died down, add the wine, bring to the boil and bubble gently for about 5 minutes. Stir in the tomatoes, with the chilli, if using, then add the potatoes, rosemary and thyme. Simmer for 5 minutes.

4 Pour in the fish stock and season well. Cover the pan and simmer for 20–30 minutes, stirring occasionally. The octopus and potatoes should be very tender, and the sauce should have thickened slightly. At this stage, you can leave the stew to cool, then put it in the refrigerator overnight.

5 Preheat a medium-hot grill (broiler). To make the croûtes, cut the garlic clove in half and rub both sides of the bread slices with the cut side. Crush the garlic, stir it into the oil and brush the mixture over both sides of the bread. Grill (broil) on both sides until the croûtes are golden brown and crisp.

6 To serve the stew, reheat it gently if it has been in the refrigerator overnight, check the seasoning and stir in the parsley leaves. Serve piping hot in individual warmed bowls, garnished with rosemary sprigs and accompanied by the warm garlic croûtes.

1 Cut the octopus into large pieces, put these in a pan and pour in cold water to cover. Season with salt, bring to the boil, then lower the heat and simmer for 30 minutes to tenderize. Drain and cut into bitesize pieces.

2 Heat the oil in a large shallow pan. Cook the onion for 2–3 minutes, until lightly coloured, then add the garlic and cook for 1 minute more. Add the octopus and cook for 2–3 minutes, stirring and tossing to colour it lightly.

Energy 325kcal/1369kJ; Protein 32.7g; Carbohydrate 20.5g, of which sugars 8.2g; Fat 8.4g, of which saturates 1.5g; Cholesterol 80mg; Calcium 86mg; Fibre 2.8g; Sodium 24mg.

FISH PLAKI

EVERY MEDITERRANEAN COUNTRY HAS A SLIGHTLY DIFFERENT VERSION OF THIS SIMPLE BUT VERY DELICIOUS DISH, WHICH MAKES THE MOST OF THE LOCAL FRESH FISH. A WHOLE FISH CAN BE USED INSTEAD OF A LARGE FILLET, IF YOU PREFER. THIS DISH ALSO WORKS WELL WITH SEA BASS OR BREAM, JOHN DORY, TURBOT, HALIBUT OR BRILL.

SERVES FOUR

INGREDIENTS

150ml/¼ pint/⅔ cup olive oil
2 large Spanish onions, chopped
2 celery sticks, chopped
4 fat garlic cloves, chopped
4 potatoes, peeled and diced
4 carrots, cut into small dice
15ml/1 tbsp caster (superfine) sugar
2 bay leaves
1 thick middle-cut fillet of grouper or cod, about 1kg/2¼lb
16–20 large black olives (optional)
4 large ripe tomatoes, peeled, seeded and chopped
150ml/¼ pint/⅔ cup dry white wine or vermouth
salt and ground black pepper
fresh herb leaves, to garnish
saffron rice, to serve

1 Preheat the oven to 190°C/375°F/ Gas 5. Heat the olive oil in a large frying pan, add the chopped onions and celery and sauté until they are transparent. Add the garlic and cook for 2 minutes more. Stir in the potatoes and carrots and cook for about 5 minutes, stirring occasionally. Sprinkle with the sugar and season to taste with salt and ground black pepper.

2 Spoon the vegetable mixture into an oval or rectangular ovenproof dish slightly larger than the fish and tuck in the bay leaves. Season the fish and lay it on the bed of vegetables, skin side up. Sprinkle the olives around the edge, if using. Spread the chopped tomatoes over the fish, pour over the wine or vermouth and season.

3 Bake for 30–40 minutes, until the fish is cooked through. Serve straight from the dish. Garnish with herb leaves. Saffron rice would be the ideal accompaniment.

COOK'S TIP
If you use a whole fish, be sure to season it inside as well as outside.

SALMON ESCALOPES WITH WHISKY AND CREAM

THIS DISH COMBINES TWO OF THE FINEST FLAVOURS OF SCOTLAND — SALMON AND WHISKY. IT TAKES VERY LITTLE TIME TO MAKE, SO COOK IT AT THE LAST MOMENT WHEN YOU ARE READY TO SERVE. YOUR GUESTS WILL DEEM IT WORTH THE WAIT. SERVE WITH NEW POTATOES AND GREEN BEANS.

SERVES FOUR

INGREDIENTS

4 salmon escalopes (scallops), about 175g/6oz each
5ml/1 tsp chopped fresh thyme leaves
50g/2oz/¼ cup butter
75ml/5 tbsp whisky
150ml/¼ pint/⅔ cup double (heavy) cream
juice of ½ lemon (optional)
salt and ground black pepper
fresh dill sprigs, to garnish

1 Season the salmon with salt, pepper and thyme. Melt half the butter in a frying pan large enough to hold two escalopes side by side. When the butter is foaming, cook the first two escalopes for about 1 minute on each side, until they are golden on the outside and just cooked through.

2 Pour in 30ml/2 tbsp of the whisky and ignite it. When the flames have died down, carefully transfer the salmon escalopes to a plate and keep them hot. Heat the remaining butter and cook the second two escalopes in the same way. Keep them hot.

3 Pour the cream into the pan and bring to the boil, stirring constantly and scraping up the cooking juices from the base of the pan. Allow to bubble until reduced and slightly thickened, then season and add the last of the whisky and a squeeze of lemon if you like.

4 Place the salmon escalopes on individual warmed plates, pour the sauce over and serve garnished with dill.

Top: Energy 557kcal/2322kJ; Protein 48.8g; Carbohydrate 24.3g, of which sugars 10.2g; Fat 27.3g, of which saturates 3.9g; Cholesterol 115mg; Calcium 74mg; Fibre 3.3g; Sodium 179mg.
Bottom: Energy 667kcal/2760kJ; Protein 36.1g; Carbohydrate 0.8g, of which sugars 0.8g; Fat 53g, of which saturates 24.5g; Cholesterol 174mg; Calcium 61mg; Fibre 0g; Sodium 164mg.

FILLETS OF TURBOT WITH OYSTERS

THIS LUXURIOUS DISH IS PERFECT FOR SPECIAL OCCASIONS. IT IS WORTH BUYING A WHOLE TURBOT AND ASKING THE FISHMONGER TO FILLET AND SKIN IT FOR YOU. KEEP THE HEAD, BONES AND TRIMMINGS FOR STOCK. SOLE, BRILL AND HALIBUT CAN ALL BE SUBSTITUTED FOR THE TURBOT.

SERVES FOUR

INGREDIENTS

12 Pacific (rock) oysters
115g/4oz/½ cup butter
2 carrots, cut into julienne strips
200g/7oz celeriac, cut into
    julienne strips
the white parts of 2 leeks, cut into
    julienne strips
375ml/13fl oz/generous 1½ cups
    champagne or dry white sparkling
    wine (about ½ bottle)
105ml/7 tbsp whipping cream
1 turbot, about 1.75kg/4–4½lb,
    filleted and skinned
salt and ground white pepper

1 Using an oyster knife, open the oysters over a bowl to catch the juices, then carefully remove them from their shells, discarding the shells, and place them in a separate bowl. Set aside until required.

2 Melt 25g/1oz/2 tbsp of the butter in a shallow pan, add the vegetable julienne and cook over a low heat until tender but not coloured. Pour in half the champagne or sparkling wine and cook very gently until all the liquid has evaporated. Keep the heat low so that the vegetables do not colour.

3 Strain the oyster juices into a small pan and add the cream and the remaining champagne or sparkling wine. Place over a medium heat until the mixture has reduced to the consistency of thin cream. Dice half the remaining butter and whisk it into the sauce, one piece at a time, until smooth. Season to taste, then pour the sauce into a blender and process until velvety smooth.

4 Return the sauce to the pan, bring it to just below boiling point, then drop in the oysters. Poach for about 1 minute, to warm but barely cook. Keep warm, but do not let the sauce boil.

5 Season the turbot fillets with salt and pepper. Heat the remaining butter in a large frying pan until foaming, then cook the fillets over a medium heat for about 2–3 minutes on each side until cooked through and golden.

6 Cut each turbot fillet into three pieces and arrange on individual warmed plates. Pile the vegetable julienne on top, place three oysters around the turbot fillets on each plate and pour the sauce around the edge.

Energy 752kcal/3125kJ; Protein 66.7g; Carbohydrate 9.2g, of which sugars 8g; Fat 44.1g, of which saturates 23.9g; Cholesterol 106mg; Calcium 252mg; Fibre 1.4g; Sodium 370mg.

JOHN DORY WITH LIGHT CURRY SAUCE

THIS EXCELLENT COMBINATION OF FLAVOURS ALSO WORKS WELL WITH OTHER FLAT FISH LIKE TURBOT, HALIBUT AND BRILL, OR MORE EXOTIC SPECIES LIKE MAHI-MAHI OR ORANGE ROUGHY. THE CURRY TASTE SHOULD BE VERY SUBTLE, SO USE A MILD CURRY POWDER. SERVE THE FISH WITH PILAU RICE AND MANGO CHUTNEY. IT LOOKS WONDERFUL ARRANGED ON BANANA LEAVES, IF YOU CAN FIND SOME.

SERVES FOUR

INGREDIENTS

- 4 John Dory fillets, each about 175g/6oz, skinned
- 15ml/1 tbsp sunflower oil
- 25g/1oz/2 tbsp butter
- salt and ground black pepper
- 15ml/1 tbsp fresh coriander (cilantro) leaves and 1 small mango, peeled and diced, to garnish

For the curry sauce
- 30ml/2 tbsp sunflower oil
- 1 carrot, chopped
- 1 onion, chopped
- 1 celery stick, chopped
- white of 1 leek, chopped
- 2 garlic cloves, crushed
- 50g/2oz creamed coconut (coconut cream), crumbled
- 2 tomatoes, peeled, seeded and diced
- 2.5cm/1in piece fresh root ginger, grated
- 15ml/1 tbsp tomato purée (paste)
- 5–10ml/1–2 tsp mild curry powder
- 500ml/17fl oz/generous 2 cups chicken or fish stock

1 Make the sauce. Heat the oil in a pan; add the vegetables and garlic. Cook gently until soft but not brown.

COOK'S TIP
The coconut sauce must be cooked over a very low heat, so use a heat diffuser if you have one.

2 Add the coconut, tomatoes and ginger. Cook for 1–2 minutes; stir in the tomato purée and curry powder to taste. Add the stock, stir and season.

3 Bring to the boil, then lower the heat, cover the pan and cook the sauce over the lowest heat for about 50 minutes. Stir once or twice to prevent burning. Leave the sauce to cool; pour into a food processor or blender and process until smooth. Return to a clean pan and reheat very gently, adding a little water if too thick.

4 Season the fish fillets with salt and pepper. Heat the oil in a large frying pan, add the butter and heat until sizzling. Put in the fish and cook for about 2–3 minutes on each side, until pale golden and cooked through. Drain on kitchen paper.

5 Arrange the fillets on individual warmed plates, pour the sauce around the fish and sprinkle on the finely diced mango. Decorate with coriander leaves and serve immediately.

Energy 333kcal/1391kJ; Protein 34.9g; Carbohydrate 12.5g, of which sugars 11.5g; Fat 16.3g, of which saturates 4.9g; Cholesterol 13mg; Calcium 102mg; Fibre 2.6g; Sodium 291mg.

GRILLED HALIBUT WITH SAUCE VIERGE

ANY THICK WHITE FISH FILLETS CAN BE COOKED IN THIS VERSATILE DISH; TURBOT, BRILL AND JOHN DORY ARE ESPECIALLY DELICIOUS, BUT THE FLAVOURSOME SAUCE ALSO GIVES HUMBLER FISH LIKE COD, HADDOCK OR HAKE A REAL LIFT.

SERVES FOUR

INGREDIENTS
105ml/7 tbsp olive oil
2.5ml/½ tsp fennel seeds
2.5ml/½ tsp celery seeds
5ml/1 tsp mixed peppercorns
675–800g/1½–1¾lb middle cut of
   halibut, about 3cm/1¼in thick, cut
   into 4 pieces
coarse sea salt
5ml/1 tsp fresh thyme
   leaves, chopped
5ml/1 tsp fresh rosemary
   leaves, chopped
5ml/1 tsp fresh oregano or marjoram
   leaves, chopped
For the sauce
105ml/7 tbsp extra virgin olive oil
juice of 1 lemon
1 garlic clove, finely chopped
2 tomatoes, peeled, seeded
   and diced
5ml/1 tsp small capers
2 drained canned anchovy
   fillets, chopped
5ml/1 tsp chopped fresh chives
15ml/1 tbsp shredded fresh
   basil leaves
15ml/1 tbsp chopped fresh chervil

1 Heat a ridged griddle pan or preheat the grill (broiler) to high. Brush the griddle pan or grill pan with a little of the olive oil. Mix the fennel and celery seeds with the peppercorns in a mortar. Crush with a pestle, and then stir in the coarse sea salt to taste. Spoon the mixture into a shallow dish and stir in the herbs and the remaining olive oil.

2 Add the halibut pieces to the olive oil mixture, turning them to coat them thoroughly, then arrange them with the dark skin uppermost in the oiled griddle pan or grill pan. Cook or grill (broil) for about 6–8 minutes, until the fish is cooked all the way through and the skin has browned.

3 Combine all the sauce ingredients except the fresh herbs in a pan and heat gently until warm but not hot. Stir in the chives, basil and chervil.

4 Place the halibut on four warmed plates. Spoon the sauce around and over the fish and serve immediately, with lightly-cooked green cabbage.

Energy 410kcal/1709kJ; Protein 37.3g; Carbohydrate 1.8g, of which sugars 1.4g; Fat 28.3g, of which saturates 4.1g; Cholesterol 60mg; Calcium 72mg; Fibre 0.5g; Sodium 165mg.

VEGETABLE-STUFFED SQUID

SHIRLEY CONRAN FAMOUSLY SAID THAT LIFE IS TOO SHORT TO STUFF A MUSHROOM. THE SAME MIGHT BE SAID OF SQUID, EXCEPT THAT THE RESULT IS SO DELICIOUS THAT IT MAKES THE EFFORT SEEM WORTHWHILE. SMALL CUTTLEFISH CAN BE PREPARED IN THE SAME WAY. SERVE WITH SAFFRON RICE.

SERVES FOUR

INGREDIENTS

4 medium squid, or 12 small squid,
  skinned and cleaned
75g/3oz/6 tbsp butter
50g/2oz/1 cup fresh
  white breadcrumbs
2 shallots, chopped
4 garlic cloves, chopped
1 leek, finely diced
2 carrots, finely diced
150ml/¼ pint/⅔ cup fish stock
30ml/2 tbsp olive oil
30ml/2 tbsp chopped fresh parsley
salt and ground black pepper
rosemary sprigs, to garnish
saffron rice, to serve

1 Preheat the oven to 220°C/425°F/ Gas 7. Cut off the tentacles and side flaps from the squid and chop these finely. Set the squid aside. Melt half the butter in a large frying pan that can safely be used in the oven. Add the fresh white breadcrumbs and cook until they are golden brown, stirring to prevent them from burning. Using a slotted spoon, transfer the breadcrumbs to a bowl and set aside until required.

2 Heat the remaining butter in the frying pan and add the chopped and diced vegetables. Cook until softened but not browned, then stir in the fish stock and cook until it has reduced and the vegetables are very soft. Season to taste with salt and ground black pepper and transfer to the bowl with the breadcrumbs. Mix lightly together.

3 Heat half the olive oil in the frying pan, add the chopped squid and cook over a high heat for 1 minute. Remove the squid with a slotted spoon; stir into the vegetable mixture. Stir in the parsley.

4 Put the stuffing mixture into a piping (pastry) bag, or use a teaspoon to stuff the squid tubes with the mixture. Do not overfill them, as the stuffing will swell slightly during cooking. Secure the openings with cocktail sticks or toothpicks, or sew up with fine kitchen thread.

5 Heat the remaining olive oil in the frying pan, place the stuffed squid in the pan and cook until they are sealed on all sides and golden brown. Transfer the frying pan to the oven and roast the squid for 20 minutes.

6 Unless the squid are very small, carefully cut them into three or four slices and arrange on a bed of saffron rice. Spoon the cooking juices over and around the squid and serve immediately, garnished with rosemary.

Energy 356kcal/1486kJ; Protein 21.8g; Carbohydrate 15.2g, of which sugars 3.6g; Fat 23.6g, of which saturates 11.1g; Cholesterol 321mg; Calcium 55mg; Fibre 1.9g; Sodium 352mg.

SAUCES <u>FOR</u> FISH AND SHELLFISH

MANY TYPES OF FISH ARE SO DELICIOUS THAT THEY DO NOT NEED TO BE COOKED IN A SAUCE, BUT A GOOD ACCOMPANYING SAUCE WILL CERTAINLY ENHANCE PLAINLY COOKED FISH.

NEVER-FAIL MAYONNAISE

Some people find classic mayonnaise difficult to make, but this simple version takes away the mystique. The essential thing is to have all the ingredients at room temperature before you start. Be aware that this recipe contains raw eggs. If this is a concern, use bought mayonnaise instead.

<u>SERVES FOUR TO SIX</u>

INGREDIENTS
    1 egg, plus 1 egg yolk
    5ml/1 tsp Dijon mustard
    juice of 1 large lemon
    175ml/6fl oz/¾ cup olive oil
    175ml/6fl oz/¾ cup grapeseed,
        sunflower or corn oil
    salt and ground white pepper

1 Put the whole egg and yolk in a food processor and process for 20 seconds. Add the mustard, half the lemon juice and a generous pinch of salt and pepper. Process for about 30 seconds, until thoroughly mixed.

2 With the motor running, pour in the oils through the feeder tube in a thin, steady stream. Process until the oils are incorporated and the mayonnaise is pale and thick. Taste and add more lemon juice and seasoning, if necessary.

VARIATIONS

Vary the oil according to the fish the mayonnaise is to accompany. Use all olive oil for robust fish such as salmon or tuna, a mixture of olive and light vegetable oil for more delicate fish.

BEURRE BLANC

Legend has it that this exquisite sauce was invented by a cook who forgot to put egg yolks into a béarnaise sauce. Whether or not this is true doesn't matter: this light sauce goes perfectly with poached or grilled (broiled) fish.

<u>SERVES FOUR</u>

INGREDIENTS
    3 shallots, very finely chopped
    45ml/3 tbsp dry white wine or
        court-bouillon
    45ml/3 tbsp white wine or
        tarragon vinegar
    115g/4oz/½ cup chilled unsalted
        (sweet) butter, diced
    lemon juice (optional)
    salt and ground white pepper

1 Put the shallots in a small pan with the wine or court bouillon and vinegar. Bring to the boil and cook over a high heat until only about 30ml/2 tbsp liquid remains. Remove the pan from the heat and then leave to cool until the liquid is just lukewarm.

2 Whisk in the chilled butter, one piece at a time, to make a pale, creamy sauce. (Make sure each piece is fully incorporated before adding the next.) Taste the sauce, then season with salt and pepper and add a little lemon juice to taste, if you like.

3 If you are not serving the sauce immediately, keep it warm in the top of a double boiler set over barely simmering water.

HOLLANDAISE SAUCE

This rich sauce goes well with any poached fish. Serve it warm. As the egg yolks are barely cooked, do not serve to children, the elderly or invalids.

<u>SERVES FOUR</u>

INGREDIENTS
    115g/4oz/½ cup unsalted
        (sweet) butter
    2 egg yolks
    15–30ml/1–2 tbsp lemon juice or
        white wine or tarragon vinegar
    salt and ground white pepper

1 Melt the butter in a small pan Put the egg yolks and lemon juice or vinegar in a bowl. Add salt and pepper and whisk until completely smooth.

2 Pour the melted butter in a steady stream on to the egg yolk mixture, beating vigorously with a wooden spoon to make a smooth, creamy sauce. Alternatively, put the mixture in a food processor and add the butter through the feeder tube, with the motor running. Taste the sauce and add more lemon juice or vinegar, if necessary.

PARSLEY SAUCE

Forget the pallid, lumpy parsley sauce of your youth; when this classic sauce is well made it is delicious. Serve it with poached cod, haddock or any white fish. If possible, use the poaching liquid to enhance the flavour of the sauce.

SERVES FOUR

INGREDIENTS

50g/2oz/¼ cup butter
45ml/3 tbsp plain (all-purpose) flour
300ml/½ pint/1¼ cups milk
300ml/½ pint/1¼ cups poaching liquid from the fish (or an extra 300ml/½ pint/1¼ cups milk)
60ml/4 tbsp double (heavy) cream
lemon juice (see method)
90ml/6 tbsp chopped fresh parsley
salt and ground black pepper

1 Melt half the butter in a small pan, add the flour and stir for 2–3 minutes to make a smooth roux. Take the pan off the heat, add a couple of spoonfuls of milk and stir in until completely absorbed. Continue to add small quantities of milk and poaching liquid, if available, stirring until the sauce has the consistency of double cream. Add the rest of the milk and poaching liquid and whisk thoroughly to break down any lumps.

2 Return the pan to the heat and bring the sauce to the boil. Lower the heat and simmer gently for about 5 minutes, stirring frequently. Stir in the cream and lemon juice to taste, and season with salt and pepper. If the sauce is at all lumpy at this stage, whisk it thoroughly with a hand-held blender or a balloon whisk.

3 Stir in the parsley, then whisk in the remaining butter and serve hot.

MUSTARD AND DILL SAUCE

Serve this fresh-tasting sauce with any cold, smoked or raw marinated fish. Note that it contains raw egg yolk.

SERVES FOUR

INGREDIENTS

1 egg yolk
30ml/2 tbsp brown French mustard
2.5–5ml/½–1 tsp soft dark brown sugar
15ml/1 tbsp white wine vinegar
90ml/6 tbsp sunflower or vegetable oil
30ml/2 tbsp finely chopped fresh dill
salt and ground black pepper

1 Put the egg yolk in a small bowl and add the mustard with a little soft brown sugar to taste. Beat with a wooden spoon until smooth. Stir in the white wine vinegar, then gradually whisk in the oil, a little at a time, mixing well after each addition.

2 When the oil has been completely amalgamated, season the sauce with salt and pepper, then stir in the finely chopped dill. Chill for an hour or more before serving.

CRAWFISH SAUCE

This sauce, also known as Nantua sauce, is perfect for using up the shells left over from seafood recipes. It can be made with other crustaceans, such as lobster or large prawns (shrimp). Use it to enhance any white fish or shellfish.

SERVES FOUR

INGREDIENTS

1 cooked crawfish (rock lobster), about 450g/1lb
40g/1½oz/3 tbsp butter
15ml/1 tbsp olive oil
45ml/3 tbsp brandy
500ml/17fl oz/generous 2 cups fish or shellfish stock
15ml/1 tbsp plain (all-purpose) flour
45ml/3 tbsp double (heavy) cream
2 egg yolks
salt and ground white pepper

1 Remove the tail meat from the crawfish and keep for another recipe. Break up the shells and legs and crush them coarsely in a food processor.

2 Melt 25g/1oz/2 tbsp of the butter in the oil in a pan, add the shells and cook for about 3 minutes, stirring frequently. Add the brandy and stock, bring to the boil, then simmer for 10 minutes.

3 Mash the remaining butter with the flour to make *beurre manié*. Whisk this into the sauce, a small piece at a time, and cook gently until thickened. Season the sauce and strain it through a fine sieve. Stir in the cream and bring back to just below boiling point.

4 Beat the egg yolks lightly in a bowl and mix in a couple of spoonfuls of the hot sauce. Return the mixture to the pan and cook gently until smooth. Adjust the seasoning and serve.

SHOPPING FOR FISH AND SHELLFISH

Australia

De Costi Seafoods
29 Bachell Ave
Lidcombe
NSW 2141
Tel: (02) 9649 7699
www.decosti.com.au

Sydney Fish Markets
Locked Bag 247, Bank Street
Pyrmont NSW 2009
Tel: (02) 9004 1100
www.sydneyfishmarket.com.au

Poulos Bros
21–29 Bank Street
Pyrmont NSW 2009
Tel: (02) 9692 8411
www.poulosbros.com.au

The Fish Factory
363 Lytton Road
Colmslie QLD 4170
Tel: (07) 3399 9888
www.fishfactory.com.au

Queen Victoria Markets
513 Elizabeth Street
Melbourne, VIC 3000
Tel: (03) 9320 5822
www.qvm.com.au

Angelakis Bros
30 Field Street
Adelaide SA 5000
Tel: (08) 8400 1300
www.angelakis.com.au

New Zealand

Seafood New Zealand
Private Bag 24901
Manners Street
Wellington 6142
Tel: (04) 385 4005
www.seafood.co.nz

United Kingdom

Fishmongers

Corney, J. A. Ltd (kosher)
16 Hallswelle Parade
Finchley Road
London NW11 0DL
Tel: 020 8455 9588

Covent Garden Fishmongers
Phil Diamond
37 Turnham Green Terrace
London W4 1RG
Tel: 020 8995 9273

Cutty Catering Supplies
Unit 4, 57 Sandgate Street
London SE15 1LE
Tel: 020 7277 7759

Dagon's Ltd
16 Granvill Arcade
Coldharbour Lane
London SW9 8PR
Tel: 020 7274 1665

GB Filipino Foods Ltd
1 Kenway Road
London SW5 0RP
Tel: 020 7373 9992

France Fresh Fish
99 Stroud Green Road
London N4 3PX
Tel: 020 7263 9767

Good Harvest Fish and
    Meat Market
14 Newport Place, Soho
London WC2H 7PR
Tel: 020 7437 0712

Harrods Food Hall
87-135 Brompton Road
Knightsbridge
London SW1X 7XL
Tel: 020 7730 1234

Harvey Nichols Food Hall
109–125 Knightsbridge
London SW1X 7RJ
Tel: 020 7235 5000

The Fresh Fish Shop
1 Palmerston House
Commercial Square
Haywards Heath
West Sussex RH16 1DR
Tel: 01444 451830

and
A272 Cowfold Road
West Grinstead
West Sussex
RH13 8LY
Tel: 01403 865110

James Knight of Mayfair Ltd
135-138 Newport Street,
Vauxhall
London SE11 6AQ
Tel: 020 7587 3070

Moxon's
149 Lordship Lane
East Dulwich
London SE22 8HX
Tel: 020 8299 1559

and
17 Bute Street
London SW7 3EY
Tel: 020 7591 0050

and
110 Islington High Street
London N1 8EG
Tel: 020 7704 1120

Newnes, C. J. (exotic fish)
76-77 Billingsgate Market
Trafalgar Way Poplar
London E14 5TQ
Tel: 020 7515 0793

Ramus Seafood Emporium
Ocean House, Kings Road
Harrogate
North Yorkshire HG1 5HY
Tel: 0800 0355 850
www.ramus.co.uk

The Seafood Store
16 Downing Street, Farnham
Surrey GU9 7PB
Tel: 01252 715010

Selfridges
400 Oxford Street
London W1A 1AB
Tel: 0800 123 400

Shellseekers Fish & Game
Borough Market
8 Southwark Street
London SE1 1TL
Tel: 020 7407 1002

Steve Hatt
88–90 Essex Road
London N1 8LU
Tel: 020 7226 3963

The Whitby Catch
1 Pier Road, Whitby
North Yorkshire
YO21 3PT
Tel: 01947 601313
www.thewhitbycatch.co.uk

Mail Order Companies

Atlantic Harvest Limited
Pennyburn Industrial Estate
Londonderry
Co Londonderry
BT48 0LU
Tel: 028 7126 4275

Atlantis Smoked Foods
Fore Street
Grampound
Truro
Cornwall, TR2 4SB
Tel: 01726 883201

The Duchy Smoked Fish
  Company Ltd
The Causeway
Off Par Green
Par
PL24 2AF
Tel: 01726 816063
www.smokedfishcornwall.co.uk

The Fish Society
Unit 1, Coopers Place
Wormley
Surrey
GU 5TG
Tel: 01428 687768
www.thefishsociety.co.uk

Fowey Fish & Fowey Wines
37 Fore Street
Fowey
Cornwall
PL23 1AH
Tel: 01726 832422
www.foweyfish.com

Rhydlewis Fishery
West of Rhydlewis
Llandysul
Ceredigion, SA44 5QS
Tel: 01239 851224

Cooking Equipment

Divertimenti
227-229 Brompton Road
London SW3 2EP
Tel: 020 7581 8151
www.divertimenti.co.uk

United States

Alioto-Lazio Fish Company
440 Jefferson Street
San Francisco, CA 94100-1315
Tel: (888) 673-5868
www.crabonline.com

Buck Bay Shellfish Farm
77 EJ Young Road
Olga, WA 98279
Tel: (360) 376-5280
buckbayshellfishfarm.com

Citarella
1313 Third Avenue
New York, NY 10021
Tel: (212) 874-0383
www.citarella.com

The Crab Place
504 Maryland Avenue
Crisfield
Maryland 21817
Tel: (877) 328-2722
www.crabplace.com

Rosendo Fish & Meat Market
383 2nd Avenue
Manhattan
New York 10010
Tel: (212) 358-7677

The Fish House
102401 Overseas Highway
Key Largo, FL 33037
Tel: (305) 451-4665
www.fishhouse.com

Fitts Seafoods
1555 12th Street SE
Salem, Oregon 97302
Tel: (503) 364-6724
www.fitts.net

Flanders Fish Market
22 Chesterfield Road
East Lyme, CT 06333
Tel: (800) 242-6055
www.flandersfish.com

Lake Superior Fish Company
1507 North 1st Street
Superior
WI 54880-1146
Tel: (715) 392-3101
www.lakesuperiorfish.com

Pike Place Fish Market
86 Pike Place
Seattle, WA 98101
Tel: (800) 542 7732
www.pikeplacefish.com

Information Services

Alaska Seafood Marketing
  Institute
www.alaskaseafood.org

Australian Marine
  Conservation Society
www.amcs.org.au

Marine Conservation
  Society (UK)
www.fishonline.org

Picture Acknowledgements

All photographs are by William
Lingwood except those on the
following pages: p8bl Life
File/Barry Mayes, p8tr Life
file/Jeremy Hoare, p9 Tony
Stone/Joe Cornish; p51t New
Zealand Seafoods, p51b Kate
Whiteman, pp61tr and 72b
Food Features (fish supplied
by Tesco), p108 Sydney Fish
Markets, p112 Cephas/Alain
Proust, 122tl and tr Janine
Hosegood.

Publisher's Acknowledgements

The publisher would like to
thank the following companies
who kindly loaned equipment
for photography: Divertimenti,
Tel: 020 7581 8065 and
Magimix, Tel. 01252 548976

INDEX